WALKING THE GR7
IN ANDALUCÍA

About the Authors

Kirstie and Michelle both love walking and writing and taking photographs. They live in Edinburgh and take every opportunity to get out into the mountains of the north of Scotland. They both have day jobs working as campaigners for development and human rights.

Between them they have travelled throughout Europe and South America spending many happy days with their boots on in the Picos de Europa, French and Austrian Alps, Sierra de Gredos, Sierra Nevada, Alpujarras and Andes.

This is their first guidebook, but they hope it will not be their last.

To Julie,
whose many songs
helped us along the way
lots of love

WALKING THE GR7
IN ANDALUCÍA

by

Kirstie Shirra and Michelle Lowe

CICERONE

2 POLICE SQUARE, MILNTHORPE, CUMBRIA LA7 7PY
www.cicerone.co.uk

First edition 2007
ISBN-13: 978 1 85284 507 0

A catalogue record for this book is available from the British Library.

Acknowledgements
Huge thank-yous to all the patient and loving friends and family who have helped
us throughout the process of writing this book. Special thanks to Kristin, Pete,
Robin, Karen, Rachel and Esa for their great company on parts of the route.
Thanks to Pete for being wonderful as always, to Matt for technical support and to
Lyn for proofreading. Thank you to Juan Holgado for invaluable information and
advice while on the route. Thank you also to all the helpful folk throughout
Andalucía who pointed us in the right direction and offered advice (including José
in Alcalá la Real and the pharmacist in Jayena). And, finally, thank you to
Cicerone for saying yes!

Advice to readers
Readers are advised that while every effort is taken by the authors to ensure the
accuracy of this guidebook, changes can occur which may affect the contents. It
is advisable to check locally on transport, accommodation, shops, etc, but even
rights of way can be altered.
    The publisher would welcome notes of any such changes.

Front cover: Approaching La Calahorra near the end of the Granada section of the
route

CONTENTS

Overview map...8–9
Map key 10

Introduction 13
About Andalucía 13
About the route..15
   Deciding which sections to walk 16
   Northern Fork 17
   Southern Fork 18
Practical information 18
   Weather and when to go...18
   How to get there..19
   How to get back 20
   Where to stay...20
   Types of accommodation..21
   Facilities 22
   Maps 23
   What to take 24
   Safety and emergencies 25
Background information 27
   Culture 27
   Andalucian cuisine 27
   Language..29
   History...29
   Current issues 35
   Wildlife 36
   National and natural parks..38
How to use this guide 39

Part 1: Cádiz and Málaga 41
Cádiz province – Tarifa to Montejaque.............................42
   Tarifa – Los Barrios..45
     Los Alcornocales natural park 47
   Los Barrios – Castillo de Castellar 50
   Castillo de Castillar – Jimena de la Frontera 55
   Jimena de la Frontera – Ubrique 57
   Ubrique – Montejaque...60
     Sierra de Grazalema natural park 63

Málaga province – Montejaque to Villanueva del Cauche 65
Montejaque – Arriate 68
Arriate – Ardales 72
Ardales – El Chorro..76
El Chorro – Valle de Abdalajís..78
Valle de Abdalajís – Antequera 80
Antequera – Villanueva del Cauche 83
El Torcal natural park..84

Part 2: Northern Fork – Málaga, Córdoba and Jaén............................86
Málaga province – Villanueva del Cauche to Rute..............................87
Villanueva del Cauche – Villanueva del Trabuco 87
Villanueva del Trabuco – Villanueva de Tapia 90
Villanueva de Tapia – Villanueva de Algaidas 93
Villanueva de Algaidas – Cuevas de San Marcos 97
Cuevas de San Marcos – Rute 100

Córdoba province – Rute to Alcalá la Real..102
Rute – Priego de Córdoba 104
Sierra Subbética natural park...107
Priego de Córdoba – Almendinilla 109
Almedinilla – Alcalá la Real 111

Jaén province – Alcalá la Real to Puebla de Don Fadrique 115
Alcalá la Real – Frailes..118
Frailes – Carchelejo 120
Carchelejo – Cambil 124
Cambil – Torres 127
Sierra Mágina natural park 128
Torres – Bedmar 131
Bedmar – Jódar 135
Jódar – Quesada 137
Quesada – Cazorla 142
Sierras de Cazorla, Segura y las Villas natural park 144
Cazorla – Vadillo de Castril 147
Vadillo de Castril – Coto-Ríos 151
Coto-Ríos – Pontones 154
Pontones – Santiago de la Espada 158
Santiago de la Espada – Puebla de Don Fadrique................................161

Part 3: Southern Fork – Malaga and Granada 164
Málaga province – Villanueva del Cauche to Ventas de Zafarraya 165
   Villanueva del Cauche – Riogordo 165
   Riogordo – Ventas de Zafarraya 169

Granada province (and Almería) – Ventas de Zafarraya
to Puebla de Don Fadrique 173
   Ventas de Zafarraya – Alhama de Granada 176
    Sierras de Tejeda, Almijara y Alhama natural park 178
   Alhama de Granada – Arenas del Rey 181
   Arenas del Rey – Jayena 183
   Jayena – Albuñuelas 186
   Albuñuelas – Nigüelas 190
    Sierra Nevada natural park 194
   Nigüelas – Lanjarón 195
   Lanjarón – Soportújar 198
   Soportújar – Pitres 202
   Pitres – Trevélez 207
   Trevélez – Cádiar 214
   Cádiar – Yegen 221
   Yegen – Laroles 227
   Laroles – Puerto de la Ragua 234
   Puerto de la Ragua – La Calahorra 239
   La Calahorra – Narváez 243
    Sierra de Baza natural park 245
   Narváez – Zújar 251
   Zújar – Benamaurel 255
   Benamaurel – Cúllar 260
   Cúllar – Orce 262
   Orce – Huéscar 266
   Huéscar – Puebla de Don Fadrique 270

Appendices
Appendix 1: Summary of route itineraries 275
Appendix 2: Spanish–English glossary 284
Appendix 3: Further information 285

The GR7 in Andalucía

N

0 — 18 km

FRANCE

PORTUGAL

Madrid

SPAIN

MEDITERRANEAN SEA

Granada
Northern Fork
Puebla de
Don Fadrique
Tarifa
Southern Fork

CÓRDOBA

Priego
Córdol

Rute

CÁDIZ

Cuevas de
San Marcos

V
c

Villanueva
de Algaidas

Vill
de

Valle de
Abdalajís

Antequera

Ardales

Villanueva
de Cauche

Ríog

Arriate

El Chorro

Montejaque

Ronda

MÁLAGA

Ubrique

MÁLAC

CÁDIZ

Jimena
de la Frontera

COSTA DEL SOL

Los
Barrios

Castellar
de la Frontera

Algeciras

ESTRECHO DE GIBRALTAR

Tarifa

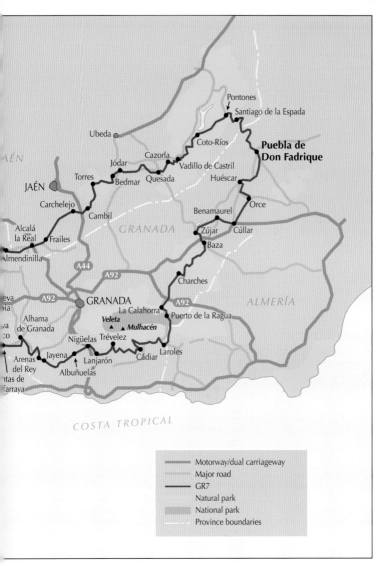

Motorway/dual carriageway
Major road
GR7
Natural park
National park
Province boundaries

MAP KEY

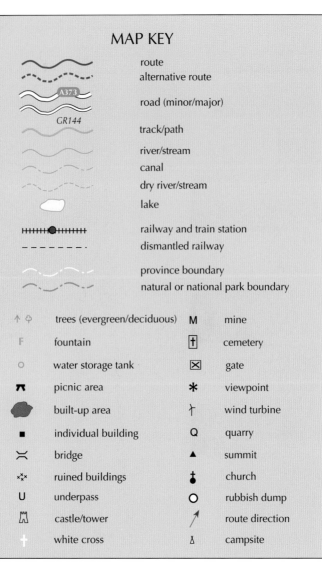

route
alternative route

road (minor/major)

track/path

river/stream

canal

dry river/stream

lake

railway and train station

dismantled railway

province boundary

natural or national park boundary

↑ ↟	trees (evergreen/deciduous)	M	mine
F	fountain	⊺	cemetery
○	water storage tank	⊠	gate
⅋	picnic area	✳	viewpoint
	built-up area	⅄	wind turbine
■	individual building	Q	quarry
≍	bridge	▲	summit
×⁎×	ruined buildings	⸸	church
U	underpass	O	rubbish dump
🏰	castle/tower	↗	route direction
✝	white cross	Å	campsite

Walking between Arenas del Rey and Jayena (Part 3)

Boulder field on the way to Priego de Córdoba (Part 2, Rute – Priego de Córdoba)

INTRODUCTION

With white sand beaches, pine forests, semi-arid desert badlands, snow-capped peaks, fertile plains, traditional agricultural villages, lush expansive river valleys, olive groves and rolling hills of cork woodland, the 1163km of the GR7 in Andalucía take you on a journey through one of the most geographically varied regions on the Iberian peninsula, and possibly even Europe.

The scenically diverse route starts at the southernmost tip of Spain on the coast at Tarifa, and meanders through the province of Cádiz before splitting into two in the Málaga province. Both routes are part of the official GR7 so here the walker has the choice of taking the Northern Fork which heads through Córdoba and Jaén provinces, or the Southern Fork which passes through Almería and Granada. The whole northern route is 711.5km long and takes 34 to 41 days. The southern route is 719.8km and takes 35 to 42 days. The routes rejoin at Puebla de Don Fadrique, the last town in the Andalucian section of the GR7 and the end of this guide. From here the route continues into the region of Murcia. On its journey through Andalucía, the GR7 crosses through seven stunning natural parks and the Sierra Nevada national park, home to mainland Spain's highest peak, Mulhacén.

Andalucía has many faces. It is perhaps most famous amongst holidaymakers for its coastline – a haven for sunseekers but now somewhat spoilt by over-development. The GR7 offers the opportunity to see another of its faces. You will explore little-visited hidden gems, enjoy the natural parks and visit unspoilt peaceful villages. And you can take part in positive rural tourism, supporting small communities by staying and eating in family-run hotels, restaurants and guesthouses.

The GR7 is also a great journey through history and cultures of the past and present. As the southernmost part of Spain, Andalucía is the cultural and geographical borderland between Europe and Africa, connecting the Mediterranean with the Atlantic Ocean. It is infused with romance as the place of the Moors' last stand and has long been an inspiration to artists and writers. Grand fortresses and watchtowers bring to life aspects of the eight centuries of Arab rule and there are also some internationally significant prehistoric sites.

ABOUT ANDALUCÍA

Andalucía is the most southerly of Spain's 17 autonomous communities and has both Mediterranean and Atlantic coastlines. It has its own regional administration, the Junta de Andalucía, based in its capital, Seville, and its other major cities are Granada and Córdoba. At 87,300km^2 it is the

Bubión, example of a whitewashed village (Part 3, Soportújar – Pitres)

second largest region and is divided into eight provinces, six of which the GR7 passes through.

Despite being the most populous of the autonomous communities (with 7.4 million people), much of the land is still uncultivated or being farmed in traditional ways. About half of Andalucía is mountainous, a third of it at altitudes greater than 600m and including 46 peaks over 1000m. It is home to two of the highest peaks of the Iberian peninsula in the Sierra Nevada mountains: Mulhacén (3481m) and Veleta (3398m).

Thanks to regional and national government initiatives over the last two decades, Andalucía now has a significant programme of environmental protection with almost a fifth of its area under some form of protection. There are 24 natural parks, 28 natural reserves, 32 natural areas and two national parks – the route passes through one of these, the Sierra Nevada, as well as through seven natural parks.

Historically, Andalucía has been a poor region, particularly as a result of the *latifundio* land ownership system, dating back to the Roman era, in which a few rich gentry owned vast tracts of land worked by poverty-stricken landless peasants. Until recently there were far sharper, more rigid class distinctions in Andalucía than in the north of the country and often class relations were marked by conflict, with many rebellions over the years.

ABOUT THE ROUTE

The GR7 is one of many waymarked long-distance routes across Europe known as 'GR', which in Spain stands for *Gran Recorrido*. Wherever possible they avoid tarmac roads and traffic, instead taking ancient routes including old trade routes, *caminos reales* (wider routes now protected by royal decree), bridlepaths and even goat tracks. There is an overview map of the route in Andalucía at the beginning of this book. There is a total of 1163km of waymarked GR7 route through the provinces of Cádiz, Málaga, Córdoba, Jaén, Granada and Almería and the route is described here from west to east.

The GR7 is the Spanish part of a much longer trans-European route, the E4, which you will sometimes see mentioned on signboards. This passes through Andalucía, Murcia and Valencia before leaving Spain for France, Switzerland, Germany, Austria, Hungary, Romania, Bulgaria, Greece and Cyprus. The E4 is over 10,000km long and one of 11 long-distance European walking routes (E1-11) which link existing national and local route networks.

The GR7 in Andalucía is a long-distance and challenging route and it is possible to walk the entire length of it (on one of the two routes) in around 40 days. However, it is also varied and versatile and can be broken into shorter sections of many different kinds, offering something for most walkers. While there are many long, strenuous days, ranging

Example of a GR7 signpost

from 15 to 35km, there are also plenty of short sections that could make pleasant day trips or be combined for longer routes. Most sections do not travel far from facilities and civilisation, but there are options to walk longer sections through natural parks with enticing diversions to climb peaks or explore some of Spain's most beautiful wild spaces further. In some of these more remote sections, or to shorten longer days, a tent becomes essential. Otherwise accommodation can be found on the rest of the route, and the remote sections avoided by using public transport if desired. The route is suitable for walkers of a reasonable level of fitness and there are only a few sections with very steep ascents. However, the possibility of high temperates, the weight of a tent and the need to be able to navigate in certain places should be taken into account when deciding which sections to walk and when.

This guide will help the walker make these decisions, dividing the route into potential day walks, detailing all the facilities available and summarising the terrain, height and landscape. A summary of all the routes, including this information, can be found in Appendix 1.

Deciding which sections to walk

Walkers need to decide which of the two GR7 routes in Andalucía to take. Both are part of the official waymarked route, which divides at Villanueva del Cauche in Málaga province. The **Northern Fork** heads through Córdoba and Jaén provinces whilst the **Southern Fork** passes through Almería and Granada. The routes rejoin at Puebla de Don Fadrique, the last town on the GR7 in Andalucía.

The book is divided into three sections: **Part 1** describes the first section of the route, before the split; **Part 2** describes the Northern Fork; and **Part 3** describes the Southern Fork. It is possible to walk the entirety of the 711.5km **Northern Route** (Part 1 plus

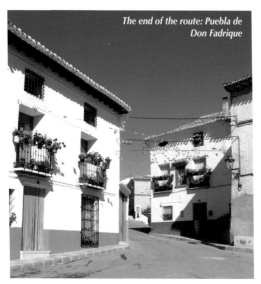
The end of the route: Puebla de Don Fadrique

NORTHERN AND SOUTHERN ROUTE STATISTICS

Route	days	distance (km)	hours	height gain/loss (m)	Tent days
PART 1	**13–17**	**268.5**	**80h30**		**2**
Cádiz province	6–9	155.5	46h00	2740/2040	2
Málaga province	7–8	113.0	34h30	2980/2940	
PART 2: NORTHERN FORK	**21–24**	**443.0**	**111h50**		**3**
Málaga province	5–6	88.0	24h30	1540/1600	1
Córdoba province	3	57.5	14h40	1560/1240	
Jaén province	13–15	297.5	72h40	7640/7400	2
NORTHERN ROUTE TOTAL	**34–41**	**711.5**	**192h20**	**16,460/15,220**	**5**
(Part 1 & Northern Fork)					
PART 3: SOUTHERN FORK	**22–25**	**451.3**	**119h25**		
Málaga province	2	43.0	11h30	1200/980	
Granada province	20–23	408.3	107h55	9940/9840	
SOUTHERN ROUTE TOTAL	**35–42**	**719.8**	**199h55**	**16,860/15,800**	**5**
(Part 1 & Southern Fork)					

the Northern Fork) in 34 to 41 days. The **Southern Route** (Part 1 plus the Southern Fork) is 719.8km long and takes 35 to 42 days to walk. The table above summarises these routes.

Northern Fork

The Northern Fork is the lesser-known of the two options and takes you into beautiful unspoilt areas not yet on the tourist trail, along winding tracks and paths through the olive groves, mountains and natural parks of Córdoba and Jaén.

In Córdoba you follow pretty, old woodland paths in the Parque Natural de la Sierra Subbética, with stunning views across the Subbética mountains, and visit the small town of Rute, famed for its liqueur – *anís* – and Priego de Córdoba, a striking historic town on a plateau. In Jaén the route takes you through the most important mountain ranges in the province: the Sierra Sur, the Sierra Mágina and the Sierras de Cazorla, Segura y las Villas. You get a taste of the beautiful natural wild spaces in the province, especially in the sections which pass through the the largest natural park in Andalucía, the Parque Natural de Cazorla, Segura y las Villas and the Parque Natural de la Sierra Mágina. You also pass through picturesque historic towns and villages including Alcalá la Real, dominated by its eighth-century castle, and the vibrant and beautiful Cazorla. The route then crosses over into the Granada province to join up with the Southern Fork of the GR7 in Puebla de Don Fadrique.

Southern Fork
At the divide in Málaga province, the Southern Fork heads into the hills along the foot of the Sierra de las Cabras and down into the province of Granada. The route in Granada is best known for the section in the Alpujarras with its pretty winding ancient paths joining the dots between tiny whitewashed Berber villages and breathtaking views of snowy peaks. However its less-walked sections are also memorable – from the wild green expanses of three natural parks to the immense sun-baked desert landscapes of the *altiplano*.

En route, you pass through towns and villages with a rich history including the beautiful town of Alhama de Granada with its dramatic gorge and relaxing *balneario* (spa bath) and the villages of the Alpujarras, such as Lanjarón. This fork also crosses briefly into Almería province, through Bayárcal, its highest village at 1255m, and then climbs further to pass over the highest part of the GR7, at the pine-forested pass of Puerto de la Ragua (2000m).

PRACTICAL INFORMATION

Weather and when to go
The climate in Andalucía is Mediterranean and the hottest and driest of anywhere in Spain. Although it varies slightly depending on whether you are inland or on the coast, in general it is very hot and dry in the summer months, especially July and August. Temperatures can exceed 40ºC inland and it is best to avoid walking during this period. Winters are mild on the coast and cool inland, but along the route there is very little in the way of tourist infrastructure open during winter (with the exception of the ski resorts in the Sierra Nevada). The best times to go therefore are spring and autumn, March to June and September to October.

While the Sierra de Grazalema natural park in Cádiz province is noted as one of the wettest places in Spain, the likelihood of consistent rainfall over consecutive days on most of the route is low even in the spring and autumn months. Temperatures in the spring and autumn are warm and make for very pleasant walking although it can still get very hot, especially in June when it may be better to avoid walking in the middle of the day. Conversely, in the higher sections of the route (the Sierra Mágina and the Cazorla, Segura y las Villas natural park in Jaén and in the Alpujarras in Granada in particular) the temperature, though warm during the day, can plummet overnight and it is worth having a warm sleeping bag if you plan to camp.

Aside from the temperature, the abundant wildflowers make spring a wonderful time to visit Andalucía (see 'Wildlife').

Most Spanish people take their holidays over Easter and in July or August and at other times many places can be extremely quiet, the natural parks, in fact, almost empty, and accommodation should be available (see 'Where to stay').

Crossing the plains to Charches (Part 3, La Calahorra – Narváez)

How to get there

You can to travel to Spain from the UK relatively inexpensively by train, aeroplane or boat.

By train: the quickest way is to take the Eurostar from London to Paris and then a connecting sleeper train from Paris to Madrid. From there you can take another sleeper to Algeciras for the start of the route at Tarifa, or a train or bus to other destinations on the route. For more information on train travel in Spain contact RENFE (☎ 902 240 202 www.renfe.es) or on international rail travel from www.raileurope.com or www.seat61.com.

By aeroplane: Málaga, Almería and Granada are the closest airports to the route and several airlines run flights direct to these destinations from the UK. Easyjet fly to Málaga from Bristol, Glasgow, London and Newcastle and to Almería from London (www.easyjet.com). Ryanair fly to Almería and Granada from London and to Madrid from Bournemouth (www.ryanair.com). Flybe fly to Málaga from Birmingham, Exeter, Norwich and Southampton (www.flybe.com).

By boat: Brittany ferries run from Plymouth to Santander and P&O from Portsmouth to Bilbao, both in the north of Spain (www.brittany-ferries.co.uk, www.poferries.com), and these may be a good option if you want to take a car and do sections of the route.

Details of how to get to the start of the route in each province can be found in the respective chapters.

19

Leaving Jimena (Part 1, Jimena de la Frontera – Ubrique)

How to get back

There are local transport links connecting most places on the route back to Granada, Jaén or Málaga, from where you can fly back to the UK (see 'How to get there'). From Puebla de Don Fadrique, the endpoint of both the Northern and Southern Forks, there is a daily (not weekends) bus to Granada (3h45) and Málaga (5h15).

Where to stay

The accommodation you will encounter varies depending on the area you are in. In most areas, accommodation of all types is plentiful but on a few sections of the route there are some quite long stretches without anywhere to stay and you really need to take a tent and camping gear. The following seven routes are those where it would be useful or essential to have a tent.

Cádiz
- Tarifa – Los Barrios (41.5km, essential)
- Jimena de la Frontera – Ubrique (36km and 720m of ascent, useful (can hitch the final 10km))

Málaga
- Villanueva del Trabuco – Villanueva de Tapia (28km, useful (can shortcut to reduce to 20km))

Jaén
- Frailes – Carchelejo (35km and 1280m of ascent, essential)
- Jódar – Quesada (34.5km, useful, camping allowed at Hornos de Peal)

Granada
- Jayena – Albuñuelas (31.5km, useful, could be skipped by bus)
- La Calahorra – Narváez (49km and 1060m of ascent, essential)

The rest of the route can easily be walked between hostels and hotels, although, if you do choose to take a tent, there are also options throughout for camping (official campsites are indicated by a 🏕 symbol in accommodation boxes and the route table in Appendix 1). There are more campsites on the Southern Fork than the Northern Fork.

Hotels have a star rating from one to five according to facilities. The stars are supposed to indicate price bands but are set by local authorities and vary from province to province. *Pensiónes* and *hostales* are also star-rated, from one to three. Accommodation is only likely to be booked up in August, Easter and for other local fiestas. However, if you're doing a long day and planning to arrive late, you may want to call ahead to have the comfort of knowing a bed is waiting for you.

Types of accommodation
Albergue – A basic hostel often with dormitories, but sometimes only available to groups and need to be booked in advance.

Apartamento – self-catering apartments often let for a minimum period of two days.

Camping – There are three types of camping ground:

- Free *permitted camping areas* in national and natural parks, often without any facilities but sometimes with a drinking fountain and benches. Further information on this is provided, where available, in each of the natural park information boxes.
- *Registered campsites* for which you have to pay. These are divided into three categories according to facilities, from showers and toilets to swimming pools, bar/restaurants, shop and laundry. Many campsites also have bungalows.
- It is also worth asking about *camping on private land* as people are often amenable to you putting up a tent, as long as you ask permission first.

Casas rurales – country houses let out as whole self-catering houses or by the room. Many of them are tastefully renovated traditional buildings. They are often family-run businesses and can have real character. Those let on a whole-house basis are often only available for a minimum of two nights but it is worth asking if you only want a night.

Hostal – simple small guesthouse or hotel with fewer facilities and services and therefore generally cheaper than a hotel (and not to be confused with a hostel).

Hotel – likely to be slightly more expensive and more comfortable than a *hostal* with the same number of stars.

*View of Sierra del Palo (highest peak 1400m) en route to Montejaque
(Part 1, Ubrique – Montejaque)*

Pensión – standard budget accommodation, usually small places offering rooms for the night, often above a bar.

Refugio – hostel in mountain areas and natural parks, as with *albergues* not always open access. They sometimes need booking ahead and are only for groups.

Facilities

Depending on which section of the route you are walking, the frequency of refreshment stops, accommodation and other facilities varies quite significantly. It is possible to walk the vast majority of the route in manageable day walks which take you from one village with accommodation and food to another. In some sections of the route, particularly the Alpujarras, you will pass through several villages each day, all with drinking fountains, and most with cafés, bars and grocers.

However, there are a few sections which are more remote, mainly those which go through natural parks. These require you to stock up on supplies and carry a tent. If you prefer not to carry camping gear these sections can be avoided by taking public transport (see each section for details of bus times and routes). You can check the facilities available on each route and in each village using the symbols in the information boxes and route descriptions. They are also summarised in the table in Appendix 1.

Most facilities (shops, pharmacies, tourist offices and museums) are closed for a long lunchtime siesta of at least two hours. There is some variation but common opening hours are 9.30am–2pm and 5–8pm, although bakers and bars will often be open as early as 6.30am if you want to pick up bread or grab a quick coffee first thing. Most shops close on Saturday afternoons and shops and many bars close on Sundays, with some also closed on Mondays. There is a plethora of local public holidays, some of which can be specific to individual villages and so hard to predict. It is best to have a little extra food in case you are caught out and find everything unexpectedly shut for the day, and also worth asking locals whether there are any upcoming fiestas.

Maps

Anyone deciding to walk this route, or any part of it, should take detailed topographical maps. The sketch maps provided in this book are intended as a guide and, due to the limitations of space, can only give an indication of what the route will be like. Having said that, Spanish maps are notoriously unreliable, sometimes putting villages in the wrong place altogether.

The best option is to get the 1:50,000 Servicio Geografico del Ejercito (Spanish Military Survey) maps. These maps are accurate but some are now quite out of date and so may be missing the odd new road. You can buy them very cheaply online from Spain at www.tiendaverde.org or from the UK at

1:50,000 SERVICIO GEOGRAFICO DEL EJERCITO MAPS FOR THE ROUTE					
Part 1: Cádiz and Málaga		**Part 2: Northern Fork**		**Part 3: Southern Fork**	
13-48 **1077**	Tarifa	17-42 **1024**	Archidona	17-43 **1039**	Colmenar
13-47 **1074**	Tahivilla	17-41 **1007**	Rute	18-43 **1040**	Zafarraya
14-47 **1075**	San Roque	17-40 **989**	Lucena	19-43 **1041**	Dúrcal
14-46 **1071**	Jimena de la Frontera	18-40 **990**	Alcalá la Real	20-32 **1042**	Lanjarón
14-45 **1064**	Cortes de la Frontera	19-40 **991**	Iznalloz	21-43 **1043**	Berja
14-44 **1050**	Ubrique	19-39 **969**	Valdepeñas de Jaén	21-42 **1028**	Aldeire
15-44 **1051**	Ronda	20-38 **948**	Torres	21-41 **1011**	Guadix
15-43 **1037**	Teba	19-38 **947**	Jaén	21-40	Benalúa de Guadix
16-43 **1038**	Ardales	20-37 **927**	Baeza	22-40	Baza
16-42 **1023**	Antequera	21-37 **928**	Cazorla	22-39	Cúllar
17-43 **1039**	Colmenar	22-36 **908**	Santiago de la Espada	23-39 **973**	Chirivel
17-43 **1039**	Colmenar	21-36 **907**	Villacarrillo	23-38 **951**	Orce
		23-37 **930**	Puebla de Don Fadrique	22-38 **950**	Huéscar
				23-36 **909**	Nerpio
				23-37 **930**	Puebla de Don Fadrique

www.stanfords.co.uk. Leave at least a month for delivery from both. If you can't wait that long, you may be able to buy them in person from Stanfords in London (12–14 Long Acre, Covent Garden; call 020 7836 1321 to check stock), The Map Shop in Upton-on-Severn (15 High Street, Upton upon Severn, Worcestershire WR8 0HJ ☎ 0800 085 40 80) and from Cartográfica del Sur in Madrid (C/Valle Inclán 2, ☎ 958 204 901).

The maps that you need are listed in order in the introduction to each province and also in the table on page 23.

Waymarking
The route is marked with red-and-white markings which appear on specific sign-posts, small markers and often various landmarks, such as rocks or trees. The signposts show the next place on the route and, often, the estimated time to get there. How well the route is marked depends on the area, and the timings are also unreliable (see 'How to use this guide').

What to take
What you take will vary according to the season in which you are travelling, but, even in summer, be prepared for cold mornings and evenings at high altitude and the occasional rain storm.

Essentials
- Comfortable clothes – several thin layers for dealing with temperature changes throughout the day and at different altitudes
- Comfortable rucksack (try not to

overpack and keep the weight down)
- Waterproof jacket and trousers
- Waterproof rucksack cover (not essential) and plastic bags for organising the contents of your rucksack and keeping them dry
- Strong waterproof walking boots with ankle support and good grip (ideally ones that you have already worn in)
- Sandals
- Maps
- Compass
- Whistle
- Torch and headlamp
- Food (have emergency supplies even if you expect to pass through villages with shops and beware the 2–5pm siesta when most shops are shut)
- A water bottle big enough to carry plenty of water (fountains along the route are marked but there is no guarantee that they will have water in summer)
- Sun protection (hat, sunglasses and sun cream are essential)
- First aid kit and toiletries including a good selection of plasters and blister products, painkillers, insect repellent and antihistamine and ankle supports
- Supply of euros and a credit card
- Tent and camping equipment (essential for a few sections of the GR7, if you are not planning to skip them)

Useful extras
- Water purification tablets
- Walking poles to ease the weight of your pack and to fend off dogs

The view on leaving Pampaneira (Part 3, Soportújar – Pitres)

- A pedometer for check your own progress against the descriptions
- A mobile phone for emergencies – there is reception along much of the route
- Camera
- Lightweight binoculars

Safety and emergencies

In general, Andalucía is a very safe place to travel through. You do not need any vaccinations and if you are an EU citizen you will be covered for healthcare by your European Health Insurance Card (EHIC), free from the post office. You should still get travel insurance to cover you for the cost of medication that you may be prescribed and also to cover you for theft or loss of belongings.

Bites and stings

There are five types of venomous snakes in Spain. The only one that you might come across in Andalucía is the Lataste's viper. Distinguished by its triangular head and distinctive zigzag pattern, it is grey and short (around 50cm) and lives in dry, rocky areas, away from human habitation. It is thankfully rare but if you are unlucky enough to be bitten, seek medical attention immediately as its bite can be fatal and you will need to be treated with a serum (stocked by most Spanish medical centres).

In the more forested sections of the route look out for hairy reddish-brown caterpillars. They can cause an allergic skin reaction if you touch them. There are also scorpions in parts of Andalucía and their sting can be extremely painful but not fatal. Check your boots in the morning!

Dogs

Most rural houses and farms in Andalucía have at least one guard dog to scare people away from the property. This means that you are likely to encounter unfriendly dogs at some point on your trip. In general, they will do little more than bark at you and they will usually back down if you bend to pick up a small stone. For the occasional dog that looks as if it might do more than bark it is sensible to carry a walking pole.

For women travellers

While instances of attacks on women in Spain are low, there is a more overtly masculine culture in Spain than in Britain and men are more likely to whistle, sound their car horns and shout comments at you. Try to take sensible precautions to keep yourself safe: don't walk about in towns or cities in the dark by yourself; carry a phone with you if possible; don't accept lifts from strangers; and, if you are wild camping near a town or village, choose your pitch carefully and don't let strangers know where it is.

General walking safety tips

- Tell someone where you are going.
- Keep to a clear path and avoid taking shortcuts unless you are absolutely confident that you know where you are going.
- Be aware that the weather can change rapidly. Bad weather

including fog, rain and storms can come in quickly and unexpectedly.
- Be aware that dry riverbeds and streams can quickly flood in storms.
- Help to protect and maintain the area you are walking through.
- Carry a whistle and torch. (The international distress call is six long blasts (or torch flashes at night) evenly spaced over a minute, followed by a minute's pause, and repeated until an answer is received. The answer is three signals per minute.)

Police

There are three different police forces in Spain:

- the **Guardia Civil** wear green uniforms and are responsible for national security and customs;
- the **Policía Nacional** normally wear a black uniform and white shirts and are responsible for guarding public buildings, the royal family and government figures. They also respond to crimes so you should contact them in the event of any trouble; and
- the **Policía Municipal** wear blue and white uniforms and spend most of their time controlling local traffic and giving parking tickets but can be a good source of local information. If you are a victim of theft the local Policía Municipal office is also the place to go to report the crime and get the police report that you will need to claim on your insurance.

Emergency contacts

The main number to call in any type of emergency is the European emergency number – 112. This is the urgent police, fire brigade or ambulance number and is also the number to call if you are lost in the mountains as they will connect you to local rescue teams.

Other useful numbers:

- Policía Nacional 091
- Policía Municipal 092
- Guardia Civil 062
- Rapid response health line (24 hour) 902 111 444
- Duty pharmacies 010
- British Consular Emergency Service 915 249 700
- British Embassy General Enquiries 917 008 200

BACKGROUND INFORMATION

Culture

Andalucians have a rich and distinct culture and a strong sense of regional identity. They are known for being gregarious and for enjoying parties and crowds. The area is particularly famous for being the home of both flamenco and bullfighting.

Flamboyant flamenco music – a fusion of Arabic, Jewish and other styles of music – originated in the southwest of the region in the 18th century and is still hugely popular today.

Bullfighting is thought to have originated in the Roman era and there are still more than 150 bullrings in Andalucía, including the famous one in Ronda. The bullfighting season, which lasts from Easter Sunday to October, is popular in Andalucía and much less controversial than it is in the north of Spain.

Andalucía is also known for its colourful *fiestas* and *ferias* (local festivals and fairs). Most villages have their own *fiesta* (and usually more than one). The main religious event is Semana Santa (Holy week) when you will encounter processions with crowds bearing huge effigies of Jesus and Mary. *Carnaval* in February or March is also important, with parties and fancy dress parades – especially in Cádiz. The main village *ferias* are usually in the summer. They originated from regional cattle markets and now often involve bullfighting, a fairground, parade and all-night singing, music, dancing and drinking.

The area is also known for having retained many of its traditional arts and crafts and these are now flourishing again with the advent of tourism. In many of the villages you will find workshops for pottery, leatherwork, rugmaking, furniture, copper, gold and silverwork, wickerwork and handmade musical instruments.

Andalucian cuisine

The region's food has been influenced by many cultures and especially Arabian cuisine, in dishes using citrus fruits, almonds, spices, mint, and also pastries and cakes.

In the villages you will visit the food tends to be simple and often based on meat (including game and ham, especially in the high mountain villages where it is cured), seafood or cheese (sheep, goat, cow and combinations of the three). Fresh local ingredients are usually on offer in the restuarants,

Eating in local bars and restaurants (Part 3, Puerto de la Ragua – La Calahorra)

including olives, lots of olive oil, oranges, lemons, chestnuts, avocados and game.

Typical Andalucian dishes include: stews using the famous *rabo de toro* (oxtail stew), fried fish, *gazpacho* (refreshing cold tomato soup), *jamón serrano* (mountain-cured ham) and prepared olives. Deserts are not a great feature of the menus – there will usually be *flan* (crème caramel) and ice cream on offer. Sometimes you will come across traditional deserts including *pestiños de miel* (honey-coated pastry fritters), *amarguillos* (almond macaroons) and *polvorónes* (almond cookies). Bread, generally white, is usually provided with your meal and most villages have their own bakeries.

There are a few vegetarian options on offer in most bars and restaurants. However, be aware that apparently vegetarian dishes may contain chopped ham or seafood. *Gazpacho*, *revueltos* (scrambled egg), cheese and lots of egg and potatoes are likely to be your standard diet.

Tapas

In many bars the main food on offer is *tapas*, often sitting warming on the bar in a glass display cabinet. These are snacks but can be combined to make up a full meal. One or two portions of tapas are sometimes offered free with your drinks. You can also ask for larger portions of them: a whole plateful is a *ración* and half a plateful is a *media ración*.

COMMON TAPAS

alchofas	artichokes
alioli	garlicy oil/mayonaise paste usually served on bread or with potatoes, fish or meat
boquerones	anchovies (often marinated in garlic olive oil and vinegar)
chocos fritos	fried battered squid
chopitos	baby squid
chorizo al vino	chorizo sausage slowly cooked in wine
ensaladilla	Russian salad of boiled vegetables with tuna, olives and mayonnaise
gambas	prawns
habas con jamón	broad beans with ham
pinchos	mini kebabs (usually pork or chicken)
patatas bravas	fried potatoes, served with a tomato salsa and mayonnaise
queso con anchoas	cheese with anchovies
rajo	pork seasoned with garlic and parsley
revuelto de esparragos	scrambled egg with asparagus
tortilla de patatas	omelette containing fried chunks of potatoes and sometimes onion
tortillitas de camarones	battered prawns

Wines and liquors

Andalucía has a long tradition of wine production (possibly dating back to the Phoenicians). It is popular and cheap and you can order it in bars by the glass (*copa*) or bottle (*botella*). Almost every village has its own local wine, but not all of them are great! Make sure you try the sherry and the other liquors of the region such as the *anís* made in Rute.

Language

If you speak Spanish it will be a great help in your travels in Andalucía, as in most of the villages you'll pass through on the route very little English is spoken (although it is more commonly spoken in tourist areas, especially the Alpujarras). Even if you don't speak any

Spanish it is worth getting hold of a phrase book and having a go as people will appreciate the effort. Appendix 2 is a glossary of Spanish words that will be useful en route.

History

Andalucía's location on the edge of Europe and Africa has made its history active, colourful and often bloody since prehistoric times. Its fertile land has also made it desirable territory for farming communities throughout history. The key periods in Andalucian history are outlined below.

Prehistoric Andalucía

During the Palaeolithic era (the last Ice Age to 8000BC) there were significant numbers of hunter-gatherer peoples living in Andalucía. Orce, in the Granada province, is famous for a bone fragment found in 1982 which holds a disputed status as a fragment of the oldest known human in Europe (possibly over a million years old) (see Part 3, Granada province, Cúllar – Orce). Along the route there are a few sites where you can see cave paintings such as the Cueva de Ardales (see Part 1, Malaga province, Arriate – Ardales) and other caves near Ronda. You can also visit some of Spain's best known dolmens (large tombs made of rocks constructed in the Chalcolithic age) near Antequera (see Part 1, Malaga province, Valle de Abdalajís – Antequera).

8th to 7th century BC: Tartessos
In the eighth and seventh centuries BC the Tartessos culture flourished in western Andalucía. It is thought to have been very rich, with advanced gold- and iron-working techniques. It was influenced by Phoenician (from present-day Lebanon) and later Greek traders, who exchanged perfumes, ivory, jewellery, oil, wine and textiles for Andalucian silver and bronze.

6th to 1st century BC: Iberians
From the sixth century BC the Phoenicians and Greeks were pushed out of Andalucía by the Iberians or Carthaginians from further north in Spain.

1st century BC to 5th century AD: Romans
The Iberians came into conflict with the growing power base of Rome and southern Spain was fought over by the two groups. In 206BC the Romans finally beat the Iberians and soon after built Italica, the first Roman town in Spain, near modern-day Seville. Andalucía became wealthy under the Romans, with Rome importing many Andalucian products such as wheat, vegetables, grapes, olives, copper, silver, lead and fish.

5th to 8th century: Visigoths
Throughout the third, fourth and fifth centuries the central authority of Rome waned and Germanic tribes invaded the territories of the Roman empire, including the Iberian peninsula. Rome was taken over by the Visigoths in 410AD and they then went on to occupy the Iberian peninsula. The Visigoths maintained many Roman institutions and did not mix with the Spanish population until the period of Muslim rule and so the Visigoth language left little trace on modern Iberian languages.

8th to 15th century: Al-Andalus
The Arabs and Islam spread through the Middle East and north Africa in the eighth century and in AD711, Arabs (Moors) landed at Gibraltar. Over the next few years they took almost all of Spain (except for areas of the northwest and Basque areas in the Pyrenees).

The Moors ruled throughout a vast area called Al-Andalus which encompassed parts of north Africa, Spain and Portugal. Their heartland was modern-day Andalucía. They were in power across most of the Iberian peninsula for four centuries and continued to be a dominant force for another three, developing the most advanced society in western Europe at the time.

Leaving Benamaurel (with Jabalcón in the distance) (Part 3, Benamaurel – Cúllar)

The Moors left behind them beautiful palaces, mosques, gardens, bathhouses and universities, and in rural areas they left impressive irrigation systems and new crops such as oranges, lemons, sugar cane and rice.

Throughout the period of Arab rule, internal conflict was rife between the rulers (made up of various Muslim groups), the Berbers (North African commoners who were often given poor quality land), and the Christians, who were allowed freedom of worship but paid extra taxes. Throughout this period power shifted from one Arab dynasty to another including the Omayyades, Almoravides, Almohades and Nasrides. There was also near-constant conflict on its borders with Christians, although for a long time they posed little threat to Al-Andalus, which was far stronger in terms of population, economy, culture and military might. As time went on intermarriage between powerful families living in the Christian north and in the Muslim south of Spain became commonplace.

8th to 15th century: Reconquista

The Reconquista, the Christian takeover of Spain, was a long, drawn-out process with internal fighting between Christian realms as well as between Christians and Muslims. Over the centuries, the Christian and Muslim populations became increasingly intermingled, making it less of a Christian crusade than a series of local, territorial conflicts.

31

In 1212, a coalition of Christian kings drove the Muslims from the centre of Spain. However, the Nasrid Emirate of Granada, whose domain included the modern provinces of Granada, Málaga and Almería as well as parts of Cádiz, Córdoba, Jaén and Sevilla, continued to be extremely powerful as a vassal state to the Christian kingdom until 1492.

The Treaty (or Capitulation) of Granada to the Catholic Monarchs, King Fernando II of Aragon and Queen Isabella of Castile, was ratified at the end of 1491 by Boabdil of Granada (Abu 'Abd Allah Muhammad). It guaranteed rights to the Moors, including religious tolerance in return for their unconditional surrender. Boabdil received the Alpujarras (through which the GR7 passes) as a fiefdom but only stayed a year or so.

For the first time since the Visigoth era, the Catholic monarchs then united most of modern Spain religiously, politically and economically under one rule and brought Spain into power and prominence in Europe. The promised religious tolerance didn't last long. Muslims were forced to convert to Christianity or deported to Africa and Jews were also persecuted. In 1499, Cardinal Cisneros, the leader of the Spanish Inquisition, forced about 50,000 Moors in Granada into mass baptisms. Islamic books were burnt, the Arabic language banned and Muslims' land confiscated.

After a quashed rebellion that started in 1500 in the Alpujarras, people who refused baptism or deportation to Africa were killed and there was a mass exodus of Muslims and Jews. In 1567 a second Alpujarran rebellion led to all *Moriscos* (Muslims converted to Christianity) being deported.

16th to 17th century: Seville, empire and the Golden Age

Through the conquest of most of South America and the West Indies, Spain began to establish itself as an empire with huge quantities of gold and silver being sent back to Spain. Seville was the premier city in Spain until the 17th century, one of the richest and largest in Europe and a world trade hub. This opened Andalucía up to new European ideas and artistic movements and its cities flourished. Rural Andalucía, however, remained extremely poor with a handful of rich landowners controlling large tracts of land on which they just kept sheep. Few peasants owned any land or property.

The Golden Age soon came to an end, with economic losses and mismanagement leading to a trade deficit. A decline in silver shipments combined with poor harvests led to the death of about 300,000 people, which, combined with the expulsion of the *Moriscos*, caused underpopulation and several economic collapses.

18th century: the Enlightenment and the Bourbons

In the 18th century, the French Bourbon Dynasty, which is Spain's ruling family again today, took control of Spain and the country enjoyed a limited economic recovery. Spanish ports traded with the Americas, stimulating the growth of Málaga, and new settlers from other parts of the country came to boost Andalucía's population.

The impressive Renaissance castle-palace at La Calahorra
(Part 3, Puerto de la Ragua – La Calahorra)

19th century: Napoleonic Wars – the reformation

During 1808–14, Spain initially sided against France in the Napoleonic Wars, but early defeats lead to a decision to shift allegiance and side with the revolutionary French. Eventually, the Spanish were defeated along with the French at the decisive Battle of Trafalgar in 1805, prompting the Spanish king to reconsider his alliance with France. This led Napoleon Bonaparte, Emperor of France, to invade Spain in 1808 and depose the king, thereby starting the Spanish War of Independence in which the Spanish people fought guerrilla-style against the French, finally driving them out with support from the British and Portuguese armies led by the Duke of Wellington.

Cádiz withstood a two-year siege by Napoleon's army to become the last bastion of Spain's anti-monarchist, liberal movement. During the French occupation, the national parliament was based there and, in 1812, that parliament declared the first Spanish constitution, which proclaimed the people's sovereignty and reduced the power of the monarchy, nobility and church.

However, Ferdinand VII revoked the new constitution and continued to rule in an authoritarian style, temporarily reinstating the Inquisition. Whilst he and his liberal opponents struggled in Spain, revolution then broke out in the Spanish colonies. Taking advantage of Spain's weakness, they won their independence.

In 1836 and 1855, to reduce the national debt, successive liberal governments auctioned off church and municipal lands, allowing the rich to build up bigger estates and plunging peasants deeper into poverty as they lost vital grazing land. Andalucía had a sharply divided population of rich landed gentry and poor landless seasonal workers who were mostly desperately poor and illiterate. In 1873 Spain briefly became a republic – a federation of 17 states – but it immediately came under attack from all sides and collapsed when the monarchy was reinstated by the army less than a year later.

Early 20th century: rebellion, dictatorship, republic and civil war

At the beginning of the 20th century, Andalucian peasants staged various brutally crushed uprisings against their miserable conditions. In 1910 an anarchist union, the CNT, was founded in Seville and grew to almost 100,000 Andalucian members in just nine years.

After a period of military dictatorship between 1923 and 1930, a second Spanish republic was established in 1931 but fractious, rapidly changing governing coalitions led to serious political unrest. In 1933, a right-wing government was elected and violence erupted between left-wing groups and the government, and in 1936 the country slid into civil war.

The vicious conflict between Nationalists and Republicans led to over 350,000 deaths including massacres of civilians and prisoners. In Andalucía, communist and socialist groups tried to bring about anarchist revolution, seizing land, killing church officials and burning churches. About 100 agrarian communities were established.

On 1 April 1939, this brutal war ended with the downfall of the Republic and General Francisco Franco's installation as dictator. Franco formed an alliance between all the right-wing parties and banned the left-wing and Republican parties and trade unions. About 100,000 people are thought to have been killed after he took power.

1939–75: the Franco dictatorship

During Franco's rule, Spain remained largely economically and culturally isolated from the outside world. Although supposedly neutral in World War II, Franco lent his support to the Nazis, as a result of which, after the war, Spain suffered the effects of an international blockade. The 1940s were known as the hunger years, with peasants in poor areas Andalucía barely managing to survive.

With the latter years of Franco's rule came some economic and political liberalization, the so-called Spanish Miracle, including the launch of mass foreign tourism on Andalucía's coast. However Spain remained way behind the rest of Europe.

1975 to the present day: democracy and economic boom

Franco ruled until he died on 20 November 1975 and King Juan Carlos came to power. He oversaw the shift to a new democratic state and a liberalization of society. In 1982 the centre-left PSOE were elected and Felipe Gonzalez became Prime Minster and proceeded to govern for 14 years.

In 1982, devolution created a regional government in Andalucía, which the PSOE also controlled. Both national and regional government took positive steps to tackle poverty in the

Camorro de la Isla (Part 2, Cuevas de San Marcos – Rute)

1980s with grants, community work schemes, social security support and some land reform to tackle the unjust ownership system.

By the 1990s, the PSOE were in decline and they lost the 1996 elections to centre-right Partido Popular, which then governed for eight years until 2004. After their unpopular decision to support the Iraq war, and three days after the Madrid bombings of 11 March, they were unseated in favour of a new socialist government.

Over the past few years Andalucía has experienced a huge boom in tourism and industry and has benefitted from EU subsidies for agriculture. However, the region still has high unemployment and in the rural areas, through which the GR7 passes, life can be tough. Over a fifth of the population still relies on agriculture for income.

Current issues

Immigration

Modern-day Andalucía is still the gateway between Europe and Africa and home to a significant proportion of Spain's one million Muslims. There are many Moroccan migrant workers and frequent reports of illegal immigrants' desperate and often tragic attempts to cross the Straits of Gibraltar. Illegal immigrants are open to exploitation and, in rural areas, there are many stories of immigrants being paid low wages and working in poor conditions in intensive vegetable cultivation. Although the area has a rosy reputation for positive racial integration, in the context of heightened European-wide anxiety about immigration and terrorism, the issue is becoming more politicised and debates more heated.

Drought

The combination of two water-intensive activities – agriculture and tourism – is taking a heavy toll on Andalucía. This is especially true of the tourist coast where a vast increase in the number of swimming pools and heavily watered golf courses is having a serious environmental impact.

It is also causing problems inland in some of the villages that you will visit on the GR7. Land which was once fertile is now parched and infertile. The Junta de Andalucía has a ten-year plan to combat desertification, including the reforestation of mountains, financial aid for farmers and education programmes to inform the public about environmentally friendly farming methods and water conservation. There are also ongoing debates about controversial plans to divert water from the north to the south.

Wildlife

The animal and plant life of Andalucía is heavily influenced, and made unique, by its location at the meeting point between Africa and Europe and by the area's geographic diversity. The meeting of the cold Atlantic and the warm Mediterranean at Tarifa make for a distinctive climate which is abundant in bird, reptile, and mammal and plant life.

Andalucía sits on one of two key migration routes for birds between Europe and Africa and is a paradise for birdwatchers. There are over 250 species which are resident all year round in Andalucía, with more wintering there. Of the resident species, 13 are birds of prey, one of which is the Spanish Imperial Eagle, which, as its name suggests, is only found in Spain. There are also golden eagles, black vultures (Europe's largest bird), griffon vultures and red kites. You are also likely to come across storks nesting on top of telegraph poles and church towers in the spring. In terms of smaller birds, the most distinctive and exotic to look out for is the golden oriole, which has a bight yellow body.

Lizards are extremely common in Andalucía and you will see and hear them all along the route. Some of the rustling you hear may also be one of the 13 different types of snake that can be found in Spain, five of which are venomous (see 'Safety and emergencies'). One of the most common to Andalucía is the ladder snake which is not venomous and named for the pattern along its back.

Mammals you may spot include red and roe deer, red squirrels, foxes, including the distinctive grey Spanish fox, and mountain goats or ibex. The wild boar is also common along much of the GR7 route but it is nocturnal and so harder to spot. Wolves do still live in Andalucía in small numbers and are now mainly found in northern Córdoba.

Andalucía is also host to 5000 species of plants and trees. Several types of oak, pine, ash, alder, willow and poplar trees are all common, with some very large forests. Wild olive trees survive alongside the huge olive plantations which in total cover more than 4500km of Andalucía. The plant life is unusually varied owing to the great geographic diversity. Lower regions are dominated by olives and pastures with other trees

Dandelion

Broom

Almonds

Olives

Birds of prey

Ladder snake

Limestone peak in the Sierra Subbética natural park (Part 2, Rute – Priego de Córdoba)

occupying higher slopes alongside beautiful and aromatic wild herbs such as rosemary, thyme and lavender.

National and natural parks

The route of the GR7 passes through eight natural or national parks: Los Alcornocales and Sierra de Grazalema in Cádiz province; Sierra Subbética in Córdoba province; Sierras de Cazorla, Segura y las Villas and Sierra Mágina in Jaén province; and Sierras de Tejeda, Almijara y Alhama, Sierra Nevada (a national park) and Sierra de Baza in Granada province.

In 1918, Spain was one of the first countries in Europe to establish **national parks** and the mainland is now home to ten, encompassing over 1200km² of land. The national parks are designated as areas of important ecological, scientific and educational value that, on the whole, have remain untouched by human intervention or developments. Throughout Spain there are also numerous **natural parks**. These are protected ecosystems or areas of outstanding natural beauty.

Both national and natural parks are controlled by individual autonomous regions, such as Andalucía province. Most tend to be areas of wilderness with little in the way of settlements or infrastructure, making them wonderful places to get away from it all and also for spotting wildlife. Walking routes have been developed throughout and most parks have their own tourist office or offices with full details of walks, along with other park information.

The geography of the parks varies greatly from forest to salt plains across Spain, but those through which the GR7 passes tend to be dominated by mountains (the Parque Natural de Los Alcornocales being the exception), from the rocky limestone peaks of the Sierra de Grazalema in Cádiz province, to the lush slopes of the Sierra Subbética in Córdoba province and the pines and aridity of the Sierra de Baza in Granada province.

Descriptions of the plants and animals to be found in each park are given in information boxes within the relevant province chapters.

HOW TO USE THIS GUIDE

The main body of the book is made up of detailed route descriptions. As covered in more detail in the 'About the route' section above, the route descriptions are divided into three parts: Part 1 covers the route in the provinces of Cádiz and Málaga up until the point where the route divides into two forks. Part 2 describes the Northern Fork, which continues through Córdoba and Jaén provinces, and Part 3 describes the Southern Fork, which passes through Almería and Granada. Both routes rejoin at Puebla de Don Fadrique, the last town in the Andalucian section of the GR7.

Within these three parts, the book is divided into provinces each with an introduction giving an overview of the route within that province, transport to and within the province, and further tourist information and information on walking in the area. (The small section of the route that crosses into Almería province is included in the Granada province section.) These province introductions, combined with the overall introduction to the book and the route summaries in Appendix 1, should provide you with the information you need to choose the sections that you would like to walk.

Within each province, the route is divided up into sections which, in the main, can be walked within a day and always end at a place with accommodation. These sections vary in length, reflecting the location of towns and villages along the route and also the strenuousness of the walking. A handful of sections are longer than can easily be walked in a day. To walk these sections, which are highlighted in the 'Where to stay' section above, you would need to have a tent, or be prepared to take a shortcut, hitch or take public transport to get to other accommodation. Conversely, there are many sections which include places with accommodation along the way. Details of these are included to give you the flexibility to plan short days or rest days, or put together your own itinerary altogether.

All towns and villages with accommodation have their facilities outlined in an information box. Each box describes the local facilities, sites and sources of further information. Sometimes a range of prices for accommodation indicates seasonal fluctuations or a choice of rooms. Facilities – such a drinking fountains, bars and campsites – situated in places not large enough to merit an information box, are highlighted in blue in the body of the text.

In many places, there is no tourist information office but often town halls will provide you with local information. Where this is the case, the telephone number for the town hall has been included. Facilities are shown in symbol form.

The timings given in the route headings are based on a person of average fitness. They do not include rests, which should be added in, as a five-hour route could be a full day out, especially in hot sunshine. The descriptions also include timings given on GR7 posts to give an indication of where you are on a route, although these seem to vary in accuracy depending on which area you are in. The text indicates where the timings appear inaccurate.

The route descriptions identify the different types of terrain that the route follows. 'Path' refers to something that is not

FACILITIES SYMBOLS	
⌐	accommodation (hotel, *hostal*, *casa rural* and so on)
🏕	campsite
🍴	restaurant, café or bar with food
F	drinking fountain
▲	food shop (supermarket or small grocery store)
€	cashpoint
☎	telephone
✉	post office
✚	pharmacy
①	tourist information
🚌	transport
🖥	internet access

suitable for vehicles and, generally, single file. A 'track' may be suitable for some 4x4 vehicles and a 'road' is either tarmac or concrete and suitable for all vehicles.

Where the route description refers to places or features shown on the sketch map, these features are highlighted in the text in bold.

PART 1
CÁDIZ AND MÁLAGA
Tarifa to Villaneuva del Cauche

The small village of Villaneuva del Cauche at the end of Part 1

41

CÁDIZ PROVINCE

Tarifa to Montejaque, 155.5km

The GR7 starts its trip eastwards in Cádiz province where, from Tarifa on the coast, it travels over 150km through striking and ever-changing landscapes.

From Tarifa, at the southwesternmost point of Spain, where the Atlantic meets the Mediterranean, the route takes you through beautiful rolling hills, up to the dramatic Ojén mountains and into the Parque Natural de los Alcornocales, home to one of the world's largest cork oak groves.

You pass through the small town of Los Barrios and then, within the park, you visit the village of Castillo de Castellar, almost entirely located within a medieval fortress perched on a hilltop. From there you carry on to Jimena de la Frontera dominated by its Arab castle, and then into the wilderness of the Cortes de la Frontera before arriving in the once-Roman town of Ubrique.

The route then crosses the Parque Natural de la Sierra de Grazalema, famous for the rare Spanish fir, caves and spectacular limestone gorges and cliffs. The park is home to the beautiful whitewashed villages of Benacoaz and Villaluenga del Rosario which you visit before crossing spectacular limestone peaks to enter the Málaga province, just before the village of Montejaque.

Travel

It is possible to get to the start of the route in Tarifa by a variety of means. By train, Algeciras (a very regular 30min bus journey away) is the closest station with trains going there direct from Granada (4h30) and Madrid (6h or 11h) or from Málaga, Córdoba and Seville if you change at Bobadilla. Buses also run regularly from these destinations to Algeciras, or direct to Tarifa from Seville (3h) and Málaga (2h).

HIGHLIGHTS OF THE ROUTE IN CÁDIZ PROVINCE

- the 5km stretch of white sand and blue sea that starts the route in Tarifa
- the many birds of prey and vultures circling overhead in the thermals near the coast
- the abundant cork groves of the Parque Natural de los Alcornocales
- the imposing limestone crags of the Parque Natural de la Sierra de Grazalema
- the whitewashed mountainside villages, famous throughout Andalucía

Walking amongst the wild flowers between Castillo and Jimena

Within Cádiz province, the Algeciras–Granada train route (three or four trains daily) passes through San Roque-La Linea, Almoraima and Jimena de la Frontera, and some trains also stop in Los Barrios, all of which are on, or very near, the GR7 route.

There are numerous local bus services to and from almost all of the places highlighted on the GR7 route (see the information boxes for local transport options).

More information

Trains: in Spain: ☎ 902 240 202 www.renfe.es
            for international rail travel:
            www.raileurope.com or www.seat61.com
Buses: Comes (☎ 952 684 038, 956 655 755)

Tourist information

Andalucía tourist information office: Avda Ramón de Carranza, 11005, Cádiz ☎ 956 258 646, otcadiz@andalucia.org
C/Juan de la Cierva, 11207 Algeciras, ☎ 956 572 636, otalgeciras@andalucia.org

Maps required

1:50,000 Servicio Geografico del Ejercito
13-48 **1077** Tarifa
13-47 **1074** Tahivilla
14-47 **1075** San Roque
14-46 **1071** Jimena de la Frontera
14-45 **1064** Cortes de la Frontera
14-44 **1050** Ubrique

The route

Tarifa (86m, pop. 16,500) ⚓ 🎒 🍴 F ▲ € ☎ ✉ ✚ ⓘ 🚌 🖥
A historic fishing port with a strong Moorish influence and spectacular views across to Africa from the viewpoint at the top of town. Its thriving surf scene gives it a trendier feel than many of the other traditional Andalucian villages you'll come to. It's worth spending a night here to relax on the beautiful white sand beaches and explore the old town including the Arab castle of Guzman the Bueno, the recently restored eighth-century Jerez Gate, the Gothic San Mateo church and the municipal museum.

Accommodation and food
There are plenty of places to eat – a mix of international restaurants including many with Arabic and Asian influence – and also lots of hotels, but it is worth booking in summer months. There are three campsites which you pass along the beach (all open all year).

Camping Tarifa (adult/tent € 6/3.5) large campsite near the beach with many facilities including swimming pool, bakery and restaurant (Playa de Los Lances, on the GR7, ☎ 956 684 778, camping-tarifa@camping-tarifa.com, www.camping-tarifa.com)

Hostal la Calzada (s/d/t en suite € 45/50/60) smart hotel in the heart of the old town, all rooms have TV and air conditioning (C/Justino Pertíñez 7, ☎ 956 681 492, info@hostallacalzada.com, www.hostallacalzada.com)

Misiana (s/d inc breakfast € 90/110) start your trip in very stylish surroundings, set in the centre of Tarifa, with air conditioning, its own lounge and live music (C/Sancho IV El Bravo, ☎ 956 627 083, www.misiana.com)

For more information
www.tarifa.net, www.tarifainfo.com, www.campingsdetarifa.com

Distance	41.5km
Time	12h
Height gain	560m
Height loss	500m
Highest point	240m

NB A tent is essential if you wish to break the journey.

A long beach walk along clean white sands, trying to resist the lure of swimming in the tempting blue sea, followed by a gentle climb up into the green hills and shady cork oak groves.

The walk starts at the tourist office in the centre of Tarifa where there's a signboard with information about the footpath. Head through the town down to the **Playa de los Lances**, which is to the right and north of the old stone pier.

Walk almost the entire length of this 7km beach, crossing the **Río de la Jara** on the way (the easiest and most pleasant option is to paddle across). When you reach the **Mistral**

Playa de los Lances

45

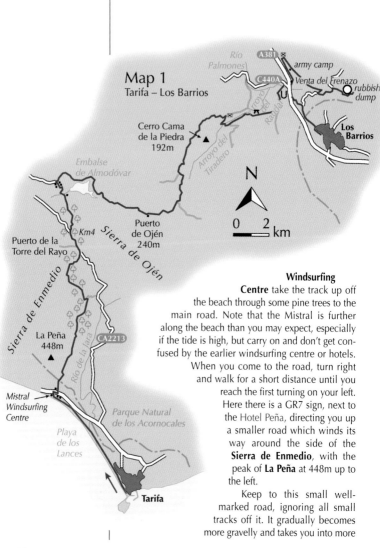

Map 1
Tarifa – Los Barrios

Río Palmones

A 381

army camp

C 440A

Venta del Frenazo

rubbish dump

Los Barrios

Cerro Cama de la Piedra 192m

Arroyo del Tiradero

Embalse de Almodóvar

N

0   2 km

Puerto de Ojén 240m

Sierra de Ojén

Km4

Puerto de la Torre del Rayo

Sierra de Enmedio

La Peña 448m

CA2213

Río de la Jara

Mistral Windsurfing Centre

Parque Natural de los Acornocales

Playa de los Lances

Tarifa

Windsurfing Centre take the track up off the beach through some pine trees to the main road. Note that the Mistral is further along the beach than you may expect, especially if the tide is high, but carry on and don't get confused by the earlier windsurfing centre or hotels. When you come to the road, turn right and walk for a short distance until you reach the first turning on your left. Here there is a GR7 sign, next to the Hotel Peña, directing you up a smaller road which winds its way around the side of the **Sierra de Enmedio**, with the peak of **La Peña** at 448m up to the left.

Keep to this small well-marked road, ignoring all small tracks off it. It gradually becomes more gravelly and takes you into more

LOS ALCORNOCALES NATURAL PARK (1678km²)

The Parque Natural de los Alcornocales is the Iberian peninsula's biggest cork oak grove and plays a large part in making Spain the world's second largest cork producer after Portugal.

Wildlife

As well as cork, the park is also home to some of the last remains of sub-tropical forest in Europe, the only others to be found in Turkey. In the humid microclimates of the *canutos* – deep, narrow valleys carved out by streams – are tropical trees and vegetation such as wild olives, pyrean oaks, rare ferns, laurel, hazel, alder and rhododendron, giving an insight into what parts of Europe would have looked like in primeval times.

Forty years ago the park would have been home to bears and wolves, but these have now been hunted to extinction and you are more likely to see red and roe deer and smaller mammals such as otters, foxes and polecats. Wild boar also inhabit the park but, as they are nocturnal, you're less likely to come across them.

The park has 226 species of birds from 56 families – including several species of eagle. It is a perfect habitat for them with its huge forests and rocky outcrops and is situated in an ideal location for a stop-off on the migratory route to Africa.

Cork

Cork comes from the cork oak tree, *Quercus suber*. It is the only tree which is able to sustain cork being taken from it. The bark is harvested from mature trees, those at least 25 years old, just once every nine years in the spring or summer. Specialised workers cut the oak's cork, *pela*, and create piles of cork, *panas*, which you can see waiting to be transported for sorting as you pass through cork groves.

Cork production has been happening in this way for up to 3000 years and nowadays the main use of cork, which is a very sustainable resource, is for bottle corks, which make up 60 per cent of the market.

For further information

There are two park visitor centres, both ☎ 956 679 161.

remote and picturesque countryside. ▸ You will pass by lots of cork trees with their barked stripped off, a sight common in this area, which is part of the Parque Natural de los Alcornocales.

The wind farm you are looking down on to the east is one of the largest in Europe.

Countryside on the way to Los Barrios

The route is straightforward to follow. The only point to watch out for is when, after about 5km, the main track heads east downhill to the **CA2213** – you don't want to go this way. Instead, keep to the smaller track and continue contouring north round the hillside. After 2.5km, you will reach the CA2213, a short distance before the pass, the **Puerto de la Torre del Rayo**. (If you do join the CA2213 too early, take a left along the road and you'll rejoin the GR7 at this point.)

At the pass, stay on the main road, ignoring a smaller track off to the left, and follow it for 1km until you reach the **Km4** sign. Here there is a track on the right (signposted Puerto de Ojén 3h). ◄ The **Sierra de Ojén**, through which you're now passing, boasts over 18 species of raptors including the short-toed eagle, the booted eagle, the griffon vulture, tawny owl, eagle owl, buzzard, goshawk and sparrow hawk.

The track takes you through beautiful countryside with a high possibility of seeing birds of prey in the crags up to the right.

This section is less well marked, but if you keep to the main track it is fine. You should pass a water works building and then cross a small river with the dam of the **Embalse de**

Almodóvar up to your right. Continue following the track up from the other side of the river through a few farms until you reach the gravel road. A few metres to your left, a GR7 sign directs you to turn right along the road and around the far side of the reservoir, heading east.

From here markings are few and far between, but keep going and after 6km you will reach the beautiful **Puerto de Ojén** where there was a bar which, sadly, has now shut down. Carry on, at first downhill, passing the **Cerro Cama de la Piedra** on your right, until you reach a small track with a **gate** off to the right after about 8km, where you leave the main track. This could be hard to spot as at the time of writing half of the GR7 signpost here was missing.

Through the gate, head downhill through a maze of little paths keeping a close eye for frequent markings and small stone cairns. After about 5–10min you should pass through a marked gap in a fence.

A couple of small paths run from here until another fence, and both end up at the same gate. Go through this and carry on along a marked but overgrown path with the **Arroyo del Raudal** to your right. A little path takes you down to, and across, the stream where you may need to paddle depending on the season. If you miss the path to the stream you will very quickly reach a GR7 sign indicating that you've gone the wrong way. (It is worth persevering with this section as it is very pretty, but should you prefer to avoid its complications, don't take the initial turning to the right at the gate and stay on the main track until you reach the **C440A**, turn right and follow it into **Los Barrios**.)

Across the stream, the path quickly turns into a wider track and, when you reach a junction, you turn left. There are then no markings for a while, but continue on this track. You will pass a shady **picnic area** on your left and then leave the park. The track then crosses the **Río Palmones** and passes under the **A381** motorway. Here you will find yourself on the C440A road at the **Venta del Frenazo**.

To get to Los Barrios turn right for an uninspiring 3km walk down the road. A short distance after turning right you will see a turning to the left. This is the start of the next section of the route and if you choose to head into Los Barrios to sleep or for refreshments, you will need to return to here to rejoin the route.

Los Barrios (23m, pop. 13,700) ⌁ 🍴 F ▲ € ☎ ✉ ✚ ⓘ 🚍 ▣

A charming small town centred around two plazas, one busy with cafés and bars, and the other, the Plaza de la Iglesia, the focus of the old town with the old church and tower, grand town hall and casino. It is also known for being the start of the bull route and has many bull farms in the vicinity. There is a good natural history museum (C/Calvarion 14, ☎ 956 621 169).

Accommodation and food

A mix of eateries including tapas, pizzas, Chinese and fast food and a couple of places to stay:

Pensión la Tinaja ★ (s/d en suite 15/26) a small bar-restaurant with a *pensión* upstairs with clean basic rooms around a hallway with balcony (C/Maldonado 36, ☎ 956 620 352/666 710 783)

Hotel Real ★ (s/d en suite €29.50–32/44.50–48) modern, smart and near the centre with 22 rooms, meals available in cosy restaurant downstairs (Avda Pablo Picasso 7, ☎ 956 620 024)

For more information

Tourist information: Avda Chamizo de la Rubia, ☎ 956 628 013 delegacionturismo@aytolosbarrios.es, www.losbarrios.es

Los Barrios – Castillo de Castellar

Distance	34km
Time	10h30
Height gain	400m
Height loss	180m
Highest point	244m

Good hill tracks start the route followed by a long road walk with the reward of the beautiful view of the hill-top castle of Castellar to end the day. A kilometre detour at Almoraima on the route would take you to Castellar de la Frontera and shorten the route by 4km and 1h30 or you could stop at a hotel along the way.

Return along the road to the point 3km north of Los Barrios where there is a GR7 post before you reach the **Venta del Frenazo**. This directs you up a quieter tarmac road back into cork oaks, with the boundary of the Parque Natural de los Acornocales running alongside the road. As you climb you will pass an **army camp** on the right and, after 2km, you come to **gates** blocking the road directly ahead. Keep following the dirt road which takes you steeply up to your right. At the cattle grid at the top, your climb is rewarded with spectacular views including the Embalse de Charco del Redondo in the distance.

Don't take the turning to the left after the cattle grid, keep following the potholed tarmac road despite the lack of signs and at a second cattle grid you'll finally reach a sign at a T-junction telling you that you've come 2h20 from Los Barrios. Turn right and you'll soon reach another sign (Castellar 5h50). (Note that there are two places called Castellar – the new town Castellar de la Frontera, and the old town, Castillo de Castellar – and the signs all refer to the former, which is 1h40 before the old town on the hill.)

Turn right again and continue to pass a huge **rubbish dump** – teeming with bird life but not a pleasant place to linger. Just past it, turn left at another signpost (Los Barrios 3h40, Castellar 4h50). The path leads you round the back of the tip (keep it on your left) and then divides. Make sure you stay on the middle fork head-ing downhill. There are no markings, but after about 20 minutes you should emerge at

Camping Alcornocales
204m
Río Hozgarganta
Jimena de la Frontera
Rancho los Lobos
Los Angeles

Map 2
Beyond Los Barrios – Camping Alcornocales

Embalse de Guadarranque
Castillo de Castellar
venta

La Jacardilla campsite

Parque Natural de los Acornocales

Castellar de la Frontera
Almoraima

N

0   2 km

Hotel los Timbales

rubbish dump
Río Guadalcortes
Río Guadarranque

another T-junction where you turn right at a sign (4h30 to Castellar).

The route then takes you northeast then heads southeast for several kilometres. At the point when you cross the **Río Guadalcortes**, go through a gate and stay on the road up to a second gate where you turn left along the **C512**. Here you'll come across another sign (Los Barrios 4h25, Castellar 4h). The road climbs over the hill and a few kilometres further on you reach a bridge over the **Río Guadarranque** and a junction with the busier **A369**, where there are two bar-restaurants, a pleasant refreshment stop and one of them is also a hotel (**Hotel los Timbales** (s/d €12/25) ☎ 956 786 046/956 786 543).

From here it is a 2h walk along a busy road to **Castellar** and the road again follows the park boundary. ◀ There are a couple of bars along the way that might be open.

After 6km you will reach **Almoraima**, the area by the station on the outskirts of Castellar which is a protected natural area that is rich in wildlife. Continue round on the main road to carry on to **Castillo de Castellar** or, if you want to stay in the new town, you can turn off to the right at the junction from which it is a 1km walk.

The plethora of storks' nests on the tops of the electricity pylons are a pleasant distraction.

Castellar de la Frontera (25m, pop. 2940 with Castillo) ⌁ ⚊ F ☎ ✚ ①

This neat modern town 8km from Castillo de Castellar was planned and built in the late 1960s to provide better living conditions for families living in the historic but cramped Castillo. Many moved to Castellar in 1971 and the wide streets and modern houses are a big contrast to its hilltop neighbour.

Accommodation and food

With tourism focused on Castillo de Castellar, there is little in the way of accommodation, but try:

Pensión-Restuarante Casa Convento la Almoraima ★ (s/d en suite €59/95) once a convent, now a bar/restaurant with 17 rooms (Finca la Almoraima, ☎ 956 693 002)

To carry on to Castillo de Castellar take the left fork at the junction where a sign says 'Castillar (sic) 1h40'. Follow the road, but to cut out a section of road walking look out

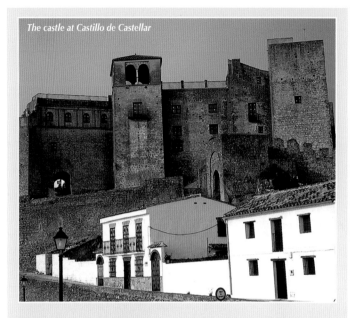

The castle at Castillo de Castellar

Castillo de Castellar (240m, pop. 2940 with Castellar) ⤴ 🏕 🍽 F ▲ ☎ ① 🚐

This beautiful hilltop village has been inhabited since prehistoric times and has a rich history as a medieval fortress and throughout the conflict between the Christians and the Muslims. It has impressive views down over the Embalse de Guadarranque. In 1983, the Government declared village and castle a 'Historical and Artistic Monument' and invested in their restoration.

Accommodation and food

Most accommodation is in much sought after *casas rurales* and there are a couple of places to eat, a few local bars and the restaurant inside the castle walls:

La Jacardilla campsite (tent/person € 10/4) pleasant green campsite with power, BBQs, clean toilet and shower blocks and activity centre, chalets also available to rent (☎ 956 647 006/693 223)

Casas rurales (s/d/t/quad € 50/65/95/115) a range of beautiful whitewashed houses inside the castle walls (C/Rosario, ☎ 956 236 620, castillo-de-castellar@tugaso.com, www.tugaso.com)

Storks nesting

for a small turn off to the right at Km3, marked with a sign claiming 1h to Castillo de Castellar. The pretty path through the trees brings you back onto the road further up where you can turn left for **La Jacaradilla campsite**, or continue along the road past the Venta of the same name.

Just after the bar, take a marked shortcut up to the left, which brings you back onto the road briefly before you leave it again on the historic cobbled route up to the castle. After a steep climb with panoramic views, you rejoin the road just at the entrance to the village and from here make the final climb up to the castle gates.

Distance	18km
Time	6h
Height gain	160m
Height loss	200m
Highest point	244m

After leaving behind the castle of Castillo, the route to Jimena is a long flat one following the railway line most of the way through rural landscapes with the opportunity of seeing many eagles overhead.

From the castle head back to the road and follow it out in the opposite direction from which you arrived and down, ignoring a smaller track to the left which takes you down to an old fountain. From here you will catch glimpses of the huge **Embalse de Guadarranque** to the west above which the castle is perched. After 1.5km the tarmac comes to an end, but the unpaved road continues on into the trees.

Follow this pleasant track, looking out for birds of prey. About 5km from Castillo you reach the **railway line** near the old Castellar **train station**. Cross the railway tracks and turn left along a path running next to the train line. You'll follow this almost all the way into **Jimena**: if in doubt, where the

Approaching Jimena

55

track divides stick to the branch closest to the railway line.
After about 8km, all unmarked, you come to a signpost
(Jimena 1h45, Castellar 4h15).

Here the wide track that you were on crosses the railway, but you turn off down a narrow path to the right that continues alongside the railway. After crossing a wooden bridge you reach another sign (1h15) directing you along a wider track. Keep following the railway, but don't cross it until you reach a mark and a sign to **Ranchos los Lobos** (1km after joining the wider track). Follow this to the left and soon cross the railway line. Jimena appears on the hill in front of you and you remain on the same road as its winds over the **Río Hozgarganta** and steeply up into the village.

If you don't want to enter the village, turn left 100m after the bridge and follow the signposted Río Hozgarganta footpath round the back of the village to rejoin the road on the other side at the white cross on the hill.

Jimena de la Frontera (200m, pop. 9000) 🔀 🏕 🍴 F ▲ € ☎ ✉ ✚ ⓘ 🚌
Dominated by its castle, an Arab fortress built on Roman ruins, Jimena is a delightful ancient village built on a steep hillside and looking down over fertile green valleys with orange groves and cork forested hills. Many British residents enjoy its sunshine and relaxed pace of life. From the castle you can see as far as Algeciras and Gibraltar.

Accommodation and food
A selection of *casas rurales*, a few *hostales* and a campsite:

Camping los Alcornocales (tent/person/cabins €4.50/4.05/from 55) just off the road out of the village on the GR7 route, a large campsite with bar-restaurant, shop, swimming pool and power (☎ 956 640 060, reserves@campinglosalcornocales.com, www.campinglosalcornocales.com)

Casa Rural Posada la Casa Grande (d €50) Norwegian-run with a good atmosphere (C/Fuente Nueva 42, ☎ 956 640 578, www.posadalacasagrande.com, tcag@retemail.es)

Hostal el Anon (s/d en suite €37/60) 12 rooms, rooftop swimming pool, sun terrace and restaurant with home-cooked food, including great vegetarian options, vibrant place with an American owner who is knowledgeable about walking and bird watching in the area (C/Consuelo 30-40, ☎ 956 640 113, reservas@elanon.net)

Distance	36km
Time	10h
Height gain	720m
Height loss	600m
Highest point	860m

NB A tent is essential if you wish to break the journey.

A beautiful route almost entirely on small paths taking you far from civilization to lofty passes and remote cork tree groves. With almost 40km separating the two places, you will either need to wild camp en route to avoid a very long day, or plan to hitch hike when you arrive at the road, about 10km from Ubrique. Alternatively, you could skip this section altogether by taking a bus to Ubrique.

To get onto the route to Ubrique, leave Jimena on the main road north. Just after you pass **Camping Alcornocales** you will reach a junction in the road and directly opposite is the well-marked GR7 path heading steeply uphill. Climb this initially cobbled path, which is known as the Sendero Vereda Ubrique – Asomidallas, until you reach a wide track after about a kilometre. Cross over and carry on up the hill-side as marked, following the line of the stone wall. Be sure to look back at the great views of Jimena.

When you reach the brow of the hill and a GR7 sign-post (Jimena 1h, Ubrique 9h) go through the gate and carry on upwards on small paths until you come to a second gate through which is a wider track again. Follow this, and when

Leaving Jimena

you come to an unmarked junction take the right fork. Pass one turning on the right but take the second one (which has a post further on).

At the next junction, about 1.5km further on, you don't take either of the forks, but instead head steeply up to the right again following a wall. The rocky tops of the **Altos de Paneron** and **Cerro de Marín** are up to your left. The path here is vague and disappears entirely in places amongst the rocks, but after about 10min of ascent there is a gate on your right with a GR7 post clearly visible.

Go through the gate and follow the now clear track left up to the top of the hill (in the Campo de Gibraltar). Follow a signpost (Ubrique 7h30) left along the top of a shoulder with stunning views over the barren hills on either side.

The track brings you to two gates, take the left one and carry on down through cork oaks. You'll then reach a gate marked 'private property', but this is the route so go through. After a short distance you will come to a post directing you right into some more dense woodland and onto an attractive path.

This section is well marked. At the only uncertain divide take the left fork to emerge a few minutes later at the **Puerto de la Venta** with a gate ahead of you. Go through the gate and then downhill gently through more corks. The scenery opens out a bit when you reach a sign for Ubrique (6h).

Contour round the hillside on a wide track and then head left, and westwards, still on the track through pine trees. When you meet another track turn right, crossing into Málaga province, although you leave it again before arriving in Ubrique. There are two more well-marked right turns after this, taking you past the halfway mark, and then you arrive at a pass signposted **Carrera del Caballo** (16km from the start). Carry on from here on the main track, contouring round with **El Castillo** (hilltop with phone masts on it) up to your right.

As you pass by the summit you'll come to a cow shelter, **Albergue la Calderone**. From there start heading downwards past an annoying sign claiming that it is 4h15 to Ubrique (when the one you walked past half an hour ago said 4h). If you have a tent and want to stop for the night, wild camping is permitted in this area.

As you head downwards crossing over an intersection, the distinctive peak of **Peñón del Berrueco** dominates the horizon, Ubrique lies beyond and to west of it. Ignore two right turns and soon you should reach the **A373** Cortes to Alcála de la Frontera road. Here there is a signpost and board with a route map (Jimena 7h, Ubrique 3h – though be warned that after a good half hour's walking you will meet another sign saying 2h45).

Turn left and walk on this small road until you reach a bar on your right (at the 2h45 sign). Here, just before the road junction to Ubrique, you enter the Parque Natural de la Sierra de Grazalema (see information box on page 63) and head off on a small path in front of the bar which cuts out some of the longer loops of the road. Follow this all the way to the outskirts of Ubrique, visible nestled among the hills, then join the road into the town itself.

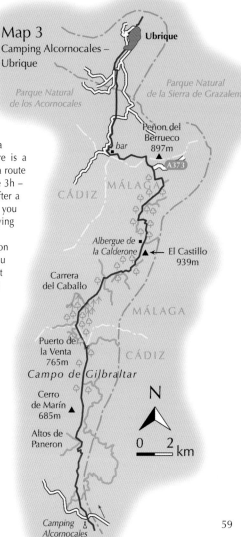

Map 3
Camping Alcornocales –
Ubrique

Ubrique

Parque Natural
de los Acornocales

Parque Natural
de la Sierra de Grazalema

Peñon del
Berrueco
897m

bar

A373

MÁLAGA

CÁDIZ

Albergue de
la Calderone

El Castillo
939m

Carrera
del Caballo

MÁLAGA

Puerto de
la Venta
765m

CÁDIZ

Campo de Gilbraltar

Cerro
de Marín
685m

N

Altos de
Paneron

0   2 km

Camping
Alcornocales

Ubrique (337m, pop. 17,900) ⌁ ⦿ F ▲ € ☎ ✉ ✚ ① 🚌 🖳

A sizeable town with all the amenities you could need, but still retaining some of the charm of a typical *pueblo blanco*. If you can manage some more walking, it is worth heading up to the old town for the views over the whole of Ubrique and the interestingly named Iglesia de Nuestro Señora de la O (Church of Our Lady of the O). Famous for its leather, produced from the livestock which are reared in the surrounding areas, every other shop seems to sell leather goods.

Accommodation and food

Good selection of eateries, but very limited accommodation for such a large place. The only hotel in the town itself is:

Hotel Occuris (s/d €35–45/50–60) clean and smart with the luxury of deep baths (Avda Solís Pascual 51, ☎ 956 463939, hotelocurris@hotelocurris.com, www.turinet.net/empresu/h.ocurris)

And on the way into Ubrique on the Cortes road:

Hotel Sierra de Ubrique (d en suite €65) very grand establishment (Ctra Ubrique-Cortes, Km33, 700, ☎ 956 466 805, www.hotelsierradeubrique.com)

A spectacular section with steep climbs that are more than worth it for the stunning views across the limestone crags and spacious valleys of the Sierra de Grazalema natural park.

Ubrique – Montejaque

Distance	26km
Time	7h30
Height gain	900m
Height loss	560m
Highest point	1060m

Ubrique – Benacoaz (3.5km, 1h)

Leave Ubrique at the north end of town on the Camino do Benacoaz, which you will find just behind the grand Convento de Capuchinos. A sign points you uphill 1h to **Benacoaz** and you climb for about 3.5km up a steep roughly cobbled Roman path.

Benacoaz (793m, pop. 680) ⚡ 🍴 F ▲ € ☎ ✉ ✚ ① 🚗 🖳

A small whitewashed village with pretty, shady little squares and a striking church tower with red decoration. If you have the energy, it's worth climbing to the top of the village to see the archaeological ruins and the impressive views.

Accomodation and food

A few nice cafés, bars and restaurants with sunny outside seating and good views and a limited selection of places to stay:

Los Chozos del Puente del Moro ★★ (4 person accommodation from €100pn) just outside Benacoaz, Los Chozos is almost a holiday camp with apartments, dorms and self-catering accommodation along with swimming pool and gardens (Finca el Lentiscal y Pereo, ☎ 956 234 163, loschozos@supercable.es)

Hostal San Anton (d en suite €40) a small, straightforward *hostal* with 5 rooms (Pza de San Anton 5, ☎ 956 125 577, hotelsananton@hotmail.com)

Benacoaz – Villaluenga del Rosario (4.5km, 1h20)

Leave Benacoaz on either the top or bottom road out of town heading south and you'll come to a sign where they meet, pointing you along the road (Villaluenga del Rosario 1h20). After 1km you reach a **picnic area** on your right and a steep path which takes you off the road with a signpost (Villaluenga 40min). Where the path disappears you rejoin the road and keep climbing, though more gently, with the 1395m peak of **Navazo Alto** of the **Sierra de la Bándera** to your left, up to the next village, passing an outdoor climbing wall on your left as you enter **Villaluenga del Rosario**.

Map 4
Ubrique – Montejaque

61

Villaluenga del Rosario (1000m, pop. 480) ⤵ ♨ F ▲ € ☎ ✉ ✚ 🛏 💻

A picturesque village with a laid back atmosphere and a dramatic setting, the highest in the province, set amongst dramatic limestone rock faces. It has the area's main caving and potholing school and is famous for its award-winning sheep and goat cheeses, which you can purchase direct from the factory on your way out. There are various short walks which leave from the village and the area is great for bird watching – look out for signboards with identification charts on the route.

Accomodation and food

A few bars and cafés and one smart restaurant which is part of the only hotel:

Hotel la Posada ★ (s/d € 33/44–55) a fairly luxurious place in a beautiful old building, 6 double rooms and 1 single, all with air conditioning, TV and telephone, with a restaurant downstairs with a range of traditional dishes from the area including cheeses (well signposted from the entrance to the village, C/Torre 1, ☎ 956 126 119, la-posada@tugasa.com)

At the time of writing a second hotel on the road out of the village was being renovated.

Villaluenga del Rosario – Montejaque (18km, 5h10)

Take the road east and, just as you reach the end of the village and a large sign for a recycling centre, turn off to the right along a path signposted as the Llanos del Republicano walking route. Climb the hill on a concrete road, admiring the views back over the village and the Sierra de Bandera behind you. Ignore the track off to the right, and 300m over the top of the hill in the shade of some trees there is a post directing you to the right (Puerto de Correo 2h).

A rare stretch of downhill walking takes you through a gate onto the valley floor (2km after Villaluenga del Rosario) surrounded by imposing limestone mountains on all sides. Follow the track down and turn left at another signpost (1h30). Go through a big metal gate and look out for a post to the right. You'll pass by two of the deep potholes (*simas*) for which the natural park is famous, the second, **Sima del Republicano**, a short detour away down a signposted path. The route soon takes you steeply uphill through the rocky terrain of the **Sierra de Libar**, part of the Parque Natural de la Sierra de Grazalema, towards the **pass**, climbing over 200m in height.

SIERRA DE GRAZALEMA NATURAL PARK (517km²)

The Parque Natural de la Sierra de Grazalema was Andalucía's first natural park, becoming so in 1984 after being designated a UNESCO Biosphere reserve seven years earlier. Located in both Cádiz and Málaga provinces, it is made up primarily of stunning cliffs and gorges carved out of limestone mountains, the highest of which is El Torreón at 1654m. The nature of limestone, combined with Spain's highest rainfall, means the park is home to some of the largest cave and pothole systems in Spain, with the largest cavern of the Hundidero-Gato system measuring 4km long.

Culturally, the area is rich too, with the mountains of the park forming the boundary between the Arab Kingdom of Granada and the Christian Kingdom, Castilla, during the 13th and 14th centuries, although evidence of human occupation dates back much further, evidenced by local cave paintings.

Wildlife
The high rainfall also makes the park rich in vegetation, with over 1300 plant species registered, including the rare Spanish fir, which dates from over 65 million years ago. Discovered in 1837 by a Swiss botanist, it is very resistant to cold and can live at an altitude up to 1700m.

The park is home to some of Europe's largest griffon vulture colonies as well as black and Egyptian vultures, five types of eagle, ospreys and peregrines along with many smaller birds such as the great spotted woodpecker and hoopoe.

Foxes, badgers, wild boar, wildcats and beech martins can all be found here as can red and roe deer which have been reintroduced for hunting.

For more information
Park visitor centre: Cortes de la Frontera, ☎ 952 154 599
Park office: El Bosque, ☎ 956 727 029
For guided walks in the park see: www.natural-images.co.uk.

The views from the top of the pass are dramatic with the rocky **Sierra del Palo** and its highest peak at 1400m ahead and the lush valley below. Descending the other side of the hill and passing through a **gate** you cross into **Málaga** province and come to a signboard and posts but with no information for those heading in this direction. Stick to the main (unmarked) path heading downhill and emerge into the expansive and beautiful valley, **Llano de Libar**. ▶

There are no markings here and the path peters out, but stick to the dry stone wall, keeping it on your right, and head towards an old gate where a signpost directs you on to

The valley is carpeted with wildflowers in spring and early summer, and, depending on the recent rainfall, can be very boggy in parts.

63

Climbing out of valley towards Montejaque

Montejaque, but with the yellow markings of the PRA 252 route. The sign says it is 5h30 but don't despair as the real timing is more like 2h45. Continue along the long flat dirt track and after about 2km you reach an **albergue**. It must be booked ahead in its entirety, but there is a camping area with toilets and picnic benches behind it which is free to use.

From here there is 3km of gentle downhill walking through shady cork oaks to a second sign, this time a red GR7 post (Montejaque 1h30), and you stay on the main track, which doesn't have many markings but is quite easy to follow. Turn around for spectacular views back over the mountains. After a further 6km, where the route divides, take the right fork downhill which takes you into **Montejaque**, which comes into view just around the corner. (See next section for description of facilities available in Montejaque.)

MÁLAGA PROVINCE

Montejaque to Villanueva del Cauche, 113km

The GR7 runs for almost 250km in Málaga. This section describes the first 113km of the route before it divides into two forks. The remaining parts of the route in the province are described in Part 2 and Part 3.

The route enters Málaga over the Puerto del Correo in the Parque Natural de la Sierra de Grazalema, descending into the Montejaque area with its rugged dolomite limestone cliffs. From here it passes through the spectacularly located Ronda and on into the idyllic mountain villages of El Chorro and Ardales.

At Villanueva del Cauche the route splits into two forks, one (the Northern Fork) heading into the northeast of Málaga province through the olive-ringed villages of Villanueva del Rosario, Villanueva del Trabuco, Villanueva de Tapia, Villanueva de Algaidas, Cuevas Bajas and Cuevas de San Marcos before crossing the Luis de Armiñán bridge over the Río Genil into Córdoba province.

The other (the Southern Fork) heads south through Colmenar and Riogordo then into the foothills of the Sierra de las Cabras and down into the province of Granada by way of an old dismantled railway line.

HIGHLIGHTS OF THE ROUTE IN MÁLAGA PROVINCE

- the dramatic limestone peaks surrounding the pretty village of Montejaque
- Ronda's beautiful architecture and precarious clifftop location
- the magnificent rock faces and gorge of El Chorro
- the 27 spires of Antequera's various churches viewed from the city's castle
- the weird and wonderful landscape of the Parque Natural El Torcal

Travel

Ronda (11km) and Antequera (20.5km) are both good places to join or leave the route with a wide range of public transport options. Other smaller places are also quite well served by local buses and trains.

Trains

The Algeciras–Granada train route (3 or 4 trains daily) passes through Banaoján (very close to Montejaque), Arriate, Ronda, and some trains stop in El Chorro. Information from ☎ 902 240 202, www.renfe.es.

Montejaque – looking back from the road to Ronda

There are also connections from Ronda with Granada via Antequera and Málaga (1 daily Mon–Sat), Cordoba (2 daily) and Madrid (1 day train, 1 night train).

Antequera is on the line to Granada (6 daily, 1h30), Seville (3 daily, 1h45) and Ronda (3 daily, 1h15).

Buses

Several bus companies serve the area with regular buses:

Comes (☎ 952 871 992) Ronda–Cádiz (5 daily, 2h), Jimena de la Frontera–Algeciras (1 daily, 1h30)

Los Amarillos (☎ 952 187 061) Ronda–Seville (5 daily, 2h30min), Ronda–Ardales–Málaga (every 2h, 1h45)

Portillo (☎ 952 872 262) Ronda–Málaga (4 daily, 1h30)

Automóviles Casado (☎ 952 841 957) Antequera–Málaga (every 50min, 1h)

Alsina Graells (☎ 952 841 365) Antequera–Granada, Córdoba, Almería

Tourist information

Andalucía tourist information office: Pasaje de Chinitas, 4, 29015, Málaga, ☎ 952 213 445, otMálaga@andalucia.org

Other walks

There is lots of walking in the hills surrounding Montejaque including a 3h circuit to the Tavizina gorge, a 2h30 ascent of the peak of Hacho (1075m) and a 14km circular route of the smaller hills around the village. A £5 guide, *Walks in Grazelema and Montejaque,* can be purchased locally or in advance from Marengo Publications (info@marengowalks.com).

The Parque Natural de Torcal has three walking routes. They are colour-coded to indicate length and difficulty, with wooden posts to follow. The green route is the shortest and easiest, 1.5km and takes about 30min. The yellow route covers most of the green area, is 2.5km long and takes you to Las Ventanillas at 1200m with dramatic views. The red route is 4.5km, taking about 3h, and climbs to 1339m, from where you can see the whole of the park and, on very clear days, over to Africa.

Maps required
1:50,000 Servicio Geografico del Ejercito
14-44 **1050** Ubrique
15-44 **1051** Ronda
15-43 **1037** Teba
16-43 **1038** Ardales
16-42 **1023** Antequera
17-43 **1039** Colmenar

The route

Montejaque (687m, pop. 1070) ⌁ ⍢ F ▲ € ☎ ① ⇌
Montejaque, which comes from the Arabic for 'lost mountain', is a pretty white village and a popular walking base with many shorter routes also departing from here. The centre of the village is the Plaza Constitution with the Santiago el Mayor church and the Hotel Palacete de Mañara, in the mansion that was once the seat of power in the area but also latterly, slightly oddly, a sausage factory.

Accommodation and food
A good selection of little places to eat and a few places to stay, mostly upmarket:
Hostal la Cabana (s/d en suite € 17/32) the cheapest option with basic rooms situated behind the restaurant of the same name (C/Santa Cruz, ☎ 952 167 158)
Hotel Palacete de Mañara ★★★ (s/d en suite € 52/66) smart with lots of useful information, swimming pool and air conditioning (Pza Constitución 2, ☎ 952 167 252, info@casitadelasierra.com, www.casitsdelasierra.com)
Casas de Montejaque (2/4/6 people € 58–75.50/74–89.50/90.50–130.50) luxurious houses set around a swimming pool (C/Manuel Ortega 16, ☎ 952 168 120, reserves@casade montejaque.net, www.casasdemontejaque.net)

Montejaque – Arriate

A short route taking you steeply up and over the El Puerto pass and into the historic town of Ronda, avoiding the infamous road there. Once you've found your way out of Ronda, this route opens out taking you across the wide valley floor to Arriate. It is worth stopping to spend some time in Ronda.

Distance	17km
Time	5h30
Height gain	360m
Height loss	440m
Highest point	740m

Montejaque – Ronda (11km, 3h30)

Come out of Montejaque on the road heading east and downhill and just under a kilometre out of town you come to a signboard listing the network of local walking routes including the GR7. Don't be tempted to turn left up this path, carry on down the road another 200m to a GR7 sign directing you off the road up the next left (Ronda 3h30).

This route soon takes you up the steep zigzagging path that is all too clear on the hill ahead of you. After about 20min

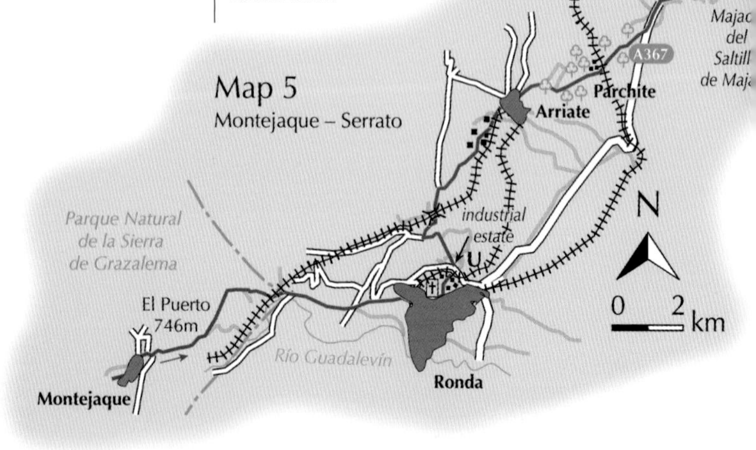

Cueva
del Becc

Majac
del
Saltill
de Maja

A367

Parchite

Arriate

Map 5
Montejaque – Serrato

*Parque Natural
de la Sierra
de Grazalema*

industrial
estate

N

El Puerto
746m

0   2 km

Río Guadalevín

Montejaque

Ronda

you should reach the top, **El Puerto**, and the route flattens out before descending the other side of the hill. ▸

Stick to the main track despite the sparse markings and on the valley floor you'll cross the Algeciras–Bobadilla **railway line**. Just after it, where the track divides, take the option closest to the river. You'll soon pass a guest house on your right (☎ 651 182 051, www.fincalosgallos.net) and, where you meet the main road, turn left onto it. After about 500m turn right along a wide dirt track with houses alongside and, when this turns into a tarmac road, turn off it onto the middle track up to the left.

As you head steeply downwards there are great views of the valley below and Ronda on the other side.

From here it's one big climb to **Ronda**. Stay on the path that takes you steeply uphill and you'll eventually emerge on the outskirts of the town and then head left along the road to get into the centre.

Cuevas del Becerro   ✝ **Serrato**

Cortijo de Santiago

Serranía de Ronda

▲ olorado 1054m

Cortijo de las Pilas

Ronda – Arriate (6km, 2h)

Ronda (744m, pop. 35,000) ↝ ⛏ ⚑ 🍴 F ▲ € ☎ ⌧ ✚ ① 🚍 🖳
Ronda is perhaps the best known of the *pueblos blancos* in the area, famous for its dramatic location atop cliffs high above the Río Guadalevín valley and straddling the 100m deep El Tajo gorge. It is much bigger and more touristy than the smaller villages surrounding it and the huge crowds of day-trippers can be a shock after the peace and space of the open countryside. But its popularity is well deserved, with beautiful architecture and great views.

Accommodation and food
A huge number of hotels and restaurants to suit every price range but still worth booking in summer months:
Campsite el Sur (person/tent € 4/4, bungalow for 2/4 € 40/80) situated just over a kilometre from Ronda, with all the facilities you would expect including a

swimming pool (Ctra Algeciras, Km1.5, ☎ 952 875 939,
info@campingelsur.com)

Pensión Gonzalez (s/d shared bathroom €14/19) small pleasant budget *hostal*
with clean rooms some with balconies (C/San Vicente de Paúl 3, ☎ 952 871
445)

Hostal Virgen del Rocio (s/d en suite €22/39) mid-range place on a bustling side
street full of restaurants, air conditioning (C/Nuevo 18, ☎ 952 877 425)

Parador de Ronda (s/d en suite €96/120) if you want to treat yourself, this luxury
hotel chain is famous in Spain and there is one right on the famous bridge,
the Puente Nuevo (Pza de Espana, ☎ 952 877 500, ronda@parador.es)

For more information
Andalucía tourist information office: Pza de Espana 1, ☎ 952 871 272,
otronda@andalucia.org
Municipal tourist information office: Paseo Blas Infante, ☎ 952 187 119,
información@turismoderonda.es, www.turismoderonda.es

Leaving Ronda is a bit tricky due to a lack of GR7 signs.
Follow the RENFE signs to the train station and then take the
road to the right of the station signposted to the **cemetery**.
Cross the level crossing into the *polígono industrial* (**industrial estate**) and then take the next right, by the Hotel
Berlonga, then almost immediately turn left. Follow this
road downhill, with it becoming more track-like, and go
over a small, and less than formal looking, **railway crossing**,
then head through an **underpass** beneath the bypass. Here
finally you come across some markings indicating (in yellow, not red) that you take the middle of three tracks back
into countryside.

Follow the track, which is concrete in places, downhill
for 1.5km slightly westwards then turn right onto a single-
lane tarmac road at a gatepost which has adverts for the
Molino and La Fuente de la Figuera hotels. Continue on this
road, which meets and passes under the railway again, until
you reach a junction. This has no GR7 markings but take the
right fork and continue on, passing a couple of bars, and you
will come into the village of **Arriate** 2h and 6km after you
left the railway station.

Arriate

Arriate (603m, pop. 3716) ↵ ⏐◉⏐ F ▲ ☎ ✉ 🚌

Arriate, which comes from the Arabic for 'the gardens', was part of the municipality of Ronda until 1630 when residents clubbed together to buy their freedom
and create the smallest municipality in Málaga province. The town itself is a
quiet *pueblo blanco* with an impressive church spire.

Accommodation and food
A range of bars and cafés, a couple of expensive hotels before you reach the village itself including:

Hotel Molino del Arco ★★★★ (d en suite/suites €96/€100) a luxurious option
   right on the GR7, on route up to Arriate about 3km before village (☎ 952
   114 017)

Hotel la Fuente de la Figuera (s/d en suite €135/€260) another option on the
   route but out of the range of most budgets, on route up to Arriate (☎ 952 114
   355)

For more information
Town hall: ☎ 952 165 096

Arriate – Ardales

A very long route through remote hilly landscapes and beneath rocky outcrops with great views, which can be split by taking a detour to spend a night in nearby Cuevas del Becerro.

Distance	38km
Time	11h
Height gain	700m
Height loss	840m
Highest point	840m

To leave Arriate follow signposts to the road to Sentenil and, once on this road, turn right up an unmarked road. After less than 500m you'll come to a signpost saying 8h30 to Serrato. After 3km uphill on the Cueva del Becerro footpath, passing lots of olive groves, you arrive at **Parchite**, a small railway station. Turn left alongside the railway tracks and before you reach the platform and the bar, turn right across the railway lines and take a path through the trees.

After 2km you emerge onto the **A367** road. Turn left and follow the road for almost 5km until a GR7 signpost takes you off to the right near a new golf course. This takes you past the **Majada del Saltillo de Majaco** on a small road. The small road continues for 3.5km until the **Cortijo de las Pilas** where it becomes a track. From here it is 9km to **Serrato** and you stay on the main track all the way, passing through pleasant farmland and meadows.

The track climbs gently for a kilometre to just over 840m, with the 1054m peak of **Colorado** on the left to the west and the start of the complicated mass of hills and gorges of the **Serranía de Ronda** to the east.

Ignore a track off to the right just before you reach the highpoint. From here the track descends all the way to Serrato. One kilometre on you pass by the **Cortijo de Santiago** and

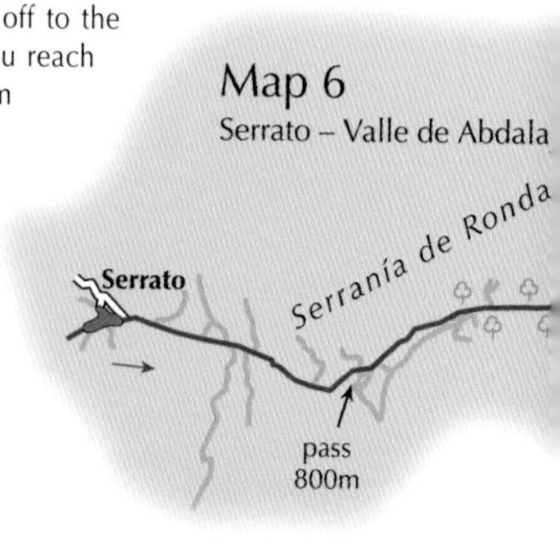

Map 6
Serrato – Valle de Abdala

Serrato

Serranía de Ronda

pass
800m

carry straight on, heading north east, ignoring smaller tracks off to either side. You will then pass by the site of an old mill before arriving at a more major junction, 3km from the high point.

Here, with less than 3km to go to Serrato, the track joins up with the route from **Cuevas del Becerro**. It is on your left and marked with a cross indicating it is the wrong way. However,

On the route to Ardales

it is worth noting at this point that there is nowhere to stay in Serrato so a detour to Cuevas may prove useful if you need a stopping place. To reach Cuevas take this left turn, heading northwest, and follow the main track for 5km/1h right into the village (accommodation is available from Bar Alfredo (s/d €15/€30) good, clean rooms in a house they let out, with shared bathroom (C/Andalucía, 31, ☎ 952 163 008)). Return to the GR7 the same way.

To carry on to **Serrato** (500m, pop. 650 🍴 **F** ▲ ☎ 🚍), take the right fork and continue downhill keeping to the main track. You arrive at the top of the small village by the **cemetery**.

To follow the GR7 from Serrato to Ardales, head down through Serrato and out past a drinking fountain and a GR7 display board. From here immediately turn left and then right onto the main but quiet road. Walk east and uphill on the road for 2km where you will find a track to the left.

The track takes you downhill and into the hill country of the **Serranía de Ronda**, away from most signs of civilisation. About halfway, ignore a turning to the right and, at the bottom, where the track divides, take the right fork to start

Ardales

climbing again. As you near the top, there is an unmarked junction in the track, turn right and continue all the way to the top of the **pass**, where you will be rewarded with great views of the valleys to come and of the **Embalse del Conde de Guadalhorce**. Ardales is 3h downhill from this point.

As you head downhill on the same track cross over another track and then turn left at the next two, well-marked, junctions. ▶ Then, 6.5km after you left the main road, you get your first view of Ardales in front of you. From here the road is very straightforward, though lacking shade, heading directly for the village. As you pass a sign saying **Ardales** is 1h away, ignore a smaller track off to the left. You'll then arrive at the bottom of the village. To enter, cross the **footbridge**.

The track here heads through an amazing patchwork of fields with neat rows of almonds and olive trees all around.

Ardales (450m, pop. 3000) ⌂ ⏻ F ▲ € ☎ ✉ ✚ ⓘ ⌨ ▯

Pleasant quiet town most known for the discovery of Neolithic and Copper Age artefacts here. Just on the outskirts of the town is the Cueva de Ardales, a cave famous not only for its geology, including massive stalagmites, but also for its history of human occupation evidenced by its cave paintings. The cave can be visited on Tue/Thu/Sat/Sun in July and August or Sat/Sun the rest of the year by calling the Ardales Museum of History and Culture on ☎ 952 458 046.

Accommodation and food
A few places to eat including the hotels:

Pensión Bobastro (s/d en suite from €12/24) situated in the centre this has no signs advertising it but locals will direct you (Pza de San Isidro 13, ☎ 952 458 081)

Hotel Restaurante el Cruce (s/d en suite €21/38) clean rooms with comfy beds and nice big balconies, although a bit near a big road, good restaurant downstairs, on the GR7 route out of town, across the bridge from the centre (Ctra Ardales-Campillos 2, ☎ 952 459 012)

La Posada del Conde (s/d en suite €49.60–56.20/67–76) upmarket establishment with comfortable rooms overlooking the reservoir and air conditioning, heating, TV and its own restaurant offering traditional dishes (Pantano del Chorro, ☎ 952 112 411/800, info@hoteldelconde.com, www.hoteldelconde.com)

For more information
www.cuevadeardales.com

Ardales – El Chorro

Great walking with the route talking you across hilltops and then down a wonderful steep zigzagging mountain path into the gorge where the small but quirky village of El Chorro sits.

Distance	13km
Time	6h
Height gain	380m
Height loss	620m
Highest point	600m

Leave Ardales on the minor road **MA442** and head out of town past the tourist information office and across the bridge, turn right at Hotel el Cruce and, after 800m, just before the slip road onto a busy road above, cut up onto a concrete track to the left. Climb the hill on this track ignoring side tracks off to houses and where the road forks go right. ◄

As you climb there are good views back to Ardales and behind it the Sierra de Alcaparain.

When you reach the top follow round the shoulder of the hill and, where the track divides again (2km since you left the road), turn left onto a tarmac minor road. To the right is the **Cueva de Ardales**.

Follow the tarmac road for 1.5km, ignoring several turnings, then turn right onto a marked gravel track. Stick to this main track and after a couple of kilometres of ups and downs and good views, turn left onto another track and follow it downhill, again keeping to this main track and not taking any of the side tracks. When the path levels out you'll pass two tracks to the right, the second signposted to Finca los Gamos, but keep left and continue down the track until you reach another small road (5km after leaving the tarmac road).

Turn right and climb on the road for just over a kilometre and then turn off left at a bend in the road and onto a forest track. (Here a sign points back to Ardales, saying 6h – pleasingly 3h30 is closer to the truth.)

Continue along through the shady pines and take the first left. When you reach a tarmac road again turn right, looking down over the stunning **El Chorro** gorge or El Desfiladero de los Gaitanes. Cut out of the limestone rock by the **Río Guadalhorce**, it is 400m deep in places and 4km long. This brings you to the huge retaining wall of the **reservoir**. From here you can look over to the **Sierra de Huma** with its highest peak of **La Huma** at 1191m. You can also see

El Chorro

a large abandoned chimney, controversial for being left *in situ* in such a beautiful location by the electricity board.

Keep a sharp eye out here as you need to turn left almost immediately down an overgrown little path running to bottom of reservoir wall. From this path you are again looking out for a little path down to the left, taking you away from the reservoir. It comes just after a wooden GR7 marking post. Follow this path steeply downhill for 3km with **El Chorro** clearly visible far below. When you meet the road at the bottom, turn right and cross the **bridge** into the village.

El Chorro (200m, pop. 100) ⌂ ♨ ⛺ ⍟ F ▲ ☎ ⛟

A tiny village dominated by sheer limestone cliffs which are a haven for rock climbers. Its amazing network of underground caves are also deservedly famous. If you're interested in other outdoor pursuits it's a good place to stop off for a while for climbing, mountain biking, horseriding, canoeing, windsurfing and other activities.

Accommodation and food
Lots of places to stay considering its size including:

Albergue-Camping el Chorro (camping per person/tent/wooden cabin/hostel bed
€3.90/3.70/42–70/9.60) set among eucalyptus and pines with a swimming
pool, bar-restaurant and *albergue*, 350m towards the gorge out of the village
(☎ 952 495 295, info@campingelchorro.com,
www.alberguecampingelchorro.com)

Finca la Campaña (tent/dorm bunk/2–8 person cottage €7pp/10/38–88) *hostal*
and camping ground offering a wide range of adventure activities, just outside village on road at top (☎ 952 112 019, www.el-chorro.com)

Apartamentos la Garganta (2/4 person apt. €60/90) old mill building converted
into classy colourful apartments round a lovely pool, heating, air conditioning, kitchens, also a pleasant bar/restaurant (Bda el Chorro (on road up to station), ☎ 952 495 000, informacion@lagaranta.com, www.lagaranta.com)

El Chorro – Valle de Abdalajís

A long steep climb
up an beneath the
imposing Sierra del
Huma is rewarded by
fantastic views before
a gentle descent
through remote
farmland into the
Valle de Abdalajís.

Distance	10km
Time	3h
Height gain	580m
Height loss	440m
Highest point	700m

From the station at the top of the village, continue along the
road 100m and a sign points you up the minor road (4h30
Valle de Abdalajís). This takes you onto a gravel track and
you join the signposted Río del Haza footpath. Where the
track divides soon after, take a left and begin zigzagging
your way up the hill, climbing through pines and eucalyptus. At a T-junction in the track take another left and continue uphill with the impressive rock face of the **La Huma**
towering above you at nearly 1200m.

After around 2km there are turnings off to the left and
right but stick to the main path and another kilometre on,

where the track divides again, keep on the main track and don't take the right turn. Soon afterwards take a right fork, diverging from the Río del Haza footpath and rising to the top of the 250m climb. Now at 500m you have great views down into the Abdalajís valley as the track levels out.

Head downhill to the right and when you meet another track, go through a gate and turn left coming to another sign-post (Abdalajís 2h30). Go uphill again briefly passing several smaller tracks off to farms but keeping to the main track. ▸

Turn right onto a track which starts off as concrete and turns to tarmac. Here, 7km from the starting point, you meet with the yellow PR85 route. Ignore a smaller turning down to the right and continue on beneath the rock face of the **Tajo del Cuervo**. When you meet the main road turn left and it takes you down into **Valle de Abdalajís**.

> The landscape turns from pines to olive groves and becomes more cultivated as you begin to descend.

Valle de Abdalajís (340m, pop. 3000) ⌁ ⍟ F ▲ € ☎ ✉ ✚ ① 🚍

Quiet village most popular with tourists who like hang-gliding. Its name is thought to have come from that of the Arab who founded it, Abd-el-Aziz.

Accommodation and food
A couple of hotels to choose from and a reasonable selection of small local bars and restaurants:

Hostal Avenida (s/d en suite € 15/30) straightforward *pensión* with busy bar beneath (Avda Blas Infante, ☎ 952 489 379/177)

Hostal Vista a la Sierra ★★ (s/d en suite € 36/25) pleasant rooms with good views and 2 flats to let at top of town, friendly owners (Prolongación C/Viento, ☎ 952 488 052)

For more information
Town hall: ☎ 952 489 100
www.valledeabdalajis.com

Valle de Abdalajís – Antequera

After some climbing to start, a relatively easy route with small sections of road walking broken up by nice tracks with views of the dramatic rock formations of the Parque Natural El Torcal.

Distance	20.5km
Time	5h
Height gain	640m
Height loss	400m
Highest point	780m

To leave Valle de Abdalajís take a track right next to the village's **garage**. This takes you down and across a small ford in the **Arroyo de las Piedras**. Just after you cross, ignore the track back to the right and then one off to the left to start climbing. Pass another track off to the right, with the **Cerro de los Perdigones** on your left, and then after 2km when you reach a crossroads carry straight on. Just around the corner you'll come to a second crossroads, at this one turn left onto a track which takes you through several fields. From here the route is very badly marked with some posts obviously missing.

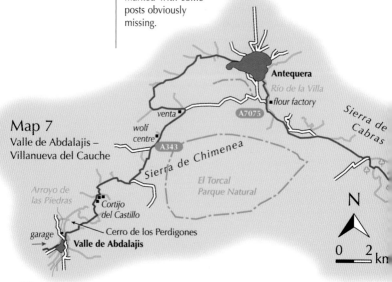

Map 7
Valle de Abdalajis –
Villanueva del Cauche

80

After another 2km you come to a T-junction. Turn right and then left, passing the **Cortijo del Castillo**, on a track which curves round the east side of a large rocky outcrop before levelling out to give you open views of the top end of the Valle de Abdalajís.

After 2.5km, this track ends at a tarmac road. Turn left here and carry on for 2km until it reaches the main **Antequera** road, the **A343**. Turn right onto this main road and walk along it for 3km, passing a **wolf centre**, until you reach the **Venta Gazpacho II**, which could be useful for a break. Here there is a small track on the left signposted for the Vereda del Cerro del Espartal (but not for the GR7). Take this track, heading briefly in the wrong direction for Antequera, and after almost 2km turn right onto an equally wide track which takes you gently uphill. When it forks

Gate to the Alcazaba, Antequera

81

turn right to walk round the east side of a small hill. From here it is 7km to Antequera.

The track heads downhill and east towards Antequera. Follow it on, passing a turning to the left, until it becomes a tarmac road and then stay on the tarmac road avoiding all turnings to reach the town, coming in by the football ground.

Antequera (577m, pop. 42,000) 🚶 🍴 F ▲ € ☎ ✉ ✚ ① 🚍 💻

A historic town whose skyline is dominated by the towers of the Moorish fortress (the Alcazaba), and its many church spires. It has layers of history, having been inhabited since the Bronze Age. If you stay here it's worth visiting the dolmens – some of Europe's oldest and biggest mass tombs made from huge rock slabs, dating from 2500bc to 1800bc, located in the park to the west of town. In the town centre you can also visit the recently excavated Roman baths, Gothic churches, the 19th-century bullring and beautiful Renaissance fountains and climb through the 16th-century Arch of the Giants up to the castle.

Accommodation and food

Wide range of places to stay and eat including Indian, Chinese and Italian cuisine for those who fancy a change:

Pensión Toril (s/d en suite €20/30) one of the cheapest options in town and still central but a little on the shabby side, TV and courtyard to sit in (C/Toril 3, ☎ 952 843 184)

Hotel Colon ★★ (s/d en suite €25/40) right in the centre of town, 25 rooms with cable TV, air conditioning and heating set around pretty courtyard, with a restaurant and internet access (C/Infante Don Fernando 31, ☎ 952 840 010, info@castelcolon.com, www.castelcolon.com)

Hotel San Sebastián ★★ (s/d en suite €25/40) less expensive than its central location and smart interior suggests, TV, internet and air conditioning, terrace seating area (Pza de San Sebastián 4, ☎ 952 844 239, informacion@hotelplazasansebastian.com, www.hotelplazasansebastian.com)

El Torcal Complejo Rural ★★ Campsite 6km from the centre of town on the GR7 in the El Torcal natural park (Ctra Comarcal C-3331, Km6, ☎ 952 111 608, www.complejoruraleltorcal.com)

For more information

Tourist information: Plaza de San Sebastián 7, ☎ 952 702 505, oficina.turismo@antequera.es, www.antequera.es

Distance	14.5km
Time	4h
Height gain	320m
Height loss	200m
Highest point	900m

To leave the town head through the historic part of town down towards the **Rió de la Villa** on the Bajada del Río. Walk out on the road with the river on your left and after about a 1.5km you come to a **flour factory** on your left, the first GR7 marking of the day and a junction with the **A7075** road.

Turn left up the road which runs alongside the beautiful **Parque Natural el Torcal** and after 2km of climbing, where the road divides, take the left fork. Very soon after that turn onto a track to the right which takes you off the road. Rejoin the road in another 1.5km and climb for a further 3km until you come to two tracks on the left and a signpost telling you that it is 2h30 to Villanueva del Cauche (more like 2h).

Take the second of the tracks and you soon emerge into beautiful open countryside. At the next divide, take the more

Small, pretty paths through fields of crops and wildflowers more than make up for an early uphill road walk. Views of the Parque Natural el Torcal accompany you for most of this route into the small village of Villanueva del Cauche.

Rooftops of Antequera

EL TORCAL NATURAL PARK (12km²)

Possibly Andalucía's strangest natural park, the Parque Natural el Torcal contains a myriad of wierd and wonderful rock formations. The whole park is a limestone plateau that originated under the sea millions of years ago. The waters of the Tetris Sea were responsible for carving out shapes in the soft, porous limestone, which was then brought to the surface, over one hundred million years ago, by movements in the Earth's crust. The limestone retained its formation and since that time has continued to be sculpted by wind and rain.

Wildlife
The rocky landscape and height of the park, in which the peak of El Torcal reaches 1336m, limits the type of vegetation and wildlife that can exist within it. However, it is known for its wildflowers, especially orchids with over 30 varieties growing in the park. Unsurprisingly rock plants and flowers are abundant and some trees manage to grow between the rocks.

In terms of wildlife, reptiles are the most numerous with many varieties of lizards and snakes to be found in the rocky crevices, including the two metre long Montpellier snake and the spine-footed lizard.

Bird life, too, is rich with the many birds of prey making the park a special protection zone for birds. Look out for griffon vultures, Bonelli's eagles, peregrines and eagle owls.

Lovers' Leap
The highest cliff within in the park, La Peña de los Enamorados (or Lovers' Leap) has been made famous by the legend that is attached to it. It is a Romeo and Juliet-like-tale that tells of an Arab girl and a Christian boy falling in love but throwing themselves from the cliff when their familes refused to accept their love.

minor one off to the left. After a kilometre this track almost peters out, becoming a small and somewhat difficult to follow, but pretty, overgrown footpath. Keep on it in a south-easterly direction, picking your way round the edges of fields towards an olive grove, and then onwards looking for small marks on rocks.

The path then turns back into a wider track. Follow this downwards until **Villanueva del Cauche** comes into sight. The view of the ancient hamlet is somewhat marred by the noisy **N331** dual carriageway between you and it. Descend towards the **Hotel las Pedrizas**, walking away from the village to cross into the hotel car park and pass under the underpass just beyond.

This is where the GR7 divides, with one fork heading north towards the province of Córdoba and the other heading south into the Granada province. From here you can follow the minor road down into the village to pick up the Southern Fork of the route or, for the northern route, carry on to Villanueva del Rosario up a marked route to the left before you enter the village.

Mountain view on the route to Villanueva del Cauche

Villanueva del Cauche (700m, pop. 298) ⤴ ⭘ F ▲ ☎ 🚌
Tiny white hamlet slightly overshadowed by the busy dual carriageway. There is not much there except a little plaza with a drinking fountain.

Accommodation and food
One bar in the village and one hotel on the major road before you enter the village:

Hotel las Pedrizas (s/d en suite € 30/50) motel-style hotel on main road (Ctra Madrid-Málaga, Km527, ☎ 952 730 850)

PART 2:

NORTHERN FORK – MÁLAGA, CÓRDOBA AND JAÉN

Villaneuva del Cauche to Puebla de Don Fadrique

This section of the book describes the Northern Fork of the GR7 from the point at which the route divides at the village of Villanueva del Cauche in Málaga province. The route up to Villanueva del Cauche is described in Part 1. The alternative route to Puebla de Don Fadrique by the Southern Fork is described in Part 3.

Mountain views on route between Carchelejo and Cambil

MÁLAGA PROVINCE

Villanueva del Cauche to Rute, 88km

An overview of the route in Málaga, and practical details such as transport information, are given at the beginning of the section 'Málaga province' (see page 65)
in Part 1.

Maps required
1:50,000 Servicio Geografico del Ejercito
17-43 **1039** Colmenar
17-42 **1024** Archidona
17-41 **1007** Rute
17-40 **989** Lucena

The route
Villanueva del Cauche – Villanueva del Trabuco

Distance	14km
Time	4h10
Height gain	160m
Height loss	160m
Highest point	760m

A gentle route passing between fields and olive groves with mountains always on the horizon distracting the walker from the busy road that the route shadows for much of the way.

Villanueva del Cauche – Villanueva del Rosario (10km, 3h)

Head out of Villanueva del Cauche on the road to the north,
cross straight over a wider road and ignore the underpass
down to the left. This takes you onto the old road up the hill,
looking down on the busy **N331** dual carriageway below. (If
you arrived at the village on the GR7, come back out on the
same road you came in on, but don't turn back down to the
underpass, instead head right and follow the road up the
hill.)

Olive fields and hills on the way to Villanueva del Trabuco

Villanueva del Rosario (670m, pop. 3300) 🚶 🍴 F ▲ € ☎ ✚ 🚌

Situated at the foot of dramatic rocky mountains, Villanueva del Rosario has a rich cultural history with several archaeological sites, two dating from the Copper Age, in the area. The Romans left much evidence of their presence in the form of Roman roads and artefacts. There is believed to be Roman treasure yet to be discovered beneath the Peñon de Solis, 3km from the centre. It is worth paying a visit to the museum in the Plaza Medieval del Saucedo if you're interested in finding out more.

Accommodation and food
A range of places to eat, mainly *tapas* bars and a couple of hotels on the main road into the village:

Hotel Cerezo ★ (s/d en suite € 20/35) just on the road into Villanueva del Rosario (Huerta del Moruno, ☎ 952 742 129)

Hotel las Delicias ★ (s/d en suite € 25/40) just on the road on the way into the village with a popular restaurant downstairs (Ctra las Pedrizas, ☎ 952 742 432)

For more information
Town hall: ☎ 952 742 008

After 2km avoid turning across a bridge instead turn right soon after a GR7 signpost (Villanueva del Rosario 3h20, 10km). Carry on up this quiet road, ignoring tracks to either side and then turning left under an **underpass**. Continue along the road until it meets another road and then turn right. You can see **Villanueva del Rosario** ahead of you amongst olives and fields of corn. Pass under another **underpass** and then take the track to the right to avoid walking in on the main road, which you rejoin just before the village.

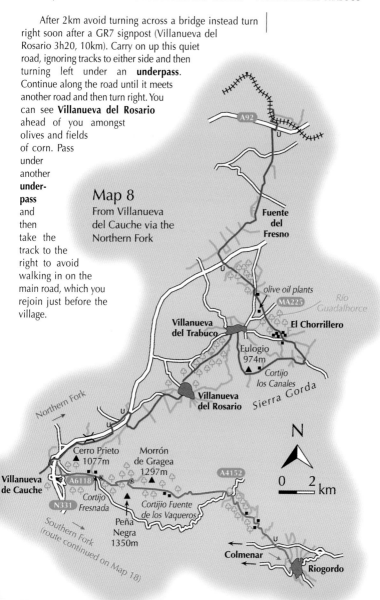

Map 8
From Villanueva del Cauche via the Northern Fork

Villanueva del Rosario – Villanueva del Trabuco (4km, 1h10)

Pass a sign up to the Nacimiento de la Villa, the source of the river – a natural spring which provides the drinking water supply for the village and has pools and waterfalls. Leave the village on a dirt track off to the right. Follow this through olive groves the entire way.

Villanueva del Trabuco (700m, pop. 5000) 🔄 🍴 F ▲ € ☎ ✉ ✚ ⓘ 🚌 💻

Villaneuva del Trabuco is an expanding but still attractive place located at the foot of the Gorda and San Jorge mountains providing the start to many walking routes. With water supplied from both the Río Guadalhorce and Río Higueral, the village's Fuente de los Tres Caños (fountain of the three pipes) is famous for never running dry even in droughts. It has a large and growing English population, so don't be surprised when you come across the 'Corner Shop'.

Accommodation and food
Several bars and restaurants but limited accommodation:

B&B (€20 per person) B&B in friendly British-run holiday flat with use of sitting room and kitchen, 4 rooms sleeping 6 in total, jacuzzi and roof terrace (C/Cádiz 4, ☎ 952 75 24 25)

Hotel Paneque (s/d en suite €25/50) big establishment on the main road a few kilometres out of the village (Ctra Málaga-Granada, Km50, ☎ 952 111 479)

Cortijo con Vistas (pppn incl breakfast €27) located 4km from the village, a house available for rent which acts as a B&B when not rented (enquiries@cortijoconvistas.co.uk, www.cortijoconvistas.co.uk)

For more information
Town hall: ☎ 952 751 021

Villanueva del Trabuco – Villanueva de Tapia

Distance	28km
Time	8h
Height gain	320m
Height loss	360m
Highest point	940m

Come out of town over a bridge with a play park on your right where there is a signboard with a map and description of the day's route. Take the road up to the left of this, Avenida Miguel Indurain, towards the hills of the **Sierra Gorda**. After 500m the road divides, and you stay on the right, tarmac branch. Climb for 2.5km on this road, then take the gravel track up to the left behind the small peak of **Eulogio**. A sign here says that it is 9h20 to Villanueva del Tapia.

Continue on the track past the **Cortijo los Canales**, ignoring a smaller track downhill, and contour round the hillside passing a track off to the left. Here you can look down over the entire village of Villanueva del Trabuco. When you meet another track turn right and carry on past two tracks, one on either side. You will come to an intersection of tracks; take the second left and begin heading downhill.

When you reach a tarmac road, turn left and stay on this until you reach the neighbourhood of **El Chorrillero**. Turn right where a signpost erroneously claims that it's 7h50 to go, 8km from the start of the route. Head up the hill past a useful drinking fountain on the right, continuing on through olive groves on a gravel track up to the road (**MA225**).

Cross over the road (or join here if you took the short-cut) turning onto the Vereda de Archidona a Alfarnate track. Pass by the Montes de Gaudalhorce Aceite de Oliva Virgen Extra **olive oil plant** on the left and, when you meet another road coming out of Villanueva del Trabuco, turn right onto it. Soon after, take a turning on the left at another **olive oil plant**, then turn immediately right onto the gravel track (rather than the tarmac one). Pass another track on the left and carry on through the olive groves.

You pass two turnings, one on either side, and take the **underpass** under the **A359**. The track from here takes you across fields before turning right at a crossroads, at which point you will have walked 15km in total. Go straight on at two more crossroads, ignoring smaller turnings, to arrive at **Fuente de Fresno** after 3km (13.8km, 4h35 to Villanueva de Tapia). From here continue along the tarmac road and after 1km carry straight on at a crossroads, ignoring yellow PR signs off to the left and right.

The track continues heading north and crosses another road after 2km. Turn right here up a smaller track. When you

A long but beautiful loop on the hillsides around the village can be bypassed by following the right branch of the road east out of the village for 1km then rejoining the route as it continues along tracks through wide open farmland and olive groves.

Poppy field along the route

approach a major road, the **A92** (a further kilometre on), take the **underpass** beneath it and turn left on the other side to get you to the **railway line**. Cross the railway line onto the Via Pecuaria Cañada Real de Seville a Granada and turn left alongside the railway tracks (signpost 2h35, 7.8km). After 1km turn right up a marked track and follow this east.

If you're in need of somewhere to stay, there is nowhere in **Villanueva de Tapia** so you might want to try the Hotel Los Borbollones at the Centro de Actividades Cinegeticas signposted off to the right along a minor road just before you reach a GR7 signpost and the main road. If not, continue down to the road and turn right towards Villanueva de Tapia. Continue along the road, following marks to take short sections away from the traffic (including turning up the side road to the bar Asador los Tres, which brings you back onto the road further up).

After 1.5km pass Hotel Rural Paloma, then continue on for another 3.5km. To enter the village head under the **underpass** and down. To continue on, turn off to the left before the underpass where a sign highlights the Ruta de Algaidas y Feria de Ganado trail.

Villanueva de Tapia (661m, pop. 1660) 🛏 🍴 F ▲ ☎ ✉ 🚍

Friendly village with busy little high street with a range of shops and a market with fresh produce. It takes its name from Pedro de Tapia, the member of the Supreme Royal Court who bought the village when King Felipe III decided it was no longer of value around the 17th century.

Accommodation and food

Nowhere to stay in the town but a couple of places on the way in and a couple of bar-restaurants to eat in:

Hotel Rural Paloma ★ (s/d en suite €35/50) a charming hotel with on-site restaurant cooking fresh produce from its own garden, all rooms en suite with air conditioning and breakfast included (Ctra Salinas a Villanueva de Tapia, ☎ 657 344 888, www.hotelrurallapaloma.com)

Hotel los Borbollones ★★★ (d en suite €50, no singles) set within a hunting centre, with a plush country club atmosphere, nice rooms set around swimming pool, breakfast included, restaurant on site, 1km up a turning just before you meet main road to Tapia (Ctra A-333, Salinas a Villanueva de Tapia, ☎ 678 730 015)

For more information

www.villanuevadetapia.org

Villanueva de Tapia – Villanueva de Algaidas

Distance	17km
Time	4h30
Height gain	620m
Highest point	920m

A pretty section of undulating tracks through seemingly endless olive groves, interrupted only occasionally by cornfields and whitewashed *cortijos*.

Head back out of village the way you entered, under the underpass and onto the track marked with a signboard for the Ruta de Algaidas y Feria de Ganado. At the time of writing there were no GR7 markings here. Climb up through olive groves, sticking to the larger track when it divides and climbing higher.

Whilst stopping to catch your breath, look back over the endless stripes of olive groves below you. As the path levels out, after about 4km, you reach several ruined buildings and the track branches at an old whitewashed farmhouse. Turn left downhill here then left again where there is a fork in the route just after the house.

Map 9
Northern Route: Hotel los Borbollones – Rute

If you want a diversion for more drinking water, turn right at the next fork in the track to a spring (which may be dry in summer), otherwise continue on the main track through more olive trees. Take the next left turn and descend slightly, ignoring the next left and continuing on the same track as it turns to tarmac.

On the way to Villanueva de Algaidas

95

Farmhouse on the way to Villanueva de Algaidas

You meet a minor road where a sign tells you it's a further 3h50 and 11km to **Villanueva de Algaidas**. Turn right along the road and after 2km head up a signposted track to the left. Turn right at a building and continue along with great views. When you meet a small tarmac road turn left and follow it downhill. Before climbing the daunting looking slope on the same road, stop off at the **Arroyo del Bebedero** for more water (again seasonal).

After 500m of climbing, turn right up the first track opposite a house and when this track splits soon afterwards, take the right fork round the hillside then downhill. Avoid tracks off to the left and pass another sign for a water point before crossing the river (both spring and river may be dry in summer). Carry on along the main track, ignoring tracks off to the left and then right. The track turns to tarmac in places after crossing another river and brings you down into the hamlet of **Albaicín**. From here it is 3km to **Villanueva de Algaidas**.

Cross straight over the road here and continue on a gravel track. Turn left and head downhill then back up through olive groves, passing a small track off to the right and making a final steep climb up to the road. Turn right down into an industrial estate and on into the village.

Villanueva de Algaidas (545m, pop. 4200) ↵ ⦿ F ▲ € ☎ ✉ ✚ ① 🚍 🖳

A large and lively village whose claim to fame is being the birthplace of internationally renowned sculptor Berrocal. There is an exhibition of his work. The church and the 16th-century Los Recoletos de San Francisco de Asís convent are also worth a visit.

Accommodation and food

Several bars and restaurants offer a choice for eating and there are a couple of hotels as well as an upmarket B&B:

Hotel Algaidas on the main street heading out at the north of the town (C/Archidona 75, ☎ 952 743 308)

Hotel la Rincona (d en suite €50) a nice enough hotel restaurant with pleasant rooms but unappealingly located in the industrial park (Polígono Industrial, Avda del Olivar, ☎ 952 745 008)

La Casa de la Fuente (en suite d from €65) British-run, luxury B&B with spacious and distinctive rooms, some with jacuzzi baths, and bar serving breakfast and evening meals (C/Málaga 18, ☎ 952 745 030/690 205 351, lacasadelafuente@yahoo.com, www.lacasadelafuente.com)

For more information
www.villanuevaadealgaidas.com

Villanueva de Algaidas – Cuevas de San Marcos

Distance	18.5km
Time	5h
Height gain	100m
Height loss	280m
Highest point	540m

This overgrown route alongside the riverbed of the Arroyo de Burriana can be a little like hacking your way through a jungle, but once you've emerged it is an easy walk along wide tracks from one Cuevas to the other.

Villanueva de Algaidas – Cuevas Bajas (10km, 3h)

Walk out of Villanueva de Algaidas heading downhill along the main street (called Archidona then Granada) and leave on the Cuevas Bajas road where there is a huge maroon sign for the route.

Soon afterwards turn right onto a small road which looks very like a dead end. Where the tarmac ends, head off

Villanueva de Algaidas

Don't be put off by the fence posts made from leftover marking posts with yellow and white crosses.

along an improbable overgrown path taking you down across a dry stream bed and up the other side where you need to search for a small path up to the left (not the more likely looking route to the road and houses on the right).

Follow the small path round the hillside and along the right-hand side of a fence. This brings you almost to the road but you turn off right along another small path next to the river. ◀ The route takes you across a small medieval bridge and then zigzags up the bank of the other side of the river into the small hamlet of La Atalaya (▲).

Once in the village walk up the main street, turn left on Calle el Pilar and follow the street up, not taking a turn-off down to the left but continuing on out of the village until you reach the last house. Then turn left downhill on a gravel track through olives to reach a road. Turn left down the road very briefly then right onto another gravel track through olive trees passing a ruin and a marked site of archeological interest.

After 2km the track disappears when it meets the riverbed of the **Arroyo de Burriana**. From here you need to pick your way alongside the river, always staying on the right (east) bank, through fields and some wilder terrain. As long as you stay near the river you can't get lost but it may take some time. There are a few markings along the way for encouragement. You rejoin a track at some solar panels. Follow this track and take the right fork when it divides. This takes you uphill and to the main road into **Cuevas Bajas**. Cross the main road at this point and walk down the old road into the village.

Cuevas Bajas (323m, pop. 1500) ⤵ ◉ F ▲ ☎ ✉ ✚ 🚌
Cuevas Bajas sits on the bank of the Río Genil which flows through the village. Thanks to the river, the land around the village is lush with vegetation, even though it is set within an arid area of scrubland. The river is also good for fishing. The centre of the village is set around the square on which Church of San Juan sits.

Accommodation and food
A couple of bars and very little in the way of accommodation:
Casa Rural Arrebola (4 person house per day during week/weekend €80/100) the GR7 runs right in front of this *casa rural* which is 1km from the village and can be rented by the day if not occupied (Paraje las Canteras, ☎ 952 729 524)

For more information
Town hall: ☎ 952 729 526

Cuevas Bajas – Cuevas de San Marcos (8.5km, 2h)
Leave Cuevas Bajas on the well-marked Riberia del Genil walking route. A sign for this on the east of the village takes you right on a wide track through the industrial estate. Where there is a divide in the track take the right fork, ignoring the walking route signs pointing left. Carry on for 3km, passing smaller tracks off to the right, then at the next divide take the right fork again (sign 1h15) to come alongside the **Río Genil**.

From here there are a few smaller tracks going off on either side but stick to the main track until a clear junction. Here you have the option of taking either the left fork, to continue on to **Rute**, or the right fork, to go into Cuevas de San Marcos.

If you choose to carry on to Rute, follow the left track until it reaches a road and then turn left to reach the bridge across the Genil (see description from Cuevas de San Marcos in the next section).

To go into **Cuevas de San Marcos** take the right fork and then, when it divides again, head left to come into the old part of the village.

Cuevas de San Marcos (360m, pop. 4500) ⤴ 🏨 F ⛰ € ☎ ✉ ✚ 🚌

Situated amidst the Sierra del Camorro mountains and valleys of olive groves, this is a small town with a few sites of interest including: the Belda cave where prehistoric remains were found and which has one of the most important bat populations in Europe; the archaeological site of Belda, a medieval town, on the top of the Sierra del Camorro; the Archaeological Museum with finds from the area; and in the town itself there's the 17th-century Church of San Marcos and the 18th-century Ermita del Carmen.

Accommodation and food
Less accommodation than its size would suggest but plenty of places to eat:

Casa Bob Guest House (s/d €22/30) British-run B&B with small but pleasant rooms, bar and good home cooking available (C/Grama 22, ☎ 952 728 212, ninagiles@wanadoo.es, www.andalucianestates.com)

At the time of writing *hostal* rooms were also being added to a restaurant on the road at the top of town.

For more information
Town hall: ☎ 952 728 102

Cuevas de San Marcos – Rute

A beautiful section crossing from Málaga into Córdoba province through pines with ancient and dramatic views across the Embalse de Iznájar.

Distance	10.5km
Time	3h
Height gain	460m
Height loss	180m
Highest point	700m

If you went into Cuevas de San Marcos leave town to the northwest on the road which leads to the bridge over the **Río Genil**. After 1.5km of walking along the road you will cross the Luis de Armiñan **bridge**, built in 1910, en route to which you will pass an odd sign indicating that Rute is 1h10 in the direction you came from – ignore this!

After you cross the bridge take the track immediately on the right and follow it along the river, ignoring another track off to the left, and into the hamlet of **Vadofresno**. From Vadofresno there are almost no markings. Take the first road on the right as you come in. This takes you along a road marked as a dead end that turns into a gravel track. When it splits into three, take the right track and, when that track then divides, take the smaller of the two tracks through a field of olive trees. One kilometre after you leave the hamlet you come back onto a small tarmac road. Carry on along this, passing a drinking fountain at **Camorro de la Isla** and continue straight on. From here a small road heads uphill, with panoramic views down over the **Embalse de Iznájar,** Andalucía's highest capacity reservoir.

After 2km, cross over a road and continue straight on. When you reach another crossroads a further 2.5km on, again carry straight on, up the long but final climb to **Rute**. The track brings you in at the south of the town. To reach the centre turn left when the track meets the road. (See next section for description of facilities available in Rute.)

Looking down on Iznájar reservoir

CÓRDOBA PROVINCE

Rute to Alcalá la Real, 57.5km

The route passes into the province of Córdoba from Málaga province, just after the village of Cuevas de San Marcos. On a scenic, winding route through olive groves, the GR7 takes you up to the small town of Rute, famed for its special liqueur, *anís*. From here you take a charming old woodland path with great views across the Subbética mountains including the highest peak in the province, La Tiñosa, at 1568m. This brings you up to Priego de Córdoba, a striking historic town on a plateau looking down over the dramatic scenery of the park.

Onwards from here you visit the tiny village of La Concepción and pass through more olive groves, with panoramic views of the Sierra de los Judios mountains and endless patterns of olives below, to reach Almedinilla. The route leaves Córdoba behind here and continues into Jaén province.

HIGHLIGHTS OF THE ROUTE IN CÓRDOBA PROVINCE

- walking through the beautiful Parque Natural de la Sierra Subbética with its peaks emerging from a sea of olive groves
- tasting locally produced *anís* in Rute
- exploring the historic, narrow streets of Priego de Córdoba

Transport

There are regular bus services from Granada to Priego de Córdoba and Almedinilla run by Alsina Graells (☎ 957 278 100, www.alsinagraells.es) Two other companies run buses within the natural park and there are also several taxi services:

Autobuses Carrera: ☎ 957 500 302/957 231 401

Autobuses Casado: ☎ 957 538 175

Taxis: ☎ 957 538 319/372/190/698

Tourist information

Andalucía tourist information office: C/Torrijos 10, 14003, Córdoba, ☎ 957 471 235, otCórdoba@andalucia.org

Other walks

There is a good network of shorter walking routes in the Subbética, including the newly restored 58km route along an old olive oil train route (Via Verde del Tren de Aceite)

which links Lucena, Cabra, Doña Mencía, Zuheros and Luque. Its stations have been turned into restaurants and the railway architecture and buildings – bridges, a tunnel, level crossings and the workers' housing – have been restored.

Many of the routes cross over, or link up with, parts of the GR7 and provide interesting extra sections if you want to spend more time in the Córdoba province or create circular routes. For further information it is worth trying to get hold of the walking guide to La Subbética from Mancomunidad de la Subbética (☎ 957 704 106, www.subbetica.es).

Maps required
1:50,000 Servicio Geografico del Ejercito
17-41 **1007** Rute
17-40 **989** Lucena
18-40 **990** Alcalá la Real

The route

Rute (637m, pop. 10,070) ⟿ 🍴 F ▲ € ☎ ✉ ✚ ① 🚌 💻
The whitewashed town overlooks the Iznájar reservoir and is dwarfed by the Sierra de Rute that looms above it. It is best known for its manufacture of *aguardiente de anís*, an aniseed-flavoured liqueur, an industry that has been thriving here since the 19th century. Try it at any of the town's *bodegas* where it is produced, or visit the Museo Anís on the Paseo del Fresno (☎ 957 538 143). Curiously, Rute is also home to a ham museum (☎ 957 539 227) – perhaps not quite as enticing a tourist attraction as the ruined Moorish castle or Baroque church.

Accommodation and food
There are two hotels as you enter and a few restaurants scattered around town:

Hotel el Mirador ★★★ (s/d en suite with breakfast €36/45) a smart hotel just around the corner from the María Luisa with balconies, air conditioning and the El Balcón restaurant (Ctra Rute-Encinas Reales, Km0.2, ☎ 957 539 404, www.miradorderute.com)

Hotel María Luisa ★★★ (s/d en suite with breakfast €50/70) upmarket hotel just as GR7 enters Rute with private balconies, indoor and outdoor swimming pools, air conditioning, bar and restaurant (Crta Luceana-Loja, Km22, ☎ 957 538 096, hotelmarialuisa@zercahoteles.com, www.zercahoteles.com)

For more information
Tourist office, Parque Nuestra Señora del Carmen, ☎ 957 532 929
www.rute.org

Rute – Priego de Córdoba

A route made up mainly of magical woodland paths passing through pine and oak trees with stunning views over Córdoba's highest peaks before it returns to olive groves as it nears Priego de Córdoba.

Distance	22.5km
Time	6h50
Height gain	580m
Height loss	560m
Highest point	920m

To leave Rute head east out of the Paseo del Fresno past the secondary school (*colegio*) and off Calle Chacarra, where a small track takes you uphill to the right into pine trees. Follow this, staying close to the right -

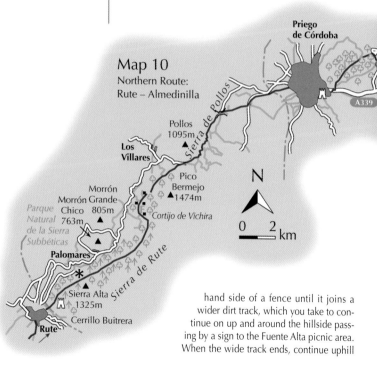

hand side of a fence until it joins a wider dirt track, which you take to continue on up and around the hillside passing by a sign to the Fuente Alta picnic area. When the wide track ends, continue uphill in the same direction on a smaller path, again through pine trees. At a clearing in the trees you can see the rocky outcrop of Sierra de la Gaulhinera (1095m), Sierra Alcaide, **Pico Bermejo** (1474m) and La Tiñosa (1570m) behind you. After another 500m you come to a **viewpoint** where you can see out across the whole valley, down to the ruins of Old Rute which was abandoned in the 15th century, and across the hills and the endless olive-clad ridges.

From the viewpoint the small, shady path continues picking its way through pine woodland on the side of the **Sierra de Rute** and you should be able to see the small village of **Palomares** down to your left. When you reach a young olive grove, be careful not to miss the path which goes up to the right (rather than into the olives) and then continues along the edge of the field passing through beautiful woods, this time with some gall oaks.

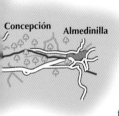

Concepción   Almedinilla

The path continues, with any small junctions clearly marked, until it reaches a gorge. Here the path divides and you should head down a rocky ridge to the left, across a boulder field heading northeast and into grassy open countryside. When the path almost disappears, follow the edge of the field marked by a broken fence and an old wall. Now, 3h20 from the start of the route, you come to a useful drinking fountain at the **Cortijo de Vichira**.

Pass the fountain and come to a signposted track. Turn right and continue along and then through a farmyard, ignoring a track off to the left. When the track divides, take the right fork uphill, passing behind a building to find a small path starting off to the right in the olive field. From here the path is patchy, but good markings take you back onto a track within 15min.

When the track meets another, turn right and then, when you enter another olive field, head left and then almost immediately right again. From here a smaller shady track takes you downhill to the road not far from the small village of **Los Villares**. Turn left for Los Villares or right to carry on with the route to **Priego de Córdoba**.

Viewpoint in the Sierra de Rute

Los Villares (612m, pop. 4970) 🔌 ⛺ 🍽 F ▲ ☎

The village of Los Villares is located deep within the beautiful surroundings of
the natural park with great views.

Accommodation and food
A campsite with *casas rurales*:

Cortijo los Villares (person/tent/casa rural €3.5/3.5/from 50) campsite with space
   for 70 people, swimming pool and restaurant (Ctra Carcabuey-Rute, Km6,
   ☎ 957 704 054, info@casadelasubbetica.com, www.casasdelasubbetica.com)

Taxis
Rural 4x4 taxis: Javier Sanchez-Sanchez ☎ 626 136 550/678 503 030

SIERRA SUBBÉTICA NATURAL PARK (320km²)

The beautiful Parque Natural de la Sierra Subbética is famous for its craggy limestone peaks which contrast sharply with the rolling lower hills covered in olive
groves and the green woodland in which it sits.

Wildlife
The park is home to many gall and holm oaks, wild olives, maples and hackber-
ries and a wide variety of wildflowers including irises, daffodils, peonies and
orchids which bring it its colour in spring.
   The area is very rich in bird life including one of the largest breeding
colonies of griffon vultures in the south of Spain, and about 70 other bird
species, including black wheatear, hoopoe, cuckoos, red-legged partridge, rock
buntings, and common and alpine swifts.
   Andalucía's largest population of peregrine falcons nest in the limestone
crags and are the symbol for the park. It is also home to many other birds of
prey – booted, Bonelli's and short-toed eagles, kestrels and several species of
owl.

For further information
Centro de Visitantes de Santa Rita: Carretera A340, Km57, ☎ 957 334 034

Stay on the small tarmac road for 4km, with great views
back to Pico Bermejo and the Sierra de Rute, then turn right
off onto a gravel track. This crosses a small **bridge** and then
divides. Take the left fork and then the second track off to the
right to go up and over a low pass before returning to a road.

Turn left along the road and then, after 600m, right onto a gravel track which takes you all the way into Priego de Córdoba. You arrive in the town at a very old and battered looking GR7 display board. To get to the centre from here turn right.

Priego de Córdoba (649m, pop. 22,900) 🔁 🐾 F ▲ € ☎ ⊠ ✚ ⓘ 🚐 🖥

Priego de Córdoba

Perched on a hill above the Sierra Subbética, this elegant old town is known for its baroque churches, and, unsurprisingly given the number of trees you'll have passed, its olive oil. To get a feel for the architecture of the place visit the Iglesia de la Asunción, the Iglesia de la Aurora and the famous Fuente del Rey, an 139-spout fountain topped by a statue of Neptune. It's also worth strolling up to the 13th-century Islamic castle and to the picturesque Barrio de la Villa, the maze-like centre of the old town with cascades of colourful flowers and bright doors and windows set off by whitewashed walls.

Accommodation and food
There's a selection of hotels and also some lovely *casas rurales* if you're thinking of staying for a while, some busy *tapas* bars and a variety of restaurants:

Hotel Río Piscina ★ a large place on the GR7 route out of town (Ctra de Granada, ☎ 957 700 186, info@hotelriopiscina.com, www.hotelriopiscina.com)

Hostal Rafi ★★ (s/d en suite €35/45) central 26-room *hostal* with restaurant and café below. Nice clean rooms with TV, air conditioning (C/Isabel la Católica 4, ☎ 957 540 749, hostalrafi@hostalrafi.net, www.hostalrafi.net)

La Posada Real (d/6-person house €48/120) typical Andalucian house in historic area of Priego, available to rent as full house or per room (C/Real, ☎ 957 541 910/619 085 167, pasador@arrakis.es, www.laposadareal.com)

For more information
www.aytopriegodecórdoba.es

Distance	10km
Time	2h40
Height gain	120m
Height loss	140m
Highest point	740m

With great views back over Priego, the route heads up through olive trees to Almedinilla.

Leave Priego on the Puerta Granada on the eastern edge of town. This small road takes you across a **bridge** and past the Hotel Río Piscina before the main **A339** road at a roundabout. Turn right and follow the road briefly in the direction of **Almedinilla** before taking the first turning on the left onto a gravel track (signposted La Concepción 55min, Almedinilla 2h55).

When this track divides take the left fork, leaving the buildings behind and beginning to get a great view back

Looking back towards Priego de Córdoba

109

Almedinilla

over Priego. At the next fork turn right as the track climbs uphill through olive trees. Stay on the main track and when it divides again, take a left and continue uphill for about a kilometre to where a signpost directs you right and east along a small path through the olive fields. After another 10min you arrive in **La Concepción** (🍴 F), 4.5km and just over an hour from the start.

Turn right into La Concepción and continue down to the bottom of the village, passing a drinking fountain. There are two roads out of the village here; take the one to the left and follow it for a kilometre keeping a close eye out for a track off to the right at a bend in the road before you would pass a house up to the left. Take this unmarked track, through olive fields turning right and then left at the two junctions. When you come to some houses turn right onto a minor tarmac road and then, when that road meets another small tarmac road, turn left.

Walk along the road for 2km and then turn right off it onto a wide gravel track, just before it goes up a small but steep hill. This takes you alongside a stream and then across it when the track divides. Follow this uphill to arrive in **Almedinilla**. Cross the main road and walk past the football ground to get to the centre of the village.

Almedinilla (622m, pop. 2500) ⚐ ⚑ F ▲ € ☎ ✉ ✚ ① 🚌

A pretty village with streets lined with orange trees. It was important in Roman times and you can visit the ruins of a large Roman villa. A former watermill in the village has now been turned into a museum and there is also an Iberian necropolis.

Accommodation and food
One place to stay and a good restaurant serving local dishes:

El Suizo Pensión-Restaurant (€10 pp) basic but friendly accommodation in the centre of the village, worth calling or asking locally if it is closed as they will open up for you (Pza Cuatro Caños 11, ☎ 957 703 021 or 957 703 012)

At the time of writing there was also a large hotel at the top of the village which was closed but it may be open when you visit.

Almedinilla – Alcalá la Real

Distance	25km
Time	5h30
Height gain	860m
Height loss	540m
Highest point	1100m

A steady climb through olive groves followed by a scenic descent to the picturesque Alcalá dominated by its impressive castle.

Follow road signs to Alcalá la Real out of Almedinilla, passing a junction off to the right with the road to Bracana next to the international school. Take the next right after this, following signs to the Museo Arqueológico. A paved footpath brings you up the impressive gorge on the left-hand side of the river.

This path brings you out onto the Bracana road at a GR7 signpost (Las Pilas 2h25). Cross over the road here and take a small track up to the right steeply uphill and over the **Cerro de la Cruz**.

A less steep, but also less attractive, option is to continue on the small local road until just after Km4 where you can take the turning to the left off the road highlighted in the directions below.

Do not turn off onto any smaller paths, and carry on through olive trees with beautiful views down to the village.

If you carry on over the hill, you climb steeply past some ruins and continue on the same path, the ancient Camino de los Canos. ◄ You come out onto the Bracana road again passing an abandoned farmhouse and another signpost (Las Pilas 1h50).

Turn right onto the road and after about 600m take a left onto a smaller tarmac road which you continue to follow downhill despite the lack of markings. After 30min and 2.5km you come to a **water storage tank** with a white tower at the ruined **Cortijo de Santa Teresa**. Pass by the tower and take the next dirt track up to the right, ignoring a track off to the left. Keep to the main track here, passing through olives and oaks and when you reach a crossroads after about 2.5km, continue straight on.

After a house on your right and then a track doubling back to the right just past it, take a right at a fork and continue on, passing a further track to the right. This main track will bring you to the road where you turn left and, after a few hundred metres, you leave the Córdoba province for Jaén. At a divide in the road 500m further on, take the right fork uphill to continue on the route (signpost Alcalá la Real 3h) or the left fork down and round the corner to visit the small village of **Las Pilas de la Fuente del Soto** (860m, ⊙| F € ☎ ⊕), 1km and about 15min further on.

If you went into Las Pilas, you can exit on the same road you came in on, taking the signposted turn up to the left in the direction of Alcalá la Real. Head uphill on this road for about 3km (40min) through olive groves. Once you start to go downhill you should come to a signpost beside a house (Alcalá 2h10), after about 300m.

This next section is very difficult to follow, taking you on small paths through olive groves and at the time of writing it was very poorly marked. It joins the road after Km3 at which point you turn right. An easier option is to leave Las Pilas on the same road you came

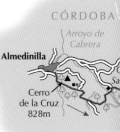

CÓRDOBA

Arroyo de Cabrera

Almedinilla

Sa

Cerro de la Cruz 828m

in on, but in the opposite direction and take its right fork when it divides. After about 4km, the GR7 joins this road and you can continue along the route from here.

After this point, follow the road as it climbs gently for about 1.5km, then head down to the left on a signposted smaller tarmac road (signed 1h25). You will come to a sign down to the right but, on the advice of the local walking club who signposted this section, ignore this post and continue to the next right turn.

Take this downhill, doubling back slightly and ignoring two tracks off to the left. When you meet another track, turn right and then right again at the next fork. A few metres before the main road, the **N432**, you turn left down another track, rejoining the marked GR7, with great views of the town ahead dominated by the Arab Castillo de la Mota. This brings you back onto the road just as you enter Alcalá la Real. (See next section for description of facilities available in Alcalá la Real.)

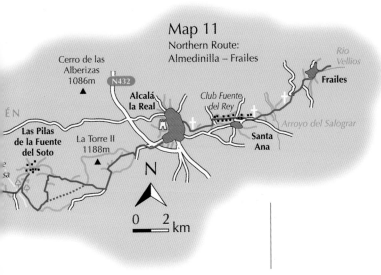

Map 11
Northern Route:
Almedinilla – Frailes

On the way to Alcalá la Real

JAÉN PROVINCE

Alcalá la Real to Puebla de Don Fadrique, 297.5km

Over 300km of route take you through Jaén province's most important mountain ranges: the Sierra Sur, the Sierra Mágina and the Sierras de Cazorla, Segura y las Villas. Jaén is full of wild spaces and is the province with the highest number of protected areas in Spain. Its protected parks and reserves cover 304,000 hectares in total, almost a third of the province.

The route crosses into Jaén from the Córdoba province at Alcalá la Real, which is the biggest place on the route in Jaén, dominated by an impressive eighth-century castle, La Mota. From there, the route passes over the imposing Sierra de Alta Coloma and down through the pretty white villages of Carchelejo and Cambil before crossing into the Parque Natural de la Sierra Mágina, home to Pico Mágina, the highest peak in the province at 2167m.

From there, the route takes you through a sea of olive groves between Bedmar, Jódar and Quesada before arriving back at the foothills of large peaks in the vibrant and beautiful Cazorla, the gateway to the largest natural park in Andalucía, the Parque Natural de Cazorla, Segura y las Villas. You get a magnificent feeling of freedom as the route winds its way around and over the pine-clad lofty peaks of the park and emerges at the source of the Río Guadalquivir.

Here the valleys and countryside have great grandeur and natural beauty and you pass through a few final villages on your way to Santiago de la Espada, the last destination of the GR7 in the Jaén province. The route then crosses over into Granada province to rejoin the Southern Fork of the GR7 in Puebla de Don Fadrique. From this point onwards, the route goes out of Andalucía and into the Murcia region of Spain.

HIGLIGHTS OF THE ROUTE IN JAÉN PROVINCE

- castles – Jaén province is home to the most castles per km^2 in Europe
- lofty peaks and stunning views of the Parque Natural de la Sierra Mágina
- the tree-covered slopes of the remote and wild Parque Natural de las Sierras de Cazorla, Segura y las Villas

Transport

Alcalá la Real and the city of Jaén itself offer the best transport options to and from places along the route of the GR7 in Jaén province, with regular buses running from both to most villages on the route. The buses are run by several companies and it is best to get in touch with them to check out up-to-date timetables. The two main companies are:

- Alsina Graells, which runs buses to/from Alcalá la Real, Carchelejo, Cazorla, Frailes, Jódar and Torres (☎ 953 255 014, www.alsinagraells.es)
- Muñoz Amezcua, which runs buses from Jaén bus station to Quesada, Jódar, Albanchez de Mágina and Bedmar stopping at many of the small places on route (☎ 953 752 157)

Futher information

Alcalá la Real bus station: ☎ 953 583 000
Alcalá la Real taxis: ☎ 953 580 507
Jaén train station: ☎ 953 270 202
Jaén bus station: ☎ 953 254 442

Tourist information

Andalucía tourist office: C/Maestra 13, Bajo, 23007, Jaén, ☎ 953 242 624, otJaén@andalucia.org

Other walks

There is a range of walking and cycling routes in the Sierra Mágina, taking in some amazing scenery. They are not very well marked, but a couple of little 'Magica Mágina' guides with descriptions and sketch maps are available from the Asociación para el Desarrollo Rural de la Sierra Mágina which has an office in Cambil (on Calle Posada above the health centre). *Rutas Saludables*, written by over 300 women who live in the area in a programme with ADR Sierra Mágina, contains shorter routes (all under 10km) some of which intersect with the GR7. *Rutas de Senderismo y Bicicleta* has longer routes, including climbing Pico Mágina and routes to Jaén and Úbeda, some of which again connect with the GR7.

In the Sierras de Cazorla, Segura y las Villas natural park there is a huge network of paths and tracks but most of them are unmarked. You can get hold of maps and route descriptions from the Cazorla tourist office or the visitor centres (see box on page 144). The Sendero Río Borosa (19km, 7h round trip) is one of the park's better known routes, starting at the Torre de Vinagre visitor centre and taking you through a spectacular gorge hewn out by the Borosa river, past waterfalls to the beautiful Laguna de Aguas Negras and the Laguna de Valdeazores. There are also shorter walks such as the 2km Sendero Cerrada de Utrero to the Linarejos waterfall.

Maps required

1:50,000 Servicio Geografico del Ejercito
18-40 **990** Alcalá la Real
19-40 **991** Iznalloz
19-39 **969** Valdepeñas de Jaén

20-38 **948** Torres
19-38 **947** Jaén
20-37 **927** Baeza
21-37 **928** Cazorla
22-36 **908** Santiago de la Espada
21-36 **907** Villacarrillo
23-37 **930** Puebla de Don Fadrique

The route

Alcalá la Real (950m, pop. 21,000) ⤴ 🍴 F ▲ € ☎ ✉ ✚ ⓘ 🚌 💻
An attractive town with an impressive eighth-century castle, La Mota, which now
houses a small museum. Also worth a visit is the imposing abbey church located
within the original city walls on the site of the original Alcalá Abbey. Built in a
combination of various architectural styles, including Gothic and Renaissance, it
has a tower which is over 40m high. It is also lovely to go for a stroll along the
exterior walkway, used for markets and fairs and evening *paseos*.

Accommodation and food
There are many places to eat, from restaurants to *tapas* bars, several hotels in the
town and lots of *casas rurales*:
Pensión Río de Oro ★★ (s/d en suite €18/35) pleasant and central (Abad Moya
   2, ☎ 953 580 337)
Hotel Torrepalma ★★★ (s/d/t en suite €25–33/37–48/50–60) upmarket and on
   way into town (Conde de Torrepalma 2, ☎ 953 581 800,
   preguntas@hoteltorrepalma.com, www.hoteltorrepalma.com)
Hospedería Zacatín ★★ (s/d en suite €25–47/40–82) friendly guest house down
   a little side street from Río de Oro with standard rooms and luxury ones with
   hydro massage in the bath, hairdryers and minibars, busy bar underneath
   (Pradillo 2, ☎ 953 580 568, zacatin@hospederiazacatin.com,
   www.hospederiazacatin.com)

For more information
Tourist information office: Palacio Abacial, Carrera de las Mercedes, ☎ 953 582
077/649 919 602/639 647 796/649 919 609

Alcalá la Real – Frailes

Climb out of Alcalá and look back on great views of the town. Pass through nearby Santa Ana and head into more open countryside, looking out on olive-covered slopes, holm oaks, walnut, cherry and almond trees and the distant Sierra Nevada as you approach Frailes.

Alcalá la Real

Distance	9km
Time	1h50
Height gain	140m
Height loss	280m
Highest point	1020m

To leave Alcalá head uphill on Calle Utrilla near the Consolación church and climb to the top of the hill, marked by a **cross**. From here take the right track signposted as the Ruta del Califato (no GR7 marking to begin with).

The small track meets a larger dirt track after 600m. Follow this round to the left along the fence line with the village of **Santa Ana** visible in front of you. There are some GR7 marks here as well as some blue marks which the local walking club also use to mark the route.

Turn left at the crossroads on the edge of Santa Ana to come round the side of an orchard and leave the Ruta del Califato. You then come to a tarmac road which you cross straight over into the suburbs of Santa Ana. At the **Club Fuente del Rey** (on your left) turn right down the road then carry straight on.

The tarmac road passes through housing then turns into a dirt track which you continue to follow, ignoring tracks back to the left and forward to right. When you meet another tarmac road, continue on in the same direction briefly and then back on a gravel track. Keep right at two forks to keep going in the same direction until you reach the edge of Santa Ana at a tarmac road. Turning right brings you to a GR7 signpost directing you left along the main road out of the village, an hour from Alcalá.

After less than half a kilometre, by a white **cross**, you leave the main road to the left on a track which takes you out into the countryside and through fields. Keep on the main track, passing straight over a crossroads and ignoring smaller tracks off into fields. At an equal divide take the left fork down to a small stream, the **Arroyo del Salograr**, and a stone wall. Ignore the track to left and head uphill on a *cañada real*.

CAÑADAS REALES AND CAMINOS REALES

Cañadas reales are old cattle tracks that were created to allow the movement of cattle between pastures. In total they cover a distance almost fifteen times the length of the Spanish railways and have a unique ecological value because, like rivers, they help the migration of a variety of species. There were the main means of getting around Spain for centuries.

Caminos reales, like *cañadas reales*, are centuries-old pathways which were designated as such by royal decree. The decree is still in force today and they are still very much in use by farmers and their animals.

Pass another white cross at the top of the hill, where you get your first view of Frailes, and start back downwards turning right when you meet a small tarmac road, which you follow into the village (7.8km, 1h50).

Frailes (780m, pop. 1800) ⤵ 🍴 F ▲ € ☎ ✉ ✚ 🚌
The village of Frailes is built around the church of Santa Lucia and has been the site for a number of important archaeological finds. Nestled into the surrounding rock faces, it is made more picturesque by the Río Vellios, which runs through the village.

Accommodation and food
A couple of small bars and one place to stay:
Mesón Hostal la Posá (d en suite € 35) bar and restaurant with spacious, bright rooms above (C/Tejar 3, ☎ 953 593 218)

Frailes – Carchelejo

Leave behind olive trees and fields to climb into wild hills where you'll have the views all to yourself, apart from the goats and the sheep. Descend through the rocky Valdearazo gorge, with impressive views of the Embalse de Quiebrajano, return to cultivated land and on into Carchelejo.

Distance	35km
Time	9h30
Height gain	1280m
Height loss	1240m
Highest point	1500m

NB A tent is essential if you want to break the journey.

You leave Frailes on the same road you came in on beside the **Río Velillos**. Follow the road through the village and out, passing by a park on the right with a GR7 display board. Passing a right turn, after just less than a kilometre take the next right fork in the road signposted to **Los Rosales** (or, for an alternative route, leave the road on a *cañada real* just after the park, which rejoins the road after the turning). This small road takes you all the way, uphill, to Los Rosales, walking next to hazels and poplars (3.5km, 40min).

To leave Los Rosales continue upwards along the road past the drinking fountain. After 500m the road forks and you take the left fork (GR7 signpost Carchelejo 8h30) onto a rough small tarmac road. This begins to take you into much wilder countryside, looking ahead to the **Sierra del Trigo**.

One kilometre further on, ignore a track to the right signposted to Las Lomillas. When you come to a divide where the left fork is signposted to **Cueva la Yedra**, head right. The road becomes much more track-like and takes you gently uphill through beautiful woodland into hillier territory.

Ignore a track back to the left and then a second one up to Cerezo Gordo as you begin to climb. Stay on the main track, past two *cortijos*, one in ruins, and head towards a hill with prominent **wind turbines (Paredón)**.

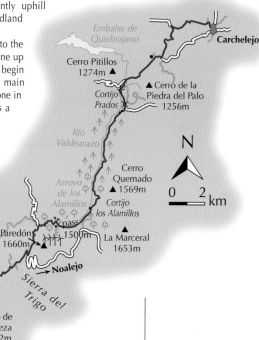

Map 12
Northern Route:
Frailes – Carchelejo

Embalse de
Quiebrajano

Carchelejo

Cerro Pitillos
1274m ▲

▲ Cerro de la
Piedra del Palo
1256m

Cortijo
Prados

Río
Valdearazo

Cerro
Quemado
▲1569m

Arroyo
de los
Alamillos

Cortijo
los Alamillos

pass

N

0   2
└──┴──┘ km

Paredón
1660m ▲   1500m   ▲ La Marceral
1653m

Cueva
la Yedra

Noalejo

Los Rosales

Sierra del
Trigo

ailes

Río
Velillos

▲ Pico de
Maleza
1462m

Climb up the first zigzag on this hill and then turn left when it divides (signpost Carchelejo 6h40). The right turn would take you to the village of Noalejo in 2h30.

After climbing gently you reach a crossroads where you turn right to curve round the side of Paredón, now up to your right. Pass through three gates on the same track then after the third, with **ruined buildings** on your left, take a smaller track up to your right. Here you will pass a small spring.

On the route to Carchelejo

After just less than a kilometre (just after the wind turbines go out of sight), the track bends sharply into a valley. Keep a close eye out here for a very small path heading steeply uphill to the right. The path is not clear on the ground but is well marked and takes you up the Sierra del Trigo heading southeast until you reach a **pass** at 1500m, where you are rewarded with panoramic views of all the surrounding mountains.

From the pass, head back downhill on a small track slightly to your right into trees and stay on it until you go through a gate (made of bedsprings at time of writing). After another 50m, head left down off the track again on a steep, unclear but well-marked path.

The path now follows the valley. Keep slightly to the right and you'll come out of the trees near a large track. Don't take the track, but instead take a path down to the left of it towards the **Cortijo los Alamillos**. This brings you back to the track at the farmhouse on a shorter route.

From here continue along the main track for 7km, descending alongside the route of the **Río Valdearazo**, ignoring one track off to the left. At a crossroads at the **Cortijo Prados** continue down and across a stone **bridge**. At the next divide take the left fork across a low **bridge/ford**.

The track continues on but you leave it at the first big hairpin bend after it starts to go up. Here a small path, with its signpost missing, heads off to the right. Follow this into the Valdearazo gorge where it clings, in places precariously, to the rocky sides. The path then crosses the river by means of a small **footbridge** before beginning the long climb on a steep zigzagging rocky path to the **Cerro de la Piedra de Palo**, a climb of around 300m with great views into the gorge and over the green water of the **Embalse de Quiebrajano** far below.

▶ Follow the path down to the **farmhouse** and then right along a track from it onto a tarmac road. Turn left along the road and carry on for 3km until a sign directs you right through olive groves onto a dirt track. Keep on the main track, ignoring two smaller ones off to either side. The track then becomes a smaller path making its way between two stone walls. Keep going downhill all the way now to **Carchelejo** only turning off to the right onto a smaller path just before you reach the village. This brings you into the centre.

When you reach the top, a signpost indicates that it is 2h to Carchelejo, most of which is mercifully downhill.

Carchelejo (820m, pop. 1480) ⌁ ◉ F ▲ € ☎ ⊠ ✚ 🚗

Carchelejo, with neighbouring Cárchel, makes up the municipality of Cárcheles. Its economic mainstays of olives and livestock are evident from the groves and pasture around. Sites to visit in the town include the 18th-century church, Nuestra Señora de los Angeles, and the Ermita de San Marcos.

Accommodation and food

There are a couple of restaurants and some lovely *casas rurales*, apartments and a hotel out of the village:

Gasparico (pppn €20) *casa rural*, sleeps up to 12 with 3 double and 2 twin rooms, kitchen and BBQ area (C/San Gregorio 2, ☎ 953 302 389, www.carcheles.es/casa_gasparico.htm)

Mezquita de Mágina Rural Apartments (5 different houses €25–70) newly refurbished, high-quality, self-contained flats/houses set around a pleasant courtyard (C/Jesus 14, ☎ 953 302 482, aptosmezquitademagina@carcheles.es)

Hotel-Restaurante Oasis (d en suite €45) at a busy road junction next to a petrol station several kilometres from the village, reached by continuing along the road out of Carchelejo instead of going under the underpass (Ctra Bailén-Motril, Km59, ☎ 953 302 083)

For more information

Town hall: ☎ 953 309 004

Carchelejo – Cambil

Half road walk, half riverside stroll, the route alongside the Río Cambil on small paths through orchards makes up for the earlier roadside trek.

Distance	15km
Time	3h30
Height gain	160m
Height loss	200m
Highest point	840m

Leave Carchelejo on the road heading east (not the road to Cárchel) and follow it for 3km until you reach a junction just before the major **N323** road. (There are no markings on this section.) Here turn left to follow the old road north as it runs parallel to the N323. Stay on this for 2km then, just before the Km61 mark, turn off to the right to go beneath the N323 through an **underpass** and across the **Río Guadalbullón** (which can be high if it has been raining).

Passing through olive groves en route to Cambil

From here you follow the **Río de Cambil** all the way into **Cambil** itself. The Río de Cambil joins the Río Guadalbullón by the underpass and you follow it upstream keeping to its left bank, heading east. There is a windmill at the start. After a kilometre of track, it becomes more of a path but you rejoin a wider track again less than 2km later. Where the track divides, after 1.5km, keep right, ignoring the left turn to Cortijo Maravadises.

Shortly after this the track starts heading north again taking you through orchards and poplars alongside the river as you approach Cambil from the south.

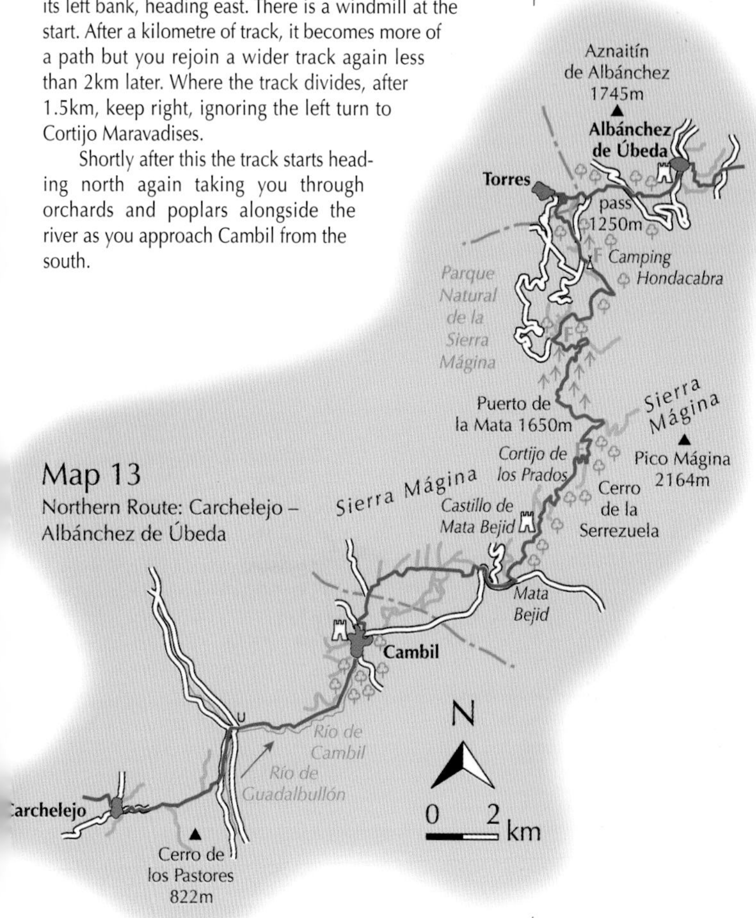

Aznaitín
de Albánchez
1745m
▲

**Albánchez
de Úbeda**

Torres

pass
1250m

Camping
Hondacabra

Parque
Natural
de la
Sierra
Mágina

Puerto de
la Mata 1650m

Sierra
Mágina

Cortijo de
los Prados

Pico Mágina
2164m

Cerro
de la
Serrezuela

Map 13
Northern Route: Carchelejo –
Albánchez de Úbeda

Sierra Mágina

Castillo de
Mata Bejid

Mata
Bejid

Cambil

Río de
Cambil

Río de
Guadalbullón

Carchelejo

Cerro de
los Pastores
822m

N

0   2 km

125

Cambil (780m, pop. 3300) 🚶 🍴 F ▲ € ☎ ✉ ✚ ① 🚌 💻

In a valley between the Engeño and Achuelo hills, Cambil is one of the villages richest in water in the area. The source of Río Arbuniel next to the village is now a picnic area. Olive cultivation is a key part of the local economy and there is a focus on using methods that avoid chemicals and minimize damage to the environment. It is also home to an ecological co-operative that produces high quality organic olive oil. Buildings of interest include the castle and the 16th-century church.

Accommodation and food

There is very little accommodation in Cambil itself but there are a few places in the surrounding area:

Hotel Monzo (s/d en suite €18/35) (Parque Municipal, ☎ 953 300 236)

Dehesa los Frailes (s/d en suite €33/45) *casa rural* 3km from town (Ctra Cambil-Huelma, ☎ 953 300 169)

Hotel las Aguas del Arbuniel ★★★ (d en suite €74) hotel complex set in gardens with attractive terrace restaurant and swimming pool a few kilometres from Cambil (Ctra Arbuniel-Cambil, Km1, ☎ 953 304 184, www.lasaguasdelarbuniel.com)

For more information

Town hall: ☎ 953 300 002

Cambil

Distance	26km
Time	6h45
Height gain	1000m
Height loss	880m
Highest point	1650m

A beautiful stretch in the heart of the Parque Natural de la Sierra Mágina, passing the ruined castle of Mata Bejid, and enjoying excellent views of the mountains including Jaén's highest peak, Pico Mágina, and El Almadén (recognisable by the communications tower on its top). There are options to climb both these peaks on routes that leave from the GR7.

Leave Cambil on the main Jaén to Huelma road. Take a small road heading off to the north signposted to Vuelta al Almadén, Bornos and Bercho Nacimiento. This leaves the village on Calle Camino de la Loma and climbs uphill. After 1.5km (around 25min) take a right fork in the road, signposted for Bornos and Almadén.

Climb more gently through olive groves staying on the main track until you reach a Sierra Mágina signpost, another 1.5km on. Here take a right turn to N324 Almáden, again staying on the main track through olive groves. The mountains of the Sierra Mágina dominate the horizon to your left and north. Carry on straight heading east (ignoring a small track off to the left) until you reach an intersection of a few tracks, where you take the one forward to the right (oddly signposted to Cambil N323). When you meet another track turn left to come down to the road (5km, 1h10).

Turn left along the road and stay on it for just under 1.5km before turning left again up a signposted gravel track just before the old settlement of **Mata Bejid**. Continue on this track heading uphill into wilder countryside. ▷ The vegetation becomes oaks and gall oaks with green slopes used to pasture sheep and goats.

The countryside changes here as a result of the much more humid climate in the valley – lots of streams from hillsides descend to fill the Río de Cambil.

After 2.5km you come to the ruins of the **Castillo de Mata Bejid** on your left. Stay on the right-hand track, passing two smaller ones off to the left. It continues uphill and you can enjoy beautiful views back over the mountains through which the route has already passed – feeling satisfied at how far you have come. The path then climbs to an area called **Cortijo de los Prados** where a signpost points you off the path to the left to a nearby fountain, 3.5km after the ruins (although it does not always have water).

Half a kilometre further on, ignore a right fork, which is a route up Pico Mágina, and stay on the main track which heads ever upwards towards the crags, passing ancient, thick-trunked oaks, and then, finally, reaching the top of the pass, **Puerto de la Mata**, at 1650m. Here there are amazing views as far as the Sierra Nevada to the southeast and over the rest of Jaén province to the north.

SIERRA MÁGINA NATURAL PARK (199km²)

The Parque Natural de la Sierra Mágina is a huge mountain massif rising out of a sea of olive groves. Although small, it has some of the highest mountains of the province. The mountains act as a barrier to the Atlantic winds and as a result produce strong climatic contrasts and varied landscapes. In the westernmost part, where the clouds break, the vegetation is lush woodland with pines and oaks. In contrast, the eastern part, which suffers from a lack of rain, has a landscape of dry white clay. This semi-desert area extends from the right bank of the Río Jandulilla to the valley of the Guadiana Menor.

During the winter months, snow covers the highest peaks of the Sierra Mágina, including Pico Mágina, which is the highest in Jaén at 2164m. The limestone rocks which make up the mountains of the Sierra Mágina act as porous sponges absorbing the water from snow melt and rain through plentiful caves and potholes. Most of the sub-soil is full of subterranean aquifers which come to the surface as springs. The water from all these springs turns into streams and rivers which run into the Jandulilla and Guadalbullón valleys and feed the Río Guadalquivir.

The area has been populated since prehistoric times and has been of great strategic importance through the ages as a route for transport and communication to the interior of the country.

Wildlife
The park has a great botanical diversity with over 1290 known plant species, some of them endemic, spread across a range of altitudes, including 300 species of wild mushrooms and 20 species of orchid.

It is also home to 240 known species of vertebrates, the majority of them protected by regional, national, or European environmental legislation and some of them, like the Iberian lynx, in danger of extinction. Only about 100 live in the wild, all of them in Andalucía. Other mammals found in the park include ibex, wildcats, foxes and wild boar. The hocicuda viper is the rarest of the snakes in the park.

There are 185 species of bird which either live permanently in the park or migrate there for a period of the year, including large raptors such as the peregrine falcon and two types of eagle.

Further information
Park visitor centre: in the castle in Jódar, ☎ 953 787 656, and open Thurs–Fri 10am–2pm, weekends and public holidays 4–6pm (October to March) and 6–8pm (April to September), www.magina.org

The track descends through pines and you can see **Torres** down in the distance. Don't take the right turn at the bend 2km from the top, but take the next right just over a kilometre further down when you meet another track. Now 19km from the start, you zigzag down the hillside. Ignore a track down to the left just after passing another fountain, then take the one to the right marked with a wooden post.

The Sierra Magina natural park

When you come to the small **Camping Hondacabra** (only open in high season) and another fountain, take the track to the right which takes you to the road into Torres. Continue down the road to enter Torres, or, if you want to continue on to Albánchez (1h20), take the signed track off to the right at the edge of the village.

Torres (900m, pop. 2000)

At foot of Cerro de la Vieja, Torres is rich in water from various different fountains and is known for its production of barley wine as well as olives. There is an open-air museum of the old rough millstones used in olive oil production and the 200-year-old large earthenware jars which were used to contain the oil. If you are staying in the village you can also visit the nearby paleolithic cave paintings at la Cueva del Morrón.

Some other good walking routes leave from here including circular routes to Aznaitín. It is worth going to the town hall to pick up information on routes.

Accommodation and food
Torres offers three fairly grand hotels, the first of which is less likely to have coach parties staying:

Hotel-Restaurante Jurinea ★★ (s/d en suite €30/50) smart, friendly place which you pass on the way in, organising outdoor and cultural activities, with good restaurant serving local dishes, air conditioning and TV (Camino de la Ladera, ☎ 953 363 121/021, 678 468 588, jurineaprunus@terra.es, www.hoteljurinea.com)

Puerto Mágina Hotel ★★★ (s/d en suite €44–49/60–67) another upmarket hotel on edge of the village which prides itself on its restaurant, swimming pool and air conditioning (Ctra Torres-Albánchez, Km3, ☎ 953 363 192/647 160 597, www.puertomagina.com)

Almoratin Hotel ★★★ (s/d en suite €50–100/50–80) very smart new hotel on the outskirts next to the Puerto Mágina with 61 rooms, bar, restaurant, free wi-fi and air conditioning (Ctra Torres-Albánchez de Mágina, Km2.8, ☎ 953 363 100, almoratin@partner-hotels.com, www.partner-hotels.com)

For more information
Town hall: Plaza de la Constitución 2, ☎ 953 494 005

Distance	16.5km
Time	5h30
Height gain	480m
Height loss	740m
Highest point	1250m

Torres – Albánchez de Úbeda (5.5km, 2h)

The route to Albánchez leaves the park at the entrance to the village on a track up to the left. It climbs steeply and is not well marked, but stay left on tracks close to the gorge, passing through cherry trees, and you will come to the road after 2km (signed Albánchez 35min).

Continue left along the road climbing gently over the Albánchez **pass** at 1250m and then leaving the road again after 1km, just after the Km5 road marking. Take a small path down to the right passing between fields of almond trees. Then take a tiny, and in places extremely overgrown, but well-marked path zigzagging down the hillside to avoid the large loops in the road.

You emerge onto a small tarmac road 2km later. Turn left to rejoin the main road, and then left again to enter the village of **Albánchez de Úbeda**, passing a viewpoint over the craggy rocks of El Torcal and Alto de la Serrezuela (1272m), the mountain behind Bedmar.

A climb through almond and cherry orchards and fields to the Albánchez pass then on along a route which contours around the very edge of the Sierra Mágina foothills, looking out across the flat expanse to Bedmar. The route is somewhat circuitous in order to take in an ancient fountain and watchtower.

Albánchez de Úbeda (860m, pop. 1700) ☞ ⛺ 🍽 F ▲ € ☎ ✉ ✚ 🚍

The village sits in the foothills of Aznaitín, its white buildings crowned by an Arab fortress, which was once, due to its strategic position, one of the most important in the region. You can visit it by climbing 300 narrow steps, but it is perhaps more spectacular from a distance. Also worth seeing are the Renaissance church, some Iberian and Roman remains, and numerous natural springs.

The village has only been called Albánchez de Úbeda since 1917 when it was bought by the Duchy of Úbeda, and many locals do not like the name and prefer Albánchez, or Albánchez de Santiago or de Mágina.

Accommodation and food
There are a few options for accommodation and food:

Camping el Ayozar (person/tent/2–4person cabin €3/10/45–60) 2km from the village this is a large campsite with a variety of options for accommodation and lots of facilities including a swimming pool and restaurant (on the road into Jimena, Km2.5, ☎ 953 358 339, www.camping-ayozar.com)

Cati (€15pppn) *casa rural* with kitchen and terrace in centre (C/Juan XXIII 25, ☎ 953 358 431)

San José de Hútar (s/d en suite €31.50/43) smart hotel with spacious rooms, air conditioning, restaurant and swimming pool (on road to Jimena, ☎ 953 357 474, sjhutar@lobaton.com)

For more information
Town hall: ☎ 953 358 339

Albánchez de Úbeda – Bedmar (11km, 3h30)

Leave Albánchez on Calle Eras heading down out of the village on a small unmarked tarmac road. From here the route has not been marked for 2km, but keep to this tarmac road and you will reach the signed route again on a track off to the right.

Take a left almost instantly, signposted to Bedmar. Stay on the main track, ignoring small tracks off into fields and one larger one off to the left just over 1.5km after leaving the road.

A kilometre on, you come to a sign for the **Abrevadero de la Fresnada**, a brief detour to a fountain up to the right. The route continues straight on, ignoring a track to the left following a white arrow on the wall.

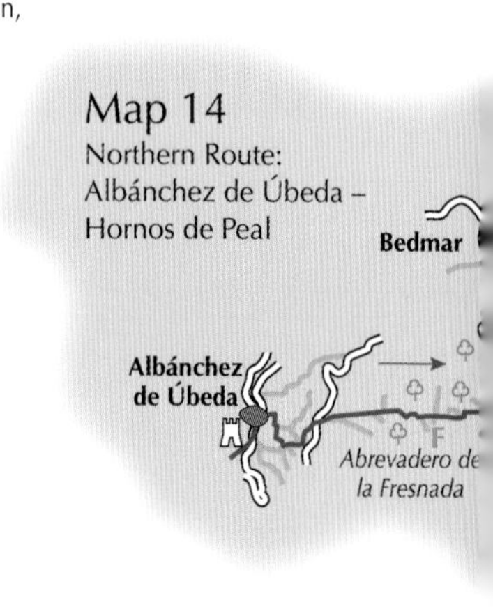

Map 14
Northern Route:
Albánchez de Úbeda –
Hornos de Peal

Bedmar

Albánchez
de Úbeda

Abrevadero de
la Fresnada

Approaching Bedmar

Continue on, ignoring little paths (feeling almost as if you're going to pass Bedmar by). When you come to a crossroads a kilometre later, carry straight on following another walking route's wooden signposts. Another 200m from

133

The ruined castle at Bedmar

here is the **Torreón de los Cuadros**, a 12m-high Arab watchtower.

After 700m, you come down to a small car park on a road and turn left (signpost Bedmar 1h55). Turn right just over 1.5km further on after passing over a small **bridge** into a field of olive trees. Take the left of the two tracks heading up towards a building. As you approach the building take a small path round the right of it and follow it along the edge of the field and then along a fence. You reach a **viewpoint** and Bedmar is 10min along the main road to the left.

Bedmar (650m, pop. 3400) ⊸ ⦿ F ▲ € ☎ ✉ ✚ ⓘ 🚍

Bedmar is dominated by the ruined castle on the hill above it, which you can walk up to for a good view down over the town. Its main economic activity is still agriculture carried out using very traditional techniques (principally olives and more recently white asparagus).

Accommodation and food

The town offers one hotel, a selection of *casas rurales*, and a few bars:

El Paraíso de Magína (s/d en suite €22/44) the only hotel in the centre of town with a good bar-restaurant beneath (Avda Virgen de Cuadros 58, ☎ 953 760 010)

La Casa del Pilar (d from €47) traditional accommodation with two bedrooms, air conditioning and open fire (C/Esparteros 21, ☎ 610 018 506, www.sierramagina.info/pag_2.htm)

La Nave de Cuadros (d en suite €60, min 2 nights) *casa rural* on the route (on the road to Cuadros, Km3.3, ☎ 953 083 237, www.riocuadros.com)

For more information

Town hall: ☎ 953 760 002

Bedmar – Jódar

Distance	7km
Time	2h20
Height gain	480m
Height loss	500m
Highest point	1133m

One of the steepest climbs in the Andalucian section of the GR7 takes you up over the Serrezuela de Bedmar and then you descend more gently through olives to Jódar.

Head out of town on the high road to the east with globe street lamps and after 1km turn up to the right onto a track (marked by a broken signpost at the time of writing) which immediately splits into two. Take the right fork and then continue straight on, following the path up by the edge of an apricot orchard and then round to the left.

135

Zigzag up the steep scree slope for about 1.5km. The path is a bit difficult to spot in places, but as long as you keep heading upwards you should reach the grassy top after about an hour of walking. The path then becomes a wider track and you curve down the other side of the hill towards **Jódar**, which is clearly visible below.

Stick to the main track until you reach a divide at the outskirts of town about 5km from the pass; here you take the left fork. Then, just before you meet the road, take the right fork and head down into town.

Jódar (627m, pop. 12,230) ↵ ⦿ F ▲ € ☎ ✉ ✚ ⓘ 🚌 🖳

Jódar was in its prime in Muslim times when it was the political, cultural and administrative capital of the area on one of the most important communication routes. It was famed for its production of high quality olive oil and also red dye. Today, it remains the largest town in the *comarca* and a key commercial and administrative centre. Its castle, which houses an information centre on the natural park, is worth a visit in itself and for the views.

Accommodation and food
A couple of hotels and plenty of choice of places to eat:

Hotel Ciudad de Jódar ★★ (s/d en suite €30/50) housed in a mock-mansion, with18 rooms all of which are ensuite with air conditioning and balcony (Prolongación Ermita Vieja, ☎ 953 785 051, correo@hotelciudaddejodar.com, www.hotelciudaddejodar.com)

Hotel los Molinos ★ (s/d en suite €18/30) central hotel with its own restaurant TV and air conditioning (C/Sanabria 47, ☎ 953 785 914)

For more information
Town hall: ☎ 953 785 086
Centro de Visitantes del Castillo de Jódar: ☎ 953 785 086
Taxis: ☎ 670 883 578/ 953 785 364/953 785 873

Distance	34.5km
Time	8h
Height gain	420m
Height loss	320m
Highest point	728m

Leave Jódar on the **A322**, passing by the **cemetery**, and stay on it for almost 10km until you reach the ruined **Estación de Quesada**. There are no markings at all for the first 5km. The landscape you pass through is dominated by olive trees with rows and rows of them on either side of the road. The mountains of Cazorla are ahead and, looking back, is the Macizo de Sierra Mágina and the Serrezuela de Bedmar, which the route crossed over to Jódar. Towards the west is the unmistakable point of Cerro Jabalcón, which the GR7 passes in Granada province.

The road crosses the **railway line** just before it reaches the station. Less than a kilometre beyond the station, the road splits and you take the right fork which is the road to Larva, leaving it 2km further on when it itself divides.

At this point you take the left fork to arrive at, and cross, the **Río Guadiana Menor**. Just after the bridge across the river, you leave the road for a track to the left heading northeast. This takes you through more olive plantations with the Alto de la Colmena up to your right. Stay on the main track ignoring tracks to the right then left after just over a kilometre, to arrive at a junction of several tracks near the large **Cortijo Mansute**. You continue heading northeast ignoring a track back to the left, one west to the right and then one left to the northwest. After this you keep left, ignoring two further tracks to the right, to arrive in the small hamlet of **Hornos de Peal** (440m, pop. 445 🏕 🍴 F ▲ ☎) where you are allowed to camp beside the village sports ground.

Leave the village heading downhill from the plaza in front of the church (with drinking fountain) towards olive fields, then at a signpost which over-optimistically tells you that it is 2h30 to **Quesada**, turn right along a gravel track that runs along the edge of a field.

A long road walk with olives as far as the eye can see before crossing the Río Guadiana Menor to head amongst the trees on tracks to Hornos de Peal – a route that may well leave you dreaming of olive trees, but a spectacular sight in its own way – followed by an easy stretch though grassland and rolling hills, passing the Arab castle La Toya and making a final steep ascent to Quesada, prominent on its hilltop. (This section can be split by camping, which is allowed beside the sports ground in Hornos de Peal.)

OLIVES AND JAÉN PROVINCE

The landscape of this area of Jaén province is dominated by olive oil production. In the Sierra Mágina alone, 180,000 tonnes of olives are grown each year producing around 40,000 tonnes of oil.

Not only are there the rows upon rows of trees but the beautiful white *cortijos* set amongst the olive groves have also been built especially for the olive oil industry. They are usually made up of one big house for the plantation owner and several more humble dwellings for the workers. Some still have old oil processing mills, although now most processing is done in larger, modern plants.

There are hundreds of different varieties of olive oil and the quality of each is determined by its acidity. The highest quality is extra virgin olive oil which is not allowed to go above 0.8 per cent acidity. Virgin olive oil has to be below two per cent acidity.

Olives have a long history in the area with the Greeks and Phoenicians first introducing them over 6000 years ago. The Romans cultivated olives but it was the Muslims who perfected oil extraction techniques and, as a result, started planting more trees across the Sierra Mágina and especially around Jódar and Garcíez. Christian conquerors paid little attention to the cultivation of the trees until the 19th century when the fall in cereal prices led to a huge expansion in olive cultivation and oil production as their incoming earning potential was realised.

When the track divides about 200m further along, stick to the wider right-hand branch and then continue on the main track avoiding smaller tracks off to the left into the fields, including a large one after another 500m.

The track comes up to meet a bigger one and you turn onto it heading left (ignoring a smaller left just before it). **Castillo de Toya** is on the hill up above you and you climb towards it, crossing a small stream and then, at a bend just after it, ignoring a track off to right and heading uphill. At the fork shortly afterwards, take the left track which bends around the side of the hill, or, if you want a short detour to climb to the castle, take the right fork.

The castle has a long history of destruction and reconstruction in battles between Christians and Muslims and the faint terraces still visible on the hill are thought to be man-made. ◀

Fragments of Roman and Medieval pottery have been found on the hillside.

You continue on walking through grassland and pines with olive groves below you and at the next fork stay right,

continuing round the hill until you come to the **Ermita de San Marcos**, a chapel built at the beginning of the 20th century.

On the route to Quesada

Cross the bridge next to the chapel and just round the corner the track meets a small tarmac road which you follow to the right into the tiny hamlet of **La Toya** (about 3.5km and 1h10 from setting off). Continue between the houses till you come to a small square with a fountain. Then turn left across the **bridge** to reach a signpost (Quesada 1h55).

Stay on the main track, bending round to the right and passing two left turns, then, when you reach some pine trees visible up to your left, stay right at the junction heading for olive groves. About 10min from leaving the village when you meet another track, turn right and continue straight on on the same track, passing another fountain on the left 1.5km and about 30min out of the village.

The track then heads uphill and you stay on it ignoring turnings to the left into olive groves and a fork to the right doubling back the way you've come. Turn right just before you reach the building that is visible ahead of you.

At a T-junction, turn right again then stay right at a fork soon after (the left fork just heads up to an abandoned

Walking up to Quesada

house, **Cortijo Cerrillo**). When you meet a bigger road after a total of about 1h40min and 8km from La Toya, cross over it onto a track almost directly opposite with large agricultural hoppers (signpost Quesada 25min).

Follow this same track up to **Quesada** whose pretty white houses and church spire are visible in the distance perched on the hillside at the foot of the Cerro de la Magdalena.

After 1.5km take the left fork and then turn right just after it at a signpost to cross over a little stone bridge. At the next fork 500m further on, continue up the right fork then turn right again at the T-junction which brings you steeply uphill into the village.

Quesada (728m, pop. 6250) ⌘ 🍴 F ▲ € ☎ ✉ ✚ ⓘ 🚗 🚌

A bustling large village with pleasant shady tree-lined plaza. There are some exciting caves to explore in the surrounding area including some of Andalucía's most important prehistoric cave paintings, in the Sierra de Quesada, in the Abrigo del Cerro de Vitar, south of the town.

Accommodation and food
There are a few eating options in and around the main plaza, some offering good *tapas*:

Hotel Restaurante Capri ★ (pppn €18–30) ask in bar to rent rooms or apartments with wood fires, TV and kitchens (some also have air conditioning and washing machine) (Pza Santa Catalina 2, ☎ 953 733 128/650, 610 070 689, turisrural@wanadoo.es)

Hotel Sierra de Quesada ★★★ (s/d en suite €22/45) good, family-run hotel (Avda de Úbeda 37, ☎ 953 733 277)

For more information
Taxi: ☎ 607 865 207

Quesada – Cazorla

Leaving the neat cultivated land and olives behind you, enter the wild woodland and exhilarating rugged mountains of the Cazorla natural park and descend into Cazorla after passing the Monasterio de Monte Sión with a stunning panorama of hills behind.

Distance	17.5km
Time	4h30
Height gain	500m
Height loss	380m
Highest point	1180m

Set off from the plaza past Bar-Restaurante Capri and head east downhill on Calle de los Espinillos. At the first junction you'll come to a sign directing you right (Cazorla 3h45).

After the right turn, take a left turn down to and across the **Río de Quesada** and then climb along the road, ignoring two tracks off to the right. Turn left when the road divides (signpost Cazorla 4h) and continue on the tarmac road, passing several dirt tracks off to either side. When the tarmac road itself divides, 1.75km out of the village, go right.

Follow this road up through terraced olive groves and reach a few pines after another 1.25km. Here the tarmac gets a bit rougher and turns into a track with great views back over Quesada. At a crossroads shortly afterwards, you are directed to turn left through a large

Map 15
Northern Route:
Hornos de Peal – Linarejos

Ermita de San Marcos
Peal de Becerro
Hornos de Peal
Castillo de Toya
La
Barranco del Castillo
Toya
Pico de Aguila 682m ▲
Río de Toya
Cortijo Cerrillo
Sierra de Toya

metal **gate** and pass round a house to climb over a mound of earth back onto the track. The alternative is to just continue straight on and this brings you up the same track, passing the house on your left.

The route is sparsely marked from here but stay on the track, curving into a gorge and crossing over a crossroads at the edge of pine forest. The track contours round the hillside then meets a tarmac road about 40min from Quesada.

Turn right up the road and pass a couple of **casas rurales** (Alojamiento Rural Casa Maria and Majuela Casa Rural, www.rinconesdelmundo.com). Cross a little **bridge** and follow the road for almost 5km to the top of the hill where you enter the Sierras de Cazorla, Segura y las Villas natural park, Spain's biggest natural park covering almost a fifth of Jaén province.

SIERRAS DE CAZORLA, SEGURA Y LAS VILLAS
NATURAL PARK (2143km²)

The area was made a natural park in 1989 after being designated a UNESCO biosphere reserve in 1983. It is hugely important from an ecological point of view, housing some of the country's wildest areas and largest forests and is extremely rich in animal and plant life. It is also home to a multitude of water sources, including two important rivers: the Guadalquivir, which carries its water 700km from the mountains to the Atlantic, and the Segura. The whole park is over 600m above sea level with its highest peak, Pico Empanada, reaching 2107m.

Wildlife
Roughly 70 per cent of the forestry in the park is pine, including some laricio pines that are estimated to be over 1300 years old. The park contains around 1300 species of plants, including fragrant herbs, beautiful wildflowers and two endemic species of daffodil.

Although one of the park's major attractions is its abundant and varied wildlife, human intervention has meant that some of the mammals that used to roam these mountains, including bears and wolves, have disappeared from the region. Wild boar, deer and mouflon – a wild sheep with distinctive large horns – have all been reintroduced following their extinction in the 1950s. Together with the Spanish ibex, stone marten, wild cat, badger, polecat, weasel and others, they make up some of the park's 51 mammal species.

Bird life is also rich, with 185 species including 29 different raptors such as griffon vultures, Bonelli's eagles and the famous and rare lammergeier, with its immense wingspan, which can still be sighted occasionally, although it no longer breeds in the park. There are 21 species of reptile (including an the endemic Valverde lizard), 12 amphibians, 11 fish and 112 butterfly species.

For further information
Cazorla tourist information office: Paseo del Santo Cristo 17, ☎ 953 710 102

Museo de Caza Centro de Interpretación de Torre del Vinagre: Ctra del Tranco, Km48.8, ☎ 953 713 040, open daily 11am–2pm and 4pm–7pm (spring) and 10am–2.30pm and 5pm–9.30pm (summer)

A couple of tour companies that provide excursions into the park also give out information and sell maps and guides:

Quercus: Pza de la Constitución 15, ☎ 953 720 115, despensa@excursiones.com, www.excursionesquercus.com

Turisnat: Paseo del Cristo 17, ☎ 953 721 351, 686 938 375, info@turisnat.org, www.turisnat.org

Here the tarmac ends and the road divides. You take the main left fork signposted Cazorla 2h45 (ignoring a smaller left track). The right fork (the continuation of the road) heads up to the Casa Forestal el Chorro (50min walk away). Now high up with great views, you follow the same track, ignoring another track to the left. The balcony track contours around the hillside with vistas through the pines all the way back to Jódar.

Stay on the main track. Around the corner from a signpost (Cazorla 1h45), turn left onto a smaller track which takes you down the stream bed of the Arroyo del Chorro towards the monastery and **Ermita de Monte Sión**. Then, just before the monastery, take a left turn to pass by it. ▶

You get your first view down onto **Cazorla** as you walk along the shoulder of the hill. The track then heads downhill and you keep following it until it turns to concrete and brings you down to a fountain and a turning off to **Ermita de San Isicio** to the left (a 500m each way detour). Otherwise take the right fork down into Cazorla, emerging into the bustling old square the Plaza de Santa Maria at the bottom of town.

The striking **Castillo de las Cinco Esquinas** up on the hill above you adds to the beautiful panoramic views.

Castillo de Cinco Esquinas

145

Cazorla (836m, pop. 9000) ⤴ 🍴 F ▲ € ☎ ✉ ✚ ① 🚌 💻

A busy little town with a dramatic setting, beneath the sheer rock faces of the hills of the natural park. Its two castles and five convents demonstrate its religious and strategic importance throughout its history under both Christian and Islamic control. It is now an important centre for trade and services for the surrounding area. The Moorish Castillo de la Yedra (ivy castle) was built on the remains of a Roman fortress and now houses El Museo de Alto Guadalquivir – a collection of local art and artefacts.

Accommodation and food

Cazorla's popularity as the gateway to the natural park means that it has a good range of places to sleep and eat. There's a great atmosphere in the evenings in some of the restaurants on the Plaza de Santa Maria:

Hotel Guadalquivir ★★ (s/d en suite €30.5/42) smart, modern rooms with air conditioning in the centre (C/Nueva 6, ☎ 953 720 268, info@hguadalquivir.com, www.hguadalquivir.com)

Hotel Parque ★★ (s/d en suite €37/53) slightly more expensive than the Guadalquivir but of a similar standard (Hilaro Marco 62, ☎ 953 721 806)

Hotel Villa de Cazorla (2/4 person apartment €41.5–71/77–119) just beneath the castle, made up of small interconnecting apartments with a shared swimming pool (Ladera San Isicio, ☎ 953 710 100, hotelvilladecazorla@spainby.com)

For more information

Tourist office: Paseo de Santo Cristo 17, Bajo, ☎ 953 720 102

Taxis: ☎ 953 710 062/659 670 592 or 953 721 511/689 638 122

www.turismoencazorla.com

Distance	16km
Time	5h30
Height gain	680m
Height loss	560m
Highest point	1400m

This highly recommended section is a great way to get a taste of the vast pine forests and dramatic rocky crags of the natural park. Most of the route follows an ancient path, looking down on views of the Guadalquivir valley, the villages of La Iruela and Cazorla.

Leave by Calle Heron, continuing up a steep concrete slope out of the houses to come to a GR7 signpost (El Vadillo 5h20) and park information board which marks the GR7 and other walking routes. Take a small steep footpath uphill and continue up to the left at a junction after 350m (but ignore smaller track marked as private down to left).

This path picks its way uphill zigzagging through lush green undergrowth and pines, and, after about 20min, brings you up to a **viewpoint**. It's worth taking a breather here to take in the panorama of contrasts – the straight neat patterns of olive groves and jagged mountains of the park, including the Cinco Esquinas castle again from the other side.

From the viewpoint, a wide track takes you uphill heading northeast and left towards the chapel, the **Ermita de la Virgen de la Cabeza**, situated high on the hill 150m above Cazorla.

At the divide, take the paved path on the left, with commanding views down over the village, towards the *ermita*. Pass the chapel (which has a fountain) and head up the little path into the pines which forks off to the right of the main wide track (signpost Vadillo 5h).

Once in the trees, curve round to the left following the edge of the woodland onto a stony path which takes you uphill before contouring round the left side of the hill. You are heading north with views down over the ruined **Castillo de la Iruela** strategically positioned on top of a rocky pinnacle.

Continue on the same undulating path, now going east through beautiful pine woodland and across meadows.
▶ It's not uncommon to see deer or mountain goats and, although sightings of wild boar are less common, there are often traces of them having been around.

There's a good chance here of seeing some exciting wildlife around here.

Climbing to the Ermita de la Virgen de la Cabeza

About 2km from the chapel, now at almost 1400m, turn left towards a ruined *cortijo* sitting in its own meadow. Then, beyond it, cross a small stream (which may be dry depending on the season) and turn left.

The path then heads out of the trees and zigzags downhill. Stay on the same path and pass a fountain, the **Fuente de Rechita**, surrounded by poplars, following an old path built into the hillside. A signpost points you uphill (Vadillo 3h20) and you continue on the same path.

It follows the contours of the hill and then climbs again. About 3km on from the signpost you take the left fork and after 500m (now 11.5km and 3h45 from Cazorla) you reach the **pass** at 1369m with great views of the rocky range of **Loma de los Castellones** to the south with its highest peak of **Gilillo** at 1848m. You can also see back to the Sierra Mágina.

From here you turn right along the ridge following the well-conserved ancient path, which was built up with stones to form an even path for horses to use. It takes you down through trees and across clearings. After 3km, turn right just after a clearing, going around the side of it rather than immediately into the woods. This path brings you down to meet a road in another 15min and you turn right to the **Fuente del Oso** (sometimes dry).

After the fountain you take a left off the road again onto a small path, signposted Sendero de la Fuente del Oso. You quickly take another left just after the fence ends, heading down to the left. Continue on this path downhill, ignoring a path doubling back on the right and one to the left and keep descending to the **Puente de las Herrerías**, a 15th-century bridge which is said to have been built in one night, thanks to divine intervention, so that the Catholic Queen Isabel could cross the river. There is a **picnic area** here and a fountain and the **Río Guadalquivir** provides a great spot for swimming in crystal-clear, turquoise waters.

Cross the little wooden **bridge** onto a small path up to the road and follow it along to the left past the **campsite** and round a bend to the right. Another 15min (2km) on from the campsite pass **Fuente de Perdy** and come to a big signboard welcoming you to the Comarca Sierra Cazorla. If you want to go into the hamlet of **Vadillo de Castril** turn left onto a little path just before it, down to the left doubling back on the

On route to
Vadillo de Castril

road. Walk along with the river on your right and cross the **bridge** towards the houses.

Vadillo de Castril (960m, pop. 60) ⤴ 🏛 🍴 F ▲
A tiny peaceful place dominated by a forestry centre and government buildings.

Accommodation and food
There is nowhere to stay in El Vadillo itself but there is a campsite on the route a couple of kilometres before you reach it and a bar-restaurant in the village itself:
Campsite Puente las Herrerías (adult/tent/2–4 person cabin €4.6/4.2/46–72)
leafy campsite next to river with bar-restaurant, swimming pool and wooden cabins (Ctra Nacimiento Río Guadalquivir, Km2, ☎ 953 727 090/111/112, www.puentedelasherrerias.com)

Distance	38km
Time	7h
Height gain	480m
Height loss	800m
Highest point	1400m

Forest tracks with glimpses of beautiful views bring you out next to the crystal clear Río Guadalquivir and onto a hidden tiny footpath for the final stretch to Coto-Ríos.

Head back to the road to continue on the route and at the junction just after the big signboard turn right uphill on road marked to **Linarejos** (signpost Coto-Ríos 8h). Just after this, turn off to the left up a steep little path signposted with a GR7 signpost to Linarejos. After just over 500m this path brings you out onto an old tarmac road, along which you turn left.

Take another left when the road divides about 800m further on. This brings you to a **bridge** which you cross, ignoring tracks off to the sides, and you continue climbing on the same forestry track. This brings you to Linarejos with its natural swimming pool built into the river, fountain, picnic ground and bar-restaurant (only open in high season). ▶

It is worth a short detour here to the famous and beautiful waterfall the Cascada de Linarejos.

The path to Coto-Ríos

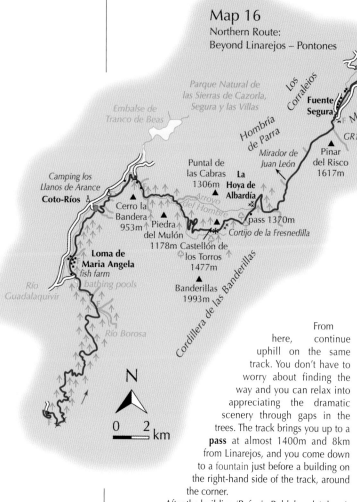

Map 16
Northern Route:
Beyond Linarejos – Pontones

Parque Natural de
las Sierras de Cazorla,
Segura y las Villas

Embalse de
Tranco de Beas

Los Corralejos

Fuente
Segura

F Monte

GR144

Hombría
de Parra

Mirador de
Juan León

Pinar
del Risco
1617m

Puntal de
las Cabras
1306m

La
Hoya de
Albardía

Camping los
Llanos de Arance
Coto-Ríos

Arroyo
del Hombre

Cerro la
Bandera
953m

Piedra
del Mulón
1178m

pass 1370m

Cortijo de la Fresnedilla

Castellón de
los Torros
1477m

Loma de
Maria Angela
fish farm

bathing pools

Banderillas
1993m

Cordillera de las Banderillas

Río
Guadalaquivir

Río Borosa

N

0   2 km

From
here, continue
uphill on the same
track. You don't have to
worry about finding the
way and you can relax into
appreciating the dramatic
scenery through gaps in the
trees. The track brings you up to a
pass at almost 1400m and 8km
from Linarejos, and you come down
to a fountain just before a building on
the right-hand side of the track, around
the corner.

After the building (Refugio Roblehondo) there's
a signpost (4h45) and you continue downhill still on the
same track (the track off to the right would take you to

Cantalar). Stay on it crossing several old stone bridges and, at a split in the track nearly 6km further on, stick to the main left fork which brings you down to the beautiful **Río Borosa**, which feeds the **Río Guadalaquivir**.

You cross it at a sign directing you downhill (1h30) past a fountain. Continue down to beautiful **bathing pools** and when you reach the **fish farm** head straight up the hill to Loma de Maria Angela.

If you have time for a detour, the fork up to the left takes you to the Centro de Interpretación de Torre del Vinagre, the park's main information centre in an old hunting lodge which has information on the park's plant and animal life as well as routes within the park. Next to it is a botanical garden with a good collection of over 300 types of plants including many endemic ones, grouped according to the altitude at which they are found. The Museo de Caza is also here, a museum about hunting, with stuffed wildlife from the park and an antler collection.

Loma de Maria Angela is a small hamlet with another fountain. Keep on the same road through the houses, not turning off until you reach the last buildings where you take the left fork. The road quickly becomes a path and you pass

Bathing pools

through a bedspring gate and follow the same winding path through olives, cork oaks, orchards and meadows until you reach denser pine woodland where you take the left path into the trees. Keep following it through the pines and **Coto-Ríos** will come into view.

Coto-Ríos (640m, pop. 340) ⬡ ⛺ ▮◀ F ▲ ☎

Because of its location on the edge of the natural park, Coto-Ríos is a popular destination for walkers and adventure sport lovers. It is a slightly strange place with the feeling of an outpost.

Accommodation and food
A few well-placed campsites and some *casas rurales*:

Camping Chopera de Coto-Ríos (person/tent €2.91–3.75/3) pleasant, shady campsite just on the edge of the village beside the river with swimming pool, bar and shop (Ctra Cazorla-Coto Ríos, Km21, ☎ 953 713 005)

Camping Llanos de Arance (person/tent/2–4 person cabins €3.40–4.50/3.55/ 50–60 plus €10 per extra person) right on the route of the GR7 just on the outskirts in the forest with swimming pool and lovely wooden cabins (Ctra Tranco, Km22, ☎ 953 713 036)

Los Villares Apartamentos (4 person apartment €70) excellent, well-equipped flats in the village with own terraces and outdoor seating (☎ 606 986 757/636 341 781)

Coto-Ríos – Pontones

Another beautiful section of natural park that leads through peaceful pinewoods (where there is a good chance of seeing Spanish ibex), past abandoned *cortijos* and between dramatic rock faces to descend into pasture land.

Distance	34km
Time	7h
Height gain	1140m
Height loss	440m
Highest point	1700m

From the plaza, head east past a GR7 signboard and a church up a gravel track to the right (signposted to Pontones). Stay on the gravel track and turn left at the fork

200m on, following it down over a little bridge and through pines (ignoring smaller tracks to both sides). Pass the cemetery on your right. After 2km the track meets a small gravel road (signpost Pontones 7h); turn right along it, walking past the Camping Los Llanos de Arance and over another **bridge**.

The track bends round to the left before curling uphill and you ignore a fork off to the left (sign Pontones 6h30) and then a second left fork a kilometre on. 500m later, after passing two buildings you come to a fountain. The same track continues past the fountain running alongside a scenic gorge.

From here the track climbs steadily for 10km and as it does you'll be able to catch glimpses through the trees of forested hills and bare rocky outcrops. After 10km it arrives at a lofty **viewpoint** with wooden rails from which you get a breathtaking 360° panoramic view of the rocky peaks around you, with eagles often circling overhead.

From the viewpoint a small path continues uphill (signposted Pontones 4h) past the ruins of **Cortijo de la Fresnedilla,** once a fertile productive *cortijo*, with green meadows and fruit trees surrounded by pines.

At this point, there is a small 'dangerous footpath' sign but don't worry – it's not. Take this small, well-marked path up through pines and rosemary bushes to a 1700m **pass** with views down to the other valley – the **Arroyo del Hombre** – and up to the peak of **Castellón de los Torros** and, below in valley, the abandoned Cortijo de Cuvero. Keep right along the ridge following a little path as it contours around the hillside. At 500m from the pass, as you're following a small dry stream bed, you meet another little path. Turn left along this to head east.

After another 500m, the path ends in an open valley beside a semi-ruined goat shed surrounded by once-cultivated land. Keep the building on your right and cross straight over the valley floor heading north towards the poplar trees where there is a GR7 post. Follow the line of the poplars on a faint path until you reach some ruined houses at **La Hoya de Albardía**, and then carry straight on through the field on an unmarked section staying by a small stream bed. After 200m it becomes a clearer path going in the same direction gently uphill to a signpost (Pontones 3h15) which directs you right on a path which heads south. You double

*On the route to
Pontones*

back on yourself briefly as you pass above the farmhouses higher on the hillside before contouring round to the east. There is a small divide in the path after a kilometre, but both forks bring you to a flat open area of grassland with a signpost (Pontones 3h).

There are two paths heading off from here; take the left one going northeast which becomes a track taking you through rocky, well-grazed landscapes with far fewer trees at about 1700m.

The track comes to another signpost after 2km with a 20min detour to the **Mirador de Juan León** straight on and the route heading downhill to the right. If you fancy a detour to the viewpoint it offers excellent views of the whole of the Valle del Guadalquivir, the Sierra de las Cuatro Villas and the Sierra de Albacete. To stick to the route, continue downhill for about 4km, ignoring a track off to the left halfway down, and you arrive at another track and an intersection with the **GR144**. Turn left along this track and after 1km it will bring you to the road on the way into **Fuente Segura** (⦿ **F**) at a picnic area.

Turn left along the road. After 300m you pass by the village itself but stay on the bottom road. 500m further on, turn off at a bend in the road to the right onto a rough track with some farm buildings on your left. This turns into a little path running along the base of some huge sloping slabs of rock before rejoining a very small road at some houses after 500m.

Follow the small tarmac road heading uphill, passing a signpost to Pontones (30min). Once up the hill and past the buildings take a gravel track to the left. This rejoins the road after 400m, but just before it does, you take a very small path off to the left passing a farm building and heading in the same direction as the road.

Ignore smaller paths through fields back to the road and when it divides take the right fork. Carry on along the little path which goes gently downhill with fields to the right and rock outcrops to the left. Where the track divides by a dry stone wall and dry stream bed carry on in the same direction keeping to the left of the stream bed on barely trodden path for 300m, at which point it divides again. Take the right fork down and across the stream bed and then up a short, steep path to meet the road, and a well-hidden post, 400m from the village. Go left along the road until you come to a signpost directing you left into **Pontones**.

Pontones (1350m, pop. 5021) ⤴ ▐◍▐ F ▲ ☎ ⊠ ✚ 🚌

Pontones is almost two villages. The lower of its two neighbourhoods (Pontones de Abajo) is situated on the banks of the Río Segura. The lushness of the gardens and fields surrounding the village provide a pretty contrast to the rocky hills that enclose it.

Accommodation and food

One hotel and a couple of *casas rurales* with a renowned restaurant in the centre:

Hotel-Restaurante Ruta del Segura ★ (s/d en suite €20/40) handy hotel as you enter the village of Pontones de Abajo with tasty food in the restaurant below, air conditioning, TV (Avda Democracia, ☎ 953 438 287)

Casa Rural Alta Segura ★ (d en suite €40) comfortable rooms in peaceful house with friendly and helpful owner, in the upper part of the village (Pontón Alto) about a kilometre up the road (☎ 953 438 328)

Pontones – Santiago de la Espada

A gentle, scenic route following tiny (sometimes hard to find) paths and streams across rolling open farmland.

Distance	15km
Time	3h15
Height gain	340m
Height loss	340m
Highest point	1620m

From the church, cross the bridge over La Rambla and turn right then left through a break in the buildings along a little path which brings you out onto the road by a GR7 display and signpost to Santiago de la Espada. (If you miss this path you can just go past the church and southeast out on the road to the same point.)

Map 17
Northern Route: Pontones – Puebla de Don Fadrique

Walk along the road for 500m/5min then turn off to the left onto a dirt track (signposted Santiago 3h) and follow it through green pastures. As you near a **goat shed**, head off to your right to reach a GR7 post (with the goat shed just up on your left). From this point there is only a faint unmarked path which is easily confused with goat tracks, but if you keep heading northeast on the right-hand side of the valley following the edge of the trees and the line of the pylons you will arrive back on a small path with some markings after 500m.

When this arrives at a small v-shaped **dry stone wall** by two pylons 100m further on, with the small hamlet of **Poyotello** directly ahead, the path seems to disappear again. Head down the right side of the dry stone wall onto a path going south leaving the line of the pylons behind. The path curves southeast between hills before doubling back up to the left (and north) to come to the farm of **Los Cerezos** and a clear gravel track. Follow the track to the right, away from the farmhouse, and onto the Poyotello road. Turn right along the road and after 700m you will come to a signpost (Santiago de la Espada 1h45). Stay on the road going in the same direction until you come to the main, but still small, road between Pontones and Santiago de la Espada, 1.5km on.

Cross over the road diagonally to the left, into a field with poplar trees. A very faint track and GR7 posts direct you across a small stream and through a gap in the poplar trees heading east-northeast. Staying roughly parallel with the road and leaving the poplars down to your left, you climb very gently uphill to a wider track which you cross

From here the path follows the stream bed of the **Arroyo de Zumeta** almost the entire way to Santiago de la Espada, making navigation easy.

over before heading downhill again on small path. When you reach another track, cross over it, still following GR7 posts, along a small path heading east.

◀ A further 500m after entering the valley, keep to the left and higher of two tracks heading into pine trees but still following the stream. After another 1km you come down and cross the stream into a clearing in the trees with the road just in front of you and a signpost (Santiago de la Espada 1h) directing you right and along the stream on its right-hand side. Pass a small dam and follow the line of the road on the other side of the gorge.

Another 3km on from the signpost, the track divides. You take the left fork, doubling back briefly downhill through a stone archway to cross over to the other side of the gorge before following a track, running beneath the road, around the hillside to the right by the edge of the trees and arriving into **Santiago de la Espada** at a roundabout and garage.

Santiago de la Espada (1340m, pop. 1500) 🛌 🍽 F ▲ € ☎ ✉ ✚ ⓘ 🚌
The last destination of the GR7 in Jaén, Santiago de la Espada is set in rocky countryside to the south of the Sierra de Segura. Its high altitude makes its climate colder and harsher than that of nearby villages and prevents the cultivation of olive trees. Instead the people of Santiago make a living from cattle and forestry.

Accommodation and food
There is just one hotel in Santiago itself:
Hotel San Francisco ★ (d en suite €40) central with spacious double or twin rooms and bar-restaurant serving traditional dishes (Avda de Andalucía 25, ☎ 953 438 072)

For more information
Town hall: Plaza de la Consititución 1, ☎ 953 438 002
Taxis: Martinez Blazquez 953 438 499, Robles Cabeza 953 438 312

Santiago de la Espada – Puebla de Don Fadrique

Distance	34km
Time	8h
Height gain	540m
Height loss	720m
Highest point	1664m

Leave Santiago de la Espada on the street with the bank and tabac, carrying on downhill towards, and then straight over, the village's lower road, where a GR7 sign directs you down a gravel track (Cortijo de las Cuevas 1h).

At a **water storage pool** 1km down, turn right, then right again at the next junction. Ignore a right turn off to a building 400m further on to pass between poplar trees on your left and fields on your right. Come to a T-junction 500m later and turn left towards the rocky hillside. Next, turn right onto a small grassy track off the main track (look out for this as it is not obvious) and continue along it, crossing a small stream then going uphill heading south. The path here is not always clear, but if you keep heading up and south you will come to a GR7 sign at the top, 2.5km from the start.

Head down from the signpost on a small rocky path passing above and around the settlement of **Cortijo de las Cuevas**, which is mainly cave-houses, many now abandoned, set into the hillside. Come down to the river, with Cuevas on your left, and cross over a wider track onto a very overgrown path which takes you around a field before rejoining a wide track. Here you come across the last GR7 sign before Puebla de Don Fadrique and the end of the Northern Fork of the GR7 in Andalucía, which it claims is 6h away.

The sign directs you along the track which crosses the **Río Zumeta** and then heads uphill to the road and into the Granada province. Turn left along the road for the long unmarked road walk to Puebla de Don Fadrique. After the first 3.5km along the road you come to a junction and take the left turn signposted to Puebla de Don Fadrique, 28km away.

The charming route to the intriguing Cortijo de las Cuevas is overshadowed by the final long road walk which is a bit of an anti-climax to the whole Northern Fork of the GR7 in Andalucía. While the road is small and picturesque it is probably still worth hitching a lift towards the end.

Cortijo de las Cuevas

As you head downwards into the valley basin in which Puebla sits, the landscape becomes drier and harsher, with scrub vegetation rather than trees.

After a further 3km, you pass by an impressive complex with helipad at the Pinar de la Vidriera. A track off to the right here looks tempting but unfortunately the route sticks to the road. From here it climbs steadily up through beautiful pines to a high point of 1664m at the **Puerto del Pinar**, 15km from your destination. While in the pines you can only catch an occasional glimpse of a view but from here the scenery starts to open out a bit as you start the long downhill into **Puebla de Don Fadrique**. ◄ Here rivers that are near-torrents in the winter dry up almost entirely in the summer months. Continue down the road passing several small tracks off to isolated farmhouses. With the end now clearly in view, you take the left fork when you arrive at another junction (2km from Puebla) to enter the village from the northwest at the Ermita Nueva and the graveyard.

From Puebla de Don Fadrique there is a daily bus (on weekdays only) to Granada (3h45) and Málaga (5h15).

Puebla de Don Fadrique (1164m, pop. 2500) 🚍 🍽 F ▲ € ☎ ✉ ✚ ① 🚌

A pleasant little town with white houses and its 16th-century church of Santa María surrounded by fields of cereals and almonds. It has a rich past, first as a Muslim settlement and later a Christian one.

Accommodation and food

The hotel is the main place to stay and eat although there are a few bars.

Hotel Puerta de Andalucía ★ (s/d en suite €20/€40) spacious, bright but characterless rooms, with bar and restaurant downstairs (Ctra Granada-Valencia 1, ☎ 958 721 340/958 721 076, p.andalucia@ribernet.es, www.ribernet.es/hostal_puerta_de_andalucia)

Apartamentos Don Fadrique well-equipped tourist flats with kitchens, heating and TV (Ctra Granada, behind petrol station, ☎ 958 721 116)

For more information

Town hall: ☎ 958 721 001

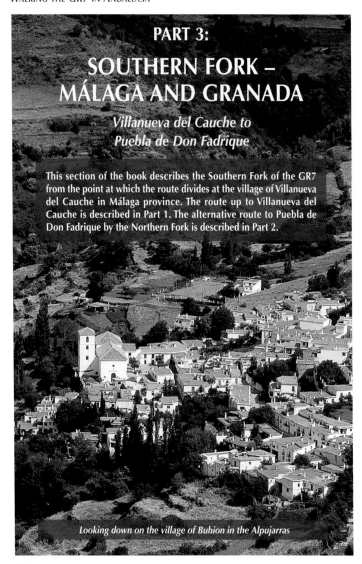

PART 3:

SOUTHERN FORK – MÁLAGA AND GRANADA

Villanueva del Cauche to
Puebla de Don Fadrique

This section of the book describes the Southern Fork of the GR7 from the point at which the route divides at the village of Villanueva del Cauche in Málaga province. The route up to Villanueva del Cauche is described in Part 1. The alternative route to Puebla de Don Fadrique by the Northern Fork is described in Part 2.

Looking down on the village of Bubion in the Alpujarras

MÁLAGA PROVINCE

Villanueva del Cauche to Ventas de Zafarraya, 43km

An overview of the route in Málaga, and practical details such as transport information, are given at the beginning of the section 'Málaga province' (see page 65)
in Part 1.

Maps required
1:50,000 Servicio Geografico del Ejercito
17-43 **1039** Colmenar

The route
Villanueva del Cauche – Riogordo

Distance	18km
Time	5h
Height gain	480m
Height loss	780m
Highest point	1160m

This whole section is unmarked but is fairly easy to follow and worth persevering with for the adventure of climbing to the pass between Peña Negra and Morrón de Gragea.

Head out of the village to the north (the same way you came
in if you arrived from Antequera on the GR7), passing a GR7
signpost which only indicates the start of the Northern Fork.
Instead of following this, turn right up the first road you
come to, the **A6118**. Walk up it for just under 2.5km until
you reach the **Cortijo Fresneda**, the first buildings on your
left. Pass one track off to your left heading into fields and
then take the second one which appears just to go to the
farmhouse and has an off-putting 'no entry' sign. This is the
route. Passing the farmhouse on your left turn right going
round another building to go uphill slightly on a track to a
gate. It is possible that this gate will be padlocked, but if it is
you can ask at the farm and they will open it.

Follow the track uphill, with the impressive rocky outcrop of **Peña Negra** getting steadily closer up on your right. After 2.7km you need to leave the track to

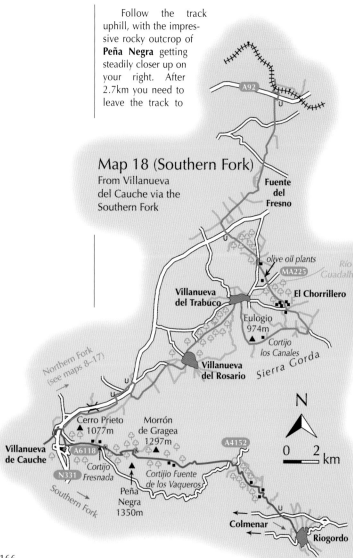

Map 18 (Southern Fork)
From Villanueva del Cauche via the Southern Fork

Peña Negra

A92

Fuente del Fresno

olive oil plants
Rio Guadalhor
MA225

Villanueva del Trabuco

El Chorrillero

Eulogio 974m
Cortijo los Canales

Northern Fork (see maps 8–17)

Villanueva del Rosario

Sierra Gorda

N

Cerro Prieto 1077m

Morrón de Gragea 1297m

A4152

0   2 km

Villanueva de Cauche

A6118

N331

Cortijo Fresnada

Cortijio Fuente de los Vaqueros

Southern Fork

Peña Negra 1350m

Colmenar

Riogordo

Leaving Villanueva del Cauche

the right and head steeply uphill (if you reach a **gate** on the track you've gone too far and need to backtrack 200m). There are only some small goat tracks to follow but if you head southeast you should come to the pass between **Peña Negra** on the right and **Morrón de Gragea** on the left, with great views ahead. There is a fence running across the pass with a crossing point where there is no barbed wire in the middle. Cross this to start heading down the other side, heading east on something more like a path.

Keep heading east for another kilometre and you will arrive at a fenced field. Follow the fence line along the top, staying on the outside and ignoring a faint car track to your right, then around the field before following the edge of an unfenced field to the **Cortijo Fuente de los Vaqueros**, another kilometre on from the start of the fence. From here the route is much easier to follow as you rejoin a track.

Take the track from the Cortijo and continue along it, ignoring smaller tracks off to other farmhouses, for just over 3km, at which point you arrive at the **A4152** road. Turn left

Pass between Peña Negra and Morrón de Gragea

up the road for 400m and then take the first track off to the right at a **water storage tank** under a power line, with a house just off the road down to the right. Stick to the main track which heads through olive trees with views across to **Colmenar** and glimpses of Riogordo. Take a left at the first fork then another left turn at another fork 1.2km further on (which may have a chain across it). This splits shortly afterwards but keep to the right-hand track from then on. After a kilometre it goes around a house, then just over another kilometre further on it heads straight through the yard of another house and on down to the left. Shortly you will see the whole length of the track to Riogordo laid out before you.

Head straight over a crossroads and steeply down a small concrete section of path which then passes through an **underpass** beneath the motorway before continuing into **Riogordo** on a track through olives and rhododendrons. You arrive at a road and a fountain on the edge of the village. Turn right to go into the centre.

Riogordo (400m, pop. 2800) ⚑ ▣ F ▲ € ☎ ✚ 🚃 🖳

Riogordo, which means 'fat river', has a colourful history. After being established by the Phoenicians and Romans, it was taken over by the Moors and the village is still laid out in an Arabic style. In the 19th century, it was best known as a haven for bandits because of its proximity to the mountains.

Accommodation and food

Very limited accommodation in the village itself, but there is a wild camping area 1.5km away on the route and a hotel-restaurant in nearby Colmenar (6km away) which can be reached by a regular bus service from the main square:

Hotel-Restaurante Belén (s/d en suite €24/42) comfortable rooms with popular bar-restaurant below serving traditional dishes and bar food/*tapas* (Urb Chorropinos, Colmenar, ☎ 952 730 031)

For more information

Town hall: ☎ 952 732 154

Museum of Popular Arts: ☎ 952 732 154, open 5pm–9pm and mornings at weekends

www.riogordo.com

Riogordo – Ventas de Zafarraya

Distance	25km
Time	6h30
Height gain	720m
Height loss	200m
Highest point	940m

Despite a disappointing 8km road walk to avoid a missing stretch of GR7 at the start, the rest of this section is very pleasant, taking you through beautiful scenery dotted with hamlets and then along an old railway line to reach your destination.

The route from Riogordo to **Cortijo de Doña Ana** is a maze of tracks with no markings, so it is preferable to follow the road to Periana for 7km and then turn off onto the **MA157** to pick up the GR7 1km on as it turns off the road to the right at **Cortijada Pulgarín**. It is 17km and 4h from here to Ventas de Zafarraya.

Turning off to the right, where there is a GR7 mark, takes you onto a dirt track and past the *cortijada*. You come to a junction after 250m and take the left up a briefly concrete

169

View towards the Embalse de la Viñuela

track and then almost immediately turn left again (not right across bridge decorated with old cartwheels). Climb for 300m, getting increasingly good views back to the peak of **Doña Ana**, then at a divide take the right fork. From here you can see all the way back to Colmenar. As the track heads southeast around the hillside the Embalse de la Viñuela comes into view with more panoramic views over the hills to the left and down to the hamlet of **Mondrón** below.

Map 19
Southern Route: Riogordo –
Ventas de Zafarraya

Looking down on Guaro

The track arrives at **Cortijo de la Cueva**, 2.5km after you left the road, where it meets another track at a T-junction. Here you come across a GR7 signpost indicating it is 5h back to Riogordo and 3h30 on to Zafarraya. Go left up the track between the buildings. At a divide 200m on take the right fork and then stay on this track, coming around the hillside and over a small rise to get your first view of **Guaro**. Go straight over the little crossroads at the top of the rise and continue to the road, where again you go straight over to enter the hamlet on a little tarmac road, passing a fountain on the way in.

Walk straight through the village, staying on the same road which becomes gravel as it leaves. Climb to meet another track with a signpost directing you left, not on the GR7, to

RANADA

Ventas de Zafarraya

Morrón de la Cuna 232m

N

0   2 km

171

Walking along the old railway line to Ventas de Zafarraya

Marchamona, and right to continue on the route to **Ventas** (it says 4h30, but it is nothing like this far). After 700m you arrive at a crossroads where you turn left, signposted to Carríon, joining a track which was once a **railway line** and which will take you all the way to Ventas, along the way passing into Granada province.

Another 1km from the crossroads, pass by a farmhouse, carrying straight on with the reservoir coming into view again, and passing by lots of broom interspersed with olives on the hillside. From here you can see a now oddly placed **railway bridge** ahead which the track goes under before carrying on through a short tunnel almost a kilometre further on. You reach the road and the village of Ventas de Zafarraya 300m after you leave the tunnel. (See next section for description of facilities available in **Ventas de Zafarraya**.)

GRANADA PROVINCE (AND ALMERÍA)

Ventas de Zafarraya to Puebla de Don Fadrique, 408.3km

The 408km of the GR7 in Granada province are some of the most varied and beautiful in the whole route. The section has everything: from breathtaking views of snowy peaks to pretty winding ancient paths joining the dots between tiny villages; and from the wild green spaces of three natural parks to the immense sun-baked desert landscapes of the *altiplano*.

Leaving Málaga province in the fertile plains around Ventas de Zafarraya, you come to the beautiful town of Alhama de Granada with its dramatic gorge and wonderfully relaxing *balneario* (spa bath). From here you pass into the green valley of Lecrín and walk beside babbling *acequias* (ancient irrigation channels) and between lush orange and lemon groves.

The route then winds its way into the Alpujarras. Passing through the villages of Albuñuelas and Nigüelas you come to Lanjarón with its famous spring water. The section that leaves here is perhaps the best-known and most-walked part of the route. It takes you right into the Alpujarras, an area known for its timeless whitewashed villages clinging to the steep hillsides.

Entering the Parque Natural de la Sierra Nevada (see information box on page 194), you walk through some genuinely wild landscapes with stunning views of the Sierra Nevada mountains and plenty of opportunities to climb them, including Mulhacén, the highest peak in the park.

The GR7 then crosses briefly into the Almería province, through Bayárcal, the province's highest village at 1255m, and then climbs further to pass over the highest part of the GR7 at the pine-forested pass Puerto la Ragua (2000m).

Back in Granada province, you head for the arid semi-desert plains landscape of the west of the province which contrasts sharply with the lush greenery that you have

HIGHLIGHTS OF THE ROUTE IN GRANADA PROVINCE

- getting lost amongst the narrow car-free streets of the traditional villages of the Alpujarras with whitewashed houses and colourful flowers pouring from balconies
- soaking tired muscles in numerous thermal spas and Arab baths including in Alhama, Baños de Zujar and Lanjarón
- the novelty of staying in a cooling cave house
- archeological sites of the Hoya de Baza area, especially the museum at Orce

already come through. The path goes through Zújar to its thermal spring baths on the shores of a beautiful reservoir and into Orce, one of the most important prehistoric sites in Europe. The final stretch is a beautiful forested walk, past the peak La Sagra with breathtaking views until you reach Puebla de Don Fadrique, the end of the route in Andalucía.

Other walks

Granada province is a popular area for walking and there are lots of options for creating circular routes from the GR7 and diversions up to peaks, especially in the three natural parks. The Alpujarras is also a particularly beautiful area to explore on foot and there are lots of marked routes linking its villages.

There are many marked routes in the parks, although marking is not always totally reliable or consistent and it is advisable to take good maps. A popular and beautiful route in the Parque Natural de Sierra Nevada, which works as a nice diversion from the Alpujarran section of the GR7, is the Sendero Siete Lagunas, an 8km route which starts in Trevélez and takes you up to seven lakes in a glacial valley at over 3000m, between the peaks of Mulhacén and Alcazaba. You can camp here and continue up to the top of Mulhacén peak the next day, or do the whole thing in one challenging day trip.

There are also opportunities to link up with other long-distance routes including the GR142 which interconnects with the GR7 in Lanjarón and goes from Lanjarón to Fiñana on the northern side of the Sierra Nevada in Almería. Further on, at Puerto de la Ragua, the route also meets the GR140, which forks off to go south to Cabo de Gata where it meets the GR92 which runs right along the south coast of Andalucía.

Transport

There are fairly regular buses between Granada and the bigger towns of the province including Lanjarón, Antequera, Cazorla and Baza. There are also connections from Málaga and Jaén. Many of them will stop at some of the smaller villages they pass through.

The buses are run by several companies and it is best to get in touch with them to check the latest timetables. The two main companies are:

- Alsina Graells: Granada–Lanjarón frequent services (every 1–2 hours weekdays and slightly reduced services at weekends and bank holidays, 1h30); Granada–Cazorla (twice daily, 4h); Granada–Antequera (three daily, 2h); Granada–Baza (twice daily, 1h40 – one of these on the same line as Granada–Puebla de Don Fadrique) ☎ 958 185 480 (Granada), 958 770 003 (Lanjarón), www.alsinagraells.es/agsur
- Maestra: buses between Benamaurel and Baza twice daily both ways (usually leaving at 8am and 3pm and then coming back, leaving Baza at 11.30am and 2pm).

At the end of the route at Puebla de Don Fadrique, there are daily buses (weekdays only) to Granada.

Tourist information
Granada tourism department: Pza Mariana Pineda 10, Granada, ☎ 958 247 146, www.turismodegranada.org, turismo@dipgra.es

Maps required
1:50,000 Servicio Geografico del Ejercito
18-43 **1040** Zafarraya
19-43 **1041** Dúrcal
20-32 **1042** Lanjarón
21-43 **1043** Berja
21-42 **1028** Aldeire
21-41 **1011** Guadix
21-40 Benalúa de Guadix
22-40 Baza
22-39 Cúllar
23-39 **973** Chirivel
23-38 **951** Orce
22-38 **950** Huéscar
23-36 **909** Nerpio
23-37 **930** Puebla de Don Fadrique

Ventas de Zafarraya (920m, pop. 1340) ⌇ ⍾ F ▲ ☎ ⊠ ⌷
As its name implies, the town started life as a *venta*, an inn, on the ancient route between Málaga and Granada. Thanks to its location on a fertile plain, it has recently experienced a revival and population growth as a result of large-scale intensive agricultural production for national and international markets.

Accommodation and food
A couple of basic places to stay both with restaurants and a handful of bars, including a traditional one in the old railway station hotel which also houses a small antiques museum:

Aquí Te Quiero Ver (s/d en suite €12/24) budget, friendly *hostal* on the main road as you enter the town, with restaurant and bar (C/Delicias 21, ☎ 958 362 222)

Restaurante-Pensión Miguel ★ (s/d without bathroom/en suite €15/26/36) just along the road from Aqui Te Quiero Ver, up for sale at the time of writing but providing an adequate, if less friendly, alternative (Pza Buenos Aire, ☎ 958 362 012/042)

For more information
Town hall: Pza de Santo Domingo de Guzmán 1, ☎ 958 362 000

Ventas de Zafarraya – Alhama de Granada

Pass through fertile agricultural land and enter the Parque Natural de las Sierras de Tejada, Almijara y Alhama then follow an ancient droving track through woodland to Alhama in its striking location below the Sierra Tejeda and above a dramatic gorge.

Distance	20km
Time	5h30
Height gain	340m
Height loss	420m
Highest point	1040m

If you want to cut a few kilometres off the route, and don't mind some roadwalking, you can leave Ventas along the A402 and turn right off it at the point that it enters the natural park, at a signpost to the Alcauca camping area, to join back up with the GR7. Otherwise, leave Ventas heading out of the southeast side of the village in the same direction as you came in, but taking the road instead of the dismantled **railway line**. Cross under the old **railway bridge** and shortly afterwards take a small, unmarked track off to the left. It divides almost immediately and you take the left fork heading around the hillside of **Morrón de la Cuna**. (The track is blocked by a chain with a 'no entry: danger' sign; but don't worry – this refers to the vehicle track which goes up the hill.)

Map 20
Southern Route:
Ventas de Zafarraya –
La Resinera

After 500m on the track, turn right down onto a small path and stay on it as it heads downhill approaching the hamlet of **Espino**. After 1km, the path meets a wider track again and you turn left down it to come into Espino 700m later at a fountain. ▶

Turn left up past the fountain, on a wide track (still unmarked) heading north-east. After 500m take the left fork at a junction,

Approaching Espino

There are no markings for any of this section.

staying close to the side of the hill. Just under a kilometre further on, turn right when the track divides again and then left almost immediately, passing through small almond orchards and lots of vegetable fields.

To your right are some of the hills of the **Parque Natural de las Sierras de Tejada, Almijara y Alhama**, whose northern border you are walking parallel to. You can see the Loma de las Víboras, Peñon del Romero and **Los Barracones**. The highest peak, **Pico La Maroma**, is further south.

SIERRAS DE TEJEDA, ALMIJARA Y ALHAMA NATURAL PARK (407km²)

This relatively new park (designated in 1999) protects an impressive mountain massif between the provinces of Málaga and Granada. Its landscape is rocky and rugged with limestone cliffs and ravines in the Sierra Tejeda, and some of the country's most important dolomite marble sites in the Sierra Almijara. Its territory is split half and half between Málaga and Granada. Its highest peak is La Maroma at 2069m. There are many caves in the park, some prehistoric.

Wildlife
There is a wide diversity of plant life across the altitude range of the park, much of it endemic. Species of note include the yew (*tejo*) which gives the park its name and used to be much more widespread until most of the trees were destroyed because yew is poisonous to livestock. You will also see: pines, including Corsican and maritime pines; boxwood; juniper; holm, cork and gall oaks; maples and rowans. In the scrub you will find broom, milk vetch and mountain cherries and there are also plentiful aromatic herbs.

The animal you are most likely to come across is the endemic mountain goat which was once endangered but whose populations are now recovering well. The bird life is impressive and, depending on the time of year, you may also spot eagles (golden, hawk, short-toed snake and booted), peregrine falcons, goshawks, woodpeckers and rock thrushes.

Camping
You are not allowed to camp in the park except in designated areas. The only one of these that the route passes near is El Robedal. This is a good base for a detour to climb La Maroma.

For further information
Consejería de Medio Ambiente, Delegación de Medio Ambiente in Málaga, Edificio Eurocom, Bloque Sur, 29071, Málaga, ☎ 951 040 058, pn.tejeda.cma@juntadeandalucia.es, www.juntadeandalucia.es/medioambiente (Spanish)

A couple of kilometres further on, the track meets another one coming up from the right and crosses over the **Arroyo de la Fuente**. It then passes between houses and climbs to meet a small road at a large **warehouse**.

Now in the natural park (this is where the shortcut along the A402 rejoins the main route), you turn right to pass by the warehouse on its south side following a signpost to the Alcauca camping area, a nice spot surrounded by oaks and elms 4km from here.

The route is still unmarked until you come to the first GR7 post of this section at the next divide, 750m on. Don't be discouraged by the fact that it marks the direction from which you have just come with a cross. This appears to be because tracks around the area have been changed recently and not yet remarked.

From here on the route is marked. Take the left fork (the camping area is up to the right). The track continues between houses and then comes to a slightly confusing intersection of five tracks. The route is uphill on the second track on your right towards a house. Walk up in front of the house, taking a track to the left heading east. Meet a small road after 400m and turn downhill to the left. Take the first track on the right which also splits soon after and you again take the left-hand option. This track seems slightly unlikely as it crosses over a pile of stones, but it does carry on and passes in front of a building. Ignore the track to the right immediately after the building, but take the next right fork. Then, when you meet another track, turn left down it to come to the main road.

Cross straight over the road, taking the gravel track directly opposite and then the right fork which passes through a field. This meets another track on the other side of the field and you turn left to continue on through fields until you meet another track after a kilometre and turn right.

Follow this track through a farmyard to a small tarmac road which you turn right onto, crossing the **Arroyo de la Madre** to arrive at the hotel-restaurant **Los Caños de la Alcaiceria**, 10.8km from the start (s/d en suite €32/53, Ctra Alhama-Vélez, Km10, ☎ 958 350 325).

The route continues left behind the hotel (GR7 signpost Alhama 1h50) on an wide cattle-droving track. This takes you almost all the way to Alhama, re-entering the natural park.

179

There's a good chance of seeing eagles here, and deer and mountain goats are also quite common.

Ignore all smaller tracks and stay on this main one passing through cork oaks and almonds and into pines. ◄ When this main track divides, the route goes left. If you head right, it is 3km to El Robedal camping area, on the mountain El Robedal, and this is also the way to follow the marked route to the top of La Maroma. (The tourist office in Alhama has information about doing this as an 8–10h, 25km route.)

Carry on through pines and poplars again staying on main track, ignoring smaller turn-offs and passing by a picnic area with a drinking fountain and then a small reservoir on your right.

Just after this you reach the road into **Alhama de Granada**. Turn left up the road for 1km with the village coming into sight. A road down to the right at this point brings you into the village.

Alhama de Granada (850m, pop. 6000) ↵ ⧉ F ▲ € ☎ ✉ ✚ ① �"

A picturesque little place in an impressive setting, Alhama is famous for the relaxing Arab thermal baths from which it gets its name (Al-Hamma, the Arabic for hot spring). The town itself is Arabic in layout with a well-preserved old quarter including the remains of a defensive wall and watchtower.

Accommodation and food
Plenty of nice places to eat with outside seating in the buzzing plaza and a few options for rooms:

Pensión San Jose ★ (s/d/t en suite €18/31/40) straightforward central accommodation with very friendly owner and little restaurant downstairs offering local fare and pizzas (Pza Constitución 27, ☎ 958 350 156)

La Seguiriya (s/d/t en suite €30/60/80 inc breakfast) beautifully decorated rooms, a terrace with a view over the gorge and a friendly owner make this a really special place to stay, with lower prices for longer stays (C/Las Peñas 12, ☎ 958 360 801, www.laseguiriya.com)

Hotel Balneario ★★★ (s/d en suite €55–60/82–95) 3km out of Alhama at the baths with access to massage, physio and pool, with comfortable rooms, the pricier ones with a living room or private terrace (Ctra Balneario, ☎ 958 350 011/366, www.balnearioalhamadegranada.com)

For more information
Town hall: ☎ 958 350 161
Tourist office: ☎ 958 360 686

Distance	20km
Time	6h
Height gain	300m
Height loss	280m
Highest point	1100m

From Calle Las Peñas leave the village heading out along the gorge, which has no GR7 marks to begin with, but is marked with a signboard for the Los Tajos y la Presa de Alhama route.

The pretty footpath takes you out past one of three abandoned old flour mills once powered by the river, and then past the **Ermita de Los Angeles**. A further 500m on, take the left fork at the split in the path and cross the little bridge into poplars before coming out onto the road at the *presa* (dam) after about 1.5km.

Turn left here, passing by the reservoir and the bird observatory on your left and El Ventorro (d/€60, once an inn

Leaving Alhama through the dramatic gorge carved out by the Río Alhama, you pass through beautiful cork oak woodland with panoramic views of the Sierras de Játar and de Almijara. After some track walking you then pick your way down to Arenas del Rey on a small path through almond orchards.

Walking out of Alhama through the gorge

for horsemen, now a comfortable hotel, ☎ 958 350 438) on your right.

After another 300m, turn right up a smaller road signposted with a GR7 sign (5h Arenas del Rey). Stay on this main track passing through poplar plantations with the **Río Alhama** alongside you on your right. Ignore all turnings, including a wide one after 3km at a building with a tennis court, but keep an eye out for a little path to the right 700m on from the building.

This footpath soon takes you up a steep climb, looking down on artichokes and across a patchwork of different crops. You then descend with views of the **Sierra de Játar** and the **Sierra de Almijara** opening up to your right.

When you meet another track, turn left and continue to a tarmac road after 10min (1km). Turn right onto it, then left onto a small path just before the **quarry**. Pass into cork oaks and climb, ignoring forks off this main track and following occasional faint marking on trees and rocks.

When you come to a house, **Cortijo de Navazo**, continue round to the left passing between it and the large greenhouse. Then, at the crossroads, carry straight on to come to the road. Turn right onto it and after 100m turn left onto a wide gravel track which you follow through almonds and cork oaks.

Ignore tracks off to either side for 3km then keep a close eye out for a small, little-trodden path to the right between two marked boulders and into oaks. You'll know you've missed it if you reach a track off to the right with a raised **water tank**.

The tiny path cuts into the trees and emerges into a dry stream bed, the **Barranco de Anguita**, which you pick your way along, through oaks, brush and long grasses, into almond groves and down to a track after about 500m.

Follow this clear track for just over 1.5km before turning off it again to the right onto an unclear path through almond trees. Posts should guide you the 300m onto another track which soon splits. You take a right and then follow this same track for a further 2km down into the **Arenas del Rey**.

Arenas del Rey (875m, pop. 2100) 🏛 🍴 F ▲ ☎ 🚌

A little village with a pleasant plaza and a church surrounded by leafy gardens. It retains some traces of Roman settlement but, like many villages in the area, Arenas was almost completely destroyed in an earthquake on Christmas Day in 1884. It was reconstructed by Alfonso XII and changed its name from Arenas de Alhama to Arenas del Rey (of the King) in his honour.

Accommodation and food

A couple of bars that serve up the usual fare but there is no accommodation in the village itself. You can either head to Los Bermejales campsite which is 7km away next to the reservoir (person/tent € 4/4, ☎ 958 35 91 90) or continue to Jayena.

For more information

Town hall: Pza Alfonso X, ☎ 958 359 103
Taxi: ask in shop for a local family who will drive walkers to Jayena or the campsite

---

Arenas del Rey – Jayena

Distance	15km
Time	4h
Height gain	300m
Height loss	260m
Highest point	1060m

From the plaza, leave the village heading downhill and east on the road out of the village in the direction of Jayena. Pass another drinking fountain and when you come to the **bridge** at the end of the village, cross it and turn right.

You soon come to a signboard for the Colada de Camino de Fornes – which is an old agricultural path to Fornes. Pass by this sign and climb on the quiet tarmac road passing some ruined buildings before branching off onto a gravel road to the left (about 2km after setting off from the village).

An hour's walking on a local road takes you to the forestry tracks which you follow back into the natural park at La Resinera and through mixed pine woodland until Jayena. There are lots of options for other routes in the natural park that leave from La Resinera.

183

Follow this round the hillside looking out across lower olive-covered hills. After 800m on this track, turn down to the left towards the large **greenhouses**, then immediately turn left again at the split just afterwards. This brings you down to a tarmac road and you turn right and cross the river.

Just after the small **bridge**, a GR7 cross on the back of a road sign indicates you should not continue up the road, but there appears to be no other option as the only other route is blocked by large locked gates to your right. It is best to ignore the marking and continue along the road for about 1.5km.

This brings you to a right turn signposted to La Resinera/Vivero. Take this turning, entering the natural park passing through poplars and, after 1.5km, come to a **picnic area** shaded by pines with barbecues and benches.

Continue on the track to come to **La Resinera** – once a factory for processing pine resin and now an **information centre** with displays about the forest fires in 1975 and 1983 which devastated the resin-processing industry in the area and forced the closure of the plant and an accompanying sawmill.

A 375m signposted detour takes you to a viewpoint, and a fork off to the right from in front of the building takes you on other routes to Puerto de Cómpeta

Map 21
Southern Route:
La Resinera – Nigüelas

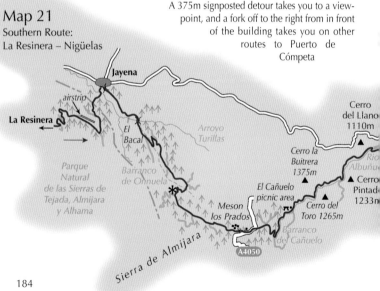

Jayena

airstrip

La Resinera

El Bacal

Arroyo Turillas

Cerro del Llano 1110m

Río Albuñu

Parque Natural de las Sierras de Tejada, Almijara y Alhama

Barranco de Onnuela

Cerro la Buitrera 1375m

Cerro Pintad 1233n

El Cañuelo picnic area

Meson los Prados

Cerro del Toro 1265m

Barranco del Cañuelo

Sierra de Almijara

A4050

(16km) and Puerto de Frigiliana (11km). You can get information about these and other routes in the centre.

The GR7 continues downhill with the information centre on the left. The track divides again shortly afterwards and you turn left down to the small Río Cebellón on a track signposted to the airstrip (Pista de Aterrizaje). Cross the little **bridge** and then stay on the main track, taking a left 100m on, walking through pines. ▸

The pines are all quite young due to replanting after the fires in the 1970s and 1980s.

Where the track divides about 1.5km after the information centre, take the fork to the left, and then ignore a smaller track off to the left. An information board here tells you about the process of extracting resin from the pines.

The track climbs, zigzagging up to a junction almost at the top of the hill (now 8.5km into the walk). The left fork goes up to the **airstrip** and the right fork, which you take, follows the south edge of it onto the firebreak between the trees. About 150m later, take the left turn into another firebreak, then 300m further on take a smaller left which brings you out onto another firebreak with the village visible down below.

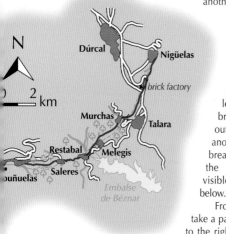

From here take a path down to the right which you can see curving ahead of you towards **Jayena**. Ignore a left turn and keep heading downhill on this winding footpath for about 2.5km until you meet a track where you turn left to head up into the village.

Jayena (912m, pop. 1300) 🛌 🏕 🍴 F ▲ € ☎ ✉ ✚ 🚌

Like many of the towns and villages in the area, archaeological finds suggest that there was a settlement here in Neolithic times. It was also inhabited in Roman times but the Islamic period was definitive in creating the town then known as Chayyana. You can see the Muslim watchtower, and the parish church is also worth a visit.

Accommodation and food

There is one place to stay in town or you can continue along the route to a campsite. For food there are also a couple of bars with standard fare:

El Bacal Camping Area a permitted camping area on La Resinera mountain, surrounded by pines with 50-person capacity, 4km beyond Jayena (signposted off the GR7)

Hospedería la Almijara (s/d/t en suite € 30/40/60) a bar-restaurant with a few rooms upstairs, somewhat chaotically run (Avda del Mediterráneo 37, ☎ 958 364 157)

For more information

Town hall: ☎ 958 364 079

Jayena – Albuñuelas

A peaceful pine forest track takes you up into hills with beautiful panoramic views across to the Sierra Nevada, and then down a riverbed into the pretty village of Albuñuelas.

Distance	31.5km
Time	7h15
Height gain	580m
Height loss	740m
Highest point	1300m

Head out of Jayena along Plaza Constitución which leaves the small plaza in front of the church (the Iglesia del Santismo Sacramento) and continues down to the right. Stay on this road down to a **bridge** which you cross and carry on climbing gently through almonds and olives towards the wooded hills ahead.

After about 15min (2km), pass a turning off to the right signposted to **El Bacal** camping area which is 2km down this turning. Continue climbing on the road and after about 500m cross the **Arroyo Turillas** just before the road turns from tarmac into a forestry track. Here you enter the **Parque Natural de las Sierras de Tejada, Almijara y Alhama**.

Follow the track up into the trees, ignoring tracks off to either side. Stay on this main track as it takes you up through shady pines and ignore a track off to the right 1.5km after entering the woods. You curve round the hill to the left on the main track. ▶ After about 45min in the woods (4km) you come out of the trees briefly for great views back across green hills to Jayena in the distance.

At a split about 300m after this clearing, stay right and keep climbing gently, back in the shady pines with glimpses out now and again to the Sierra Nevada mountains to the east. Pass a small track off to the left after 10km in the woods and stay on the main track, soon passing another turning doubling back to the right. Keep ascending gently to reach a good **viewpoint** after 12.5km and 2h15 in the woods.

For the whole of this section in the woods there are sparse paint markings on trees and occasional faded posts.

Viewpoint in the Sierra de Almijara

Just after the viewpoint, you come to a fork where you stay left. Pass a right turn and after 20min come to the first building of the **Cortijo los Prados** which you pass on your left to climb the track, through the *cortijo*. Leave through its large green metal **gate** and turn right onto another track which soon brings you to the **A4050** tarmac road at the bar-restaurant **Meson los Prados**.

A GR7 signpost here directs you left along the road known as the Carretera de la Cabra to Albuñelas. After about 250m on the road you come to a signboard for the 5km Cardel de la Venta de la Lata walk. Continue past this and walk another 500m up the road to a gravelly car park with a track leading off it. Take this, climbing through young pines, and after 500m reach another wider gravel track down which you turn right.

After just over 1km, turn left onto a smaller path running alongside the streambed of the **Barranco del Cañuelo**, passing between huge fragrant rosemary bushes. When the track bends up to the right leave it to continue along the streambed on a little-walked overgrown small path which, after 600m, emerges onto the same wider track. Follow the track for just over 1km to arrive at **El Cañuelo picnic area**.

There are two houses available to rent by contacting the town hall in advance and you can camp for free. There are also pleasant shady picnic tables to eat at and barbecues (although at the time of writing all fires had been banned in the spring and summer months due to the risk of forest fires). Water is available here too although it is not chlorinated so you may want to treat it before drinking.

Leave the picnic area on the main track heading left around the hillside and down to the stream which feeds the **Río Albuñuelas**. You then follow the riverbed (which may be dry depending on the season) for about 7.5km, starting with it on your right-hand side, but crossing over it several times. It is bordered by azaleas and pines, and the rocky crags of the **Cerro la Buitrera** and **Cerro Pintado** tower above you.

After about 3.5km, the track takes you up above the river and then another kilometre on, you descend back to its level at a junction, continuing uphill and round the bend to the left and ignoring the track away to the right.

Staying on the same track, you climb gently and above some ruined buildings. Another 7.5km after leaving the picnic

Tree bearing tasty pine nuts in the Sierra de Almijara

area, you turn right onto a smaller track that doubles back to the right taking you down to the riverbed again. Ignoring a confusing cross on the rock ahead, cross the river and climb up the track on the other side.

Albuñuelas comes into view after another kilometre and you can see the two parts of the village, the higher part (Barrio Alto) at 738m and the lower neighborhood (Barrio Bajo) below it. Turn down a track to the left towards it, leaving the pines behind and passing between almond trees and cultivated land. Pass a small track off to the left heading into fields then, a short distance on, take the track heading downhill at a junction. Continue straight on where the path divides, walking between two metal fences as the path becomes more overgrown and picks its way downhill into the valley.

Cross the narrow valley which is lush with green vegetable patches, orchards and fig trees, and climb the other side on the Camino de los Molinos – a steep cobbled path that quickly brings you up onto a narrow concrete street in the village, passing between gardens full of orange trees.

Albuñuelas (750m, pop. 1200) ⚲ ⍾ F ▲ ☎ ✉ ✚ 🚌

A charming, historic village. Buildings of note include the 16th-century watch-tower, the parish church, the Ermita de San Antonio, and the old archbishop's palace (17th and 18th centuries). There have been human settlements in the area since prehistoric times and you can visit caves just outside the village where archaeological remains have been discovered.

Accommodation and food
The village has a couple of B&Bs and a *casa rural* plus several bars which do food:

La Casa Azul (s/d en suite €30/50) an English-run B&B with rooms and apartment and a lovely roof terrace, meals available (C/Horno 8, ☎ 958 776 366, ken@fishinginspain.co.uk, www.fishinginspain.co.uk)

La Casa (s/d €45/60) another English-run B&B with internet, meals available and patio. The owners also run a holiday home (☎ 958 776 143, enquiries@casaamelia.com, www.casaamelia.com)

El Cortijo del Pino a small *casa rural* with 4 doubles and a single and a patio with beautiful views (Fernan Núñez 2, ☎ 958 776 257, cortijodelpino@eresmas.com, www.casaruralelcortijodelpino.com)

For more information
Town hall: ☎ 958 776 031

A day dominated by orange groves and the sound of water bubbling along the ancient irrigation channels. The route joins the dots between several of the small villages of the Lecrín valley before arriving at the foot of the mountains to come into Nigüelas.

Albuñuelas – Nigüelas

Distance	14km
Time	3h30
Height gain	460m
Height loss	260m
Highest point	950m

Albuñuelas – Restábal (4km, 55min)
Head out east through the Barrio Alto of Albuñuelas on the main road until you come to a GR7 display board at a bus stop. Go down Calle Alta, the last road on the right before the display board, which takes you down into Barrio Bajo, the lower part of Albuñuelas, and keep heading down to the Ermita San Sebastian and a fountain.

Here turn right down a steep street passing the village's old laundry. Take the first left after the laundry along a narrow street, with the first GR7 mark of the day, and follow it round, taking the next right along Calle Mojon to come to a small dirt path and a GR7 sign (Saleres 50min).

The small path is well marked and takes you straight into the groves of oranges, lemons, almonds, olives and grenadines, alive with the colours and smells of fruits or blossoms depending on the time of year. ▶

The path follows the routes of the *acequias*, the ancient irrigation channels built by the Moors. Stay on this small path heading east, ignoring paths off into fields. At a less clear junction, after 1.8km, take the left (marked) fork up to pass through an orange grove and onto a wider track which becomes concrete. Remain on this, avoiding turns, all the way into the small village of **Saleres** (560m, pop. 300 ▮●▮ **F**) whose winding streets still retain their medieval layout (3km, 45min). For a short detour, visit the *atalaya*, the village watchtower, which has excellent views out across the valley.

Leave the village on the road marked to Restábal, passing the Fuente de los Tres Caños, and follow it for the 1km to the village of Restábal. There was previously a route through the gorge and over the hill into Restábal from Saleres, but at the time of writing very little trace of it could be found amongst new building developments. You will come to a road junction just at the entrance to the village: take the left, signposted to Lecrín, to carry on, or right to enter **Restábal**.

This lush landscape is typical of the fertile Lecrín valley, also called the 'Valley of Happiness' (Valle de la Alegría) thanks to its temperate microclimate.

Restábal (538m, pop. 1400) ↵ ▮●▮ F ▲ ☎ ✚ ⛆
This quiet little whitewashed village surrounded by fruit orchards is the administrative centre for El Valle area (the villages of Melegis, Restábal and Saleres). The sights of the village are the remains of a Moorish castle from the Nasrid period (13th to 15th century), the C/Real market and the 16th-century San Cristóbal church.

Accommodation and food
Several bars including Bar Jovi which has a restaurant whose owners run several *casas rurales*:
Meson Dispensa del Valle a good restaurant serving local dishes which rents out a few houses (C/Santa Ana 5, ☎ 958 793 598/531)

For more information
Town hall: Avda Andalucía, 34, ☎ 958 793 181, ayuntelvalle@terra.es,
Taxi: ☎ 958 793 218

Looking back on Restábal

Restábal – Nigüelas (10km, 2h35)

To leave Restábal, return to the road junction where you
entered the village and turn right downhill. This takes you
past a GR7 display board and across a **bridge** over the **Río
Izbor**. Immediately on the other side of the bridge turn off the
road to the left (signed Murchas 50min). Left again would
take you to the **Embalse de Beznar** but, to stay on the route,
head right along a smaller track through orange trees. Soon
afterwards, take another right between some old stone walls.

Just round the bend from this divide the GR7 leaves the
track for a small path on the left, across an *acequia*. This is a
little overgrown in places, but well marked, and brings you
back to a wider track after a few hundred metres. Stay on this
wider track, not crossing the stream, and follow it round to the
right then uphill as it becomes concrete. When it splits take
the left fork and carry on to arrive at a GR7 sign for **Melegís**
(553m, pop. 580), which is a 10min diversion to the right.

You go left, then immediately right and then left again 150m on. From here there are fewer markings, but stay on this main track, ignoring turnoffs, until a major divide after 2km, on the outskirts of the village. Here you go left towards some buildings and pass by another turning to the left that would take you to an Arab castle built between the 12th and 15th centuries. Go right to enter the village of **Murchas** (660m, pop. 280 ⬤❚ F ☎).

To leave Murchas, carry on through the village passing the church and the fountain and head out on the road with **Talara** up on the hill directly ahead. Cross over the **bridge** on the road and then immediately turn left onto a track which runs alongside the (mainly dry) bed of the **Río Torrente** (GR7 sign, Nigüelas 1h). Continue alongside the river channel and after 1.3km you pass beneath a major road bridge. Turn left here to go between the buildings of a **brick factory**.

Ignore a turning up to the right, onto the road, after 700m, then pass beneath another bridge just before crossing the riverbed to continue along a track in the same direction on the other side. 500m further on, you come to the end of a tarmac road at a bridge and cross back to a track on the other side of the Río Torrente again, but still in the same direction. This track takes you all the way up to the village, which sits on a plateau above the river. When the track comes to the top and meets another, turn left to climb steeply up a street into **Nigüelas**.

Nigüelas (950m, pop. 1100) ⤳ ⬤❚ F ▲ € ☎ ⌧ ✝ 🚌
Nigüelas is a charming place with an attractive tree-lined square. It has some grand 17th- and 18th-century houses and also a number of inhabited cave houses.

Accommodation and food
There are a few *casas rurales* which are usually only available for a minimum of two nights and there is some luxury accommodation on the outskirts, but if you are stuck for a bed, head out of town on the northwest road to Dúrcal. Only half an hour away it has a few *hostales* and plenty of restaurants, but little else to recommend it.

Alquería de los Lentos (d en suite €75) highly luxurious accommodation situated in a converted mill on the outskirts of the village – rooms have private entrances, open fires, sitting area and air conditioning and it boasts a swimming pool, garden and bar/restaurant (Camino de los Molinos, ☎ 958 777 850, info@loslentos.com, www.loslentos.com)

La Solanilla 2 houses for 4–6 people (€60–77) well-equipped with private gardens with BBQs (☎ 958 780 575)

A number of *casas rurales* – only open in peak season and best booked ahead (www.casas-turismo-rural.com)

For more information
Town hall: C/Angustias 6, ☎ 958 777 607

SIERRA NEVADA NATURAL PARK (1718km²)

The Sierra Nevada is a walkers' paradise. It is the second highest mountain range in Europe with over 20 peaks at more than 3000m. Its highest peak, Mulhacén (3481m), is the highest on the Iberian peninsula.

The area has various protected statuses. It contains a national park, one of only two in Andalucía, which has the highest level of protection, and is a UNESCO biosphere reserve.

The Sierra Nevada is home to exceptionally diverse plant, bird and animal species at a range of bioclimatic levels from lush green valleys to bleak windswept mountain tops. It also has a rich cultural and historical heritage dating back to the Tartessians, Visigoths, Romans and the Moors.

Wildlife

The park boasts the highest number of endemic plant species in Europe and also many North African species. In the spring and early summer the range of wildflowers is remarkable. The vegetation you are likely to see varies hugely according to the altitude you are at, from gall oaks, maples, wild olives, and shrubs such as prickly junipers lower down, to pines, junipers, bushy thyme, rosemary and broom higher up, and lichens and grass species at the highest altitudes. Near to streams and rivers you'll find poplar, alder, ash, elms and willows.

The park is known for its population of Spanish ibex, a type of native mountain goat, and these are the mammals you are most likely to spot (often posing silhouetted on hilltops!). If you're lucky, you may also see foxes, badgers, wild boars, wild cats, beech martens and genets. On higher slopes you may come across Mediterranean pine voles and weasels. The park also has a huge variety of insect life, and is particularly interesting for its butterflies, with 120 catalogued species.

The bird life in the park is impressive, with over 60 species including important colonies of birds of prey such as golden eagles, Bonelli's eagles, peregrine falcons, griffon vultures and kestrels. In wooded areas you may see or hear hoopoes, short-toed treecreepers, green woodpeckers, great tits, goldfinches and golden orioles. And, in the highest areas, there are Alpine accentors, black redstarts, skylarks, northern wheatears, rock thrushes, rock buntings and red-billed choughs.

Further information
Park information office: Ctra de la Sierra, Km 7, 18191-Pinos Genil, Granada
☎ 958 026 300/303, pn.snevada.cma@juntadeandalucia.es
    On the route, there are also limited information points at Puerto de la Ragua and Pampaneira.

Nigüelas – Lanjarón

Distance	15km
Time	3h30
Height gain	360m
Height loss	660m
Highest point	1280m

Small paths and forest tracks take you high up through pines and almonds with expansive views over the Lecrín valley, before a long descent brings you to the spa town of Lanjarón and the start of the Alpujurras.

To leave **Nigüelas**, head northeast out of the plaza to the street you came in on. You pass a GR7 sign (Lanjarón 3h30) and the street takes you down and out of the buildings. Ignore the first track up to the left, but take the second one which is roughly cobbled in places. When this divides, turn right up a concrete track leaving the village behind you and walking between almonds.

Ignore a track off to the left just after the concrete ends, but take the next left, an unmarked dirt track which heads into an almond field. After just 20m, turn right at a marked boulder up a very small path between the almonds which looks a bit like an irrigation channel at first glance.

This becomes a delightful path that climbs steeply for 500m before meeting another path along which you turn left. It climbs steeply between the trees, giving you increasingly good views back over Nigüelas and neighbouring Dúrcal and Padul spread out on the valley floor. Stay on it as

195

it zigzags up northwards and around the hillside before coming out on a main forestry track after 1.3km.

Turn right up the main track, ignoring a smaller one heading backwards to right, and then keep right, passing a turning to the left after 1km. Keep climbing through pines with bare rock faces and water-eroded slopes above, and contrastingly neatly ordered olive groves below.

A further 1.5km on, at the next divide in the track, take the right fork. The track levels out and you walk round a deforested hillside getting views down over the villages of the Lecrín valley through which you have passed. ◄

You can also see the sea here on clear days and, on very clear days, all the way across to Africa.

After 2km, walk straight over a crossroads where there is a noticeable change in rock colour from red to grey. Another 800m on you pass the Icona drinking fountain and from there continue on the main track ignoring small ones off to various farms until 1.5km later where there is a divide in the main track. You head right, going uphill past an **albergue** and at another divide soon after, right again.

The town of Lanjarón soon comes into view far below you and the track begins to descend in large zigzags to meet it. From here it is all downhill. As you descend, you will pass several tracks off the main one signposted to *cortijos*. When the track divides after the last one to the right signposted to Albercón, take the right fork to come down further and arrive at a T-junction in amongst the trees. You head left and from here keep heading downhill, ignoring smaller tracks and keeping to the left side of a small stream. This brings

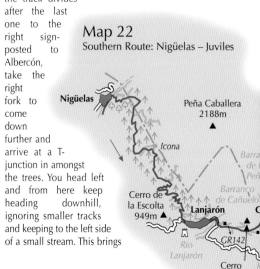

Map 22
Southern Route: Nigüelas – Juviles

Nigüelas

Peña Caballera
2188m ▲

Icona

Barran
de la
Peña

Cerro de
la Escolta
949m ▲

Barranco
de Cañuelo

Lanjarón

C

Rio
Lanjarón

GR142

Cerro
Mimbre
1072m

Lanjarón (650m, pop. 4000) ⇆ ◉ F ▲ € ☎ ✉ ✚ ① 🚌 🖥

Made famous by its natural spring, Lanjarón is still dominated by water, with many making the trip to visit its spa. This, combined with its billing as the 'gateway to the Alpujarras', makes it a busy place to visit with plenty of hotels and restaurants to choose from and lots of handicraft shops. If you have time, treat your aching muscles to a massage at the spa.

Accommodation and food

Hostal Nevada (s/d en suite €22/28) simple but smart accommodation with friendly owner (Avda Andalucía 18, ☎ 958 770 159/153)

Hotel Alcadima (s/d en suite €45/52) luxurious with swimming pool, solarium and pretty courtyard full of geraniums with views of the castle (C/Francisco Tarrega 3, ☎ 958 770 809/279)

Hotel Miramar ★★★ (s/d en suite €58/84) for those wanting a bit of the high life the Miramar has a swimming pool, large rooms some with their own lounge, air conditioning and balconies (Avda Andalucía 10, ☎ 958 770 161)

Balneario de Lanjarón

The waters here have been renowned for their health-giving properties since 1770. You can have all manner of massages, baths, facials and health consultations (☎ 958 770 137, www.balneariodelanjaron.com).

you to the main road into **Lanjarón**. Turn left along it to enter the village on its main street.

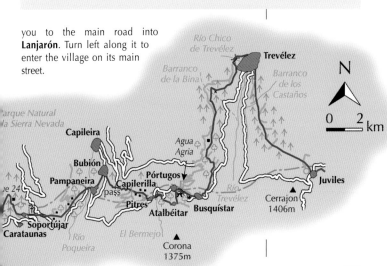

For more information
Town hall: Pza de la Constitucíon, 29, ☎ 958 770 002
Buses: ☎ 958 770 003

Lanjarón – Soportújar

A pretty climb out of Lanjarón takes you up to a path that zigzags round ravines passing Cáñar and crossing an impressive dam, Dique 24, to reach Soportújar.

Distance	12.8km
Time	4h50
Height gain	460m
Height loss	240m
Highest point	1040m

Lanjarón – Cáñar (7.8km, 2h50)

Head out of Lanjarón on the main road, past the Ermita de San Sebastian, and across the **Río Lanjarón** at the east edge of town, heading towards the rock face of the **Cerro Mimbre**. After passing a GR7 signboard, continue along the road to come to a left turn 250m further on (signposted Cáñar 2h15).

The concrete track turns rapidly into a little cobbled path passing up behind a house and onto another concrete track behind it. You cross this and continue up another steep little path, soon reaching a wide dirt track above. The route then follows this track up the hill, taking signposted short-cuts off it to cut off some of the track's loops and come to a concrete track near the top.

There are good views back down over the town and you can see the ruined Moorish **castle** down by the river, built to control access to the town. Its tower was used as part of the communication line between the watchtowers throughout the Alpujarras and the coast. When Christians took the town after an epic battle in 1490, Captain Negro, who was defending the town, is said to have jumped to his death from the tower rather than live to see the town fall into enemy hands.

Go left along the concrete track for 600m then turn off again onto a little cobbled path to come out onto a track at a farmhouse where you turn right to come to onto a concrete

track again. Turn right along it and follow it through almond and olive trees for about 600m before coming to a junction where you turn left (signposted to Caballo Blanco). Ignore a confusing mark on a rock down to the left here as this is for the **GR142**.

Climbing up out of Lanjarón

Follow this track, passing a GR142 signpost to Orgiva, but taking the next wider right track signposted to Cortijo Mesquerina. Another 800m on pass a track to the right, continuing on the main track. At the next fork go left (the right is clearly signposted as private land) and continue uphill until the next divide where you go left, then left again almost immediately onto a little path.

This takes you on a V-shaped path around a ravine. At the divide in the path nearly a kilometre on, take the left fork. The path becomes a little overgrown and difficult to follow but there are marks and you should keep heading north and uphill, passing between oaks and brambles. The path then becomes clearer and you descend to the pretty **Barranco de Cañuelo**, a pleasant and shady place to rest.

ALPUJARRAS

The Alpujarras is an area of valleys between the Sierra Nevada and the Sierras of Almijara, Contraviesa and Gádor to the south. The GR7 crosses the western part of the region which is in the province of Granada and a small section of the eastern part in the province of Almería.

The name Alpujarras comes from the Arabic *abuxarrat* meaning 'land of silk', and the area, which was the last refuge of the moors in Spain, still retains a distinctive Arab influence, evident in the cuisine, arts and crafts, sophisticated irrigation systems and Arabic place names. It is known for its Berber architecture: whitewashed flat-roofed houses with distinctive chimneys packed into steep narrow streets.

In the fertile valleys of the western Alpujarras, the main economic activity (apart from increasing tourism) is still agriculture. The land is still farmed using traditional methods as the steep terrain makes many modern agricultural techniques impractical. You'll pass through cereal crops, olives, vines, oranges and lemons, almonds, walnuts, apples and cherries.

Cross the stream and climb the hill on the other side of the gorge with **Cáñar** coming into view ahead of you. The path then takes in a loop into and out of the next gorge, crossing the **Barranco de las Peñas** which is often dry and onto the Camino de las Viñas which takes you into the village. Where it splits by a concrete bunker, you can take either the right or the left fork to bring you out at the road which you cross to enter the village.

Cáñar (1014m, pop. 350) ↵ ⦿ F ▲ ☎ 🚆

Quiet with leafy plazas, Cáñar, like other villages in the area, owes its layout and architecture to Arabic times with Berber-influenced flat-roofed whitewashed houses. In Arab times its economy was based around the production of silk. It boasts a viewpoint to Africa which is worth a detour on a clear day.

Accommodation and food
Some bars with food and a couple of options for accommodation:

Alpujarras Accommodation B&B (d/t €40) beautiful views (☎ 958 784 741/618 465 675, www.alpujarras-accommodation.com)

Casa Rural Cáñar Fernando (s/d €40/55) 2 charming houses available for rental by room when not full (☎ 696 894 799, www.lamua.com)

For more information
Town hall: Pza Santa Ana 1, ☎ 958 785 301

Cáñar – Soportújar (5km, 2h)
Leave Cáñar on the east side of the village at the Fuente de Ya Bajos and GR7 sign pointing you northeast along a concrete track with wooden handrails (Soportújar 2h). This route is also signposted to the **cemetery** and **Dique 24** which you pass by.

Follow the concrete track with great views down to the valley and Orgiva. After 300m, when it goes uphill, take the lower right fork, then shortly afterwards, a left fork. The track becomes a smaller path and you turn right at the next small divide. You can see Soportújar straight ahead across the ravine that you are about to walk round.

After 1km on the small path, you come to a divide and take the right lower fork (the left one rejoins the path later) and keep heading into the ravine. After 800m, ignore a path off to the left and stay on the lower path. At the next split both forks take you to the same place.

A further 3km later, you arrive at Dique 24, so-called because it is the 24th in a series of dams built to reduce erosion from the Río Chico, although now there are only trees and vegetation behind it, rather than any water. Cross behind the dam and down the steps on the other side where the small path zigzags upwards briefly through pines before levelling out and passing a building.

The path then follows along the side of a pretty *acequia* before crossing it at a divide in the path and heading right downhill through a lush valley with lots of camomile and fig trees. Go left when the path divides and carry on, coming to a concrete track into the village. It divides just after you join it and you go right to descend into **Soportújar** passing the Fuente del Vino/Fuente del Chorro at the entrance.

Soportújar (975m, pop. 300) ↩ F ▲ ☎

A sleepy village perched above the valley floor looking down on Orgiva. Have a look into the 16th-century parish church, Santa María la Mayor, on your way past. It was built in the Mudéjar style on top of the site of an old mosque and has a gilded wooden 18th-century altarpiece.

Accommodation and food

There are only a couple of bars that serve food, a small food shop and one place to stay:

La Huerta (2–4 person apartments €50–90) well-equipped, self-catering apartments (Camino de Carataunas, ☎ 625 811 929/669 034 657)

For more information

Town hall: ☎ 958 787 635

Soportújar – Pitres

A great day starting with a winding path into Pampaneira at the bottom of the beautiful Poquiera valley, then a climb up through Bubión over a pass with incredible views back across the valley and up to the peaks of the Sierra Nevada, before descending to Pitres.

Distance	13.9km
Time	3h45
Height gain	740m
Height loss	460m
Highest point	1600m

Soportújar – Pampaneira (7km, 2h)

Pass out of Soportújar on the east road, crossing the **bridge** then heading south and passing a fountain on the left with a GR7 signboard opposite. Continue along the road, then turn off to the left up a signed concrete track (Pampaneira 2h). At the top of the hill, the concrete track goes uphill towards the **cemetery**. Turn right at the southwest corner wall of the cemetery down a small path to a lower gravel track. Then go left along the lower track and, when it divides, take the bottom right track.

Come round the hill on a small dirt path through broom with amazing views. This takes you up to a small tarmac road along which you turn right for 400m before taking a gravel track to the left. This has a small path off it to the right which you take and carry along past a ruined building then between a house and a wall, just after which you turn right when the path divides.

From here the path enters the Poquiera valley and you can see Bubión ahead. Continue on round and into the valley now heading north. The path comes to a wider track after 3.6km and you turn right along it, then left up a concrete track, which looks like a driveway with gates at the end but actually has a small path running off to the left just before the gates. You take this overgrown path up and behind the building and carry on.

Bubión, Capileira and a GR7 mark

At the next building stay on the small path which then crosses over another track and continues. Again, at a third house, make sure you stay on the small path, ignoring its driveway. Shortly after this you reach a wide track which you follow round to the right.

Turn right at both of the next divides in the track, with views of Pampaneira now ahead. Just after the second divide, cross a small **stream** and then immediately afterwards, take a path off and up to the left. Follow this well-marked little path until you come to another track which you then follow downhill through raspberries and under cherry and chestnut trees. When you come to another little path off to the right, descend on it all the way to the road, which you come out onto just before the **bridge** over the **Río Poqueira**.

Turn left along the road and across the **bridge** heading up into the village. A small track off to the left after 200m takes you off the road and zigzags uphill behind the electricity pylons. When it meets the road again cross over it and up a track into **Pampaneira**.

Pampaneira (1050m, pop. 400) ꒰ ◉ F ▲ € ☎ ✉ ✚ ⓘ ᕦ

Pampaneira is a perfect example of the picturesque, clean, white villages for which the Alpujarras are famous. Its traditional architecture is well conserved including many *tinaos* (covered streets). It is packed with craft workshops and shops which risk tempting walkers into adding weight to their rucksacks by buying textiles, ceramics, shoes and leatherwork, and ham.

Accommodation and food

A good selection of restaurants and places to stay, many of the best are around the pretty main plaza:

Hostal Pampaneira ★ (s/d en suite €25/36) pleasant rooms and a terrace looking down on the bustling street life and the popular good value restaurant below, at the bottom of the village (Avda Alpujarra 1, ☎ 958 763 002)

Hostal Ruta del Mulhacén ★ (s/d en suite €25–35/30–45) oppostite Hostal Pampaneira, cosy rooms with a bath, many with balconies or terraces looking down into the valley (☎ 958 763 010, www.rutadelMulhacén.com)

For more information

Town hall: Pza Mirador de Poqueira 1, ☎ 958 763 001, www.pampaneira.es
Taxi: ☎ 958 763 002

Pampaneira – Bubión (1.4km, 20min)

Head out of the northeast of Pampaneira following signs to the **Camino de Bubión** which leaves the village from halfway up Calle Castillo on a small path to the left. At a T-junction 400m on, turn left and then right at a divide 50m further on at a big dead tree. The path from here goes up amongst holm oaks, chestnuts and hawthorn before arriving in **Bubión**.

Bubión (1300m, pop. 600) ⇄ 🏔 F ▲ € ☎ ⊠ ✚ ① 🚌 🖥

A lively village with a thriving handicrafts industry with little art galleries, hand-weaving workshops and souvenir shops selling traditional Alpujarran products including cheeses, ceramics and the ubiquitous legs of ham which are cured in the high mountain villages. There's also a museum, La Casa Alpujarrena, a traditional house displaying crafts, traditional life and folklore.

Capileira, the village to the north of Bubión, provides the start to many routes in the Sierra Nevada, including to the summit of Veleta. Throughout the summer there is also a bus service to within three hours' walk of the summit of Mulhacén.

Accommodation and food
Accommodation and bars/restaurants are plentiful here:

Hostal las Terrazas (s/d €22/29) comfortable hotel rooms or (2/4/6 person €50/60/78) self-catering apartments with terraces down the hill, just off the main road (Pza del Sol, ☎ 958 763 034, www.terrazasalpujarra.com)

La Sevillana (d from €55) B&B in an attractive old house with 7 light rooms (Ctra de la Sierra 3, ☎ 958 763 153/628 132 357, casalasevillana@hotmail.com)

Los Tinaos (2/4/6 €59/78/102) pleasant terraced apartments with beautiful views down to Pampaneira (C/Parras, ☎ 958 763 217/192, www.lostinaos.com)

For more information
Town hall: Pza de Iglesia 1, ☎ 958 763 032
Taxi: ☎ 958 763 148

Bubión – Pitres (4.5km, 1h25)

Leave Bubión by the road which connects Pampaneira, Bubión and Capileira on the east side of the village. A GR7 sign (Capilerilla 1h) directs you off the road up Calle Ermita past a house and a horse corral, staying on the wider track and starting to climb. Another 700m on, turn right at a junction

Looking at the view between Bubion and Pitres

and then, very soon after, leave the wide track for a little path up to the right which continues to climb.

After 500m, the path divides and you go left to carry on zigzagging up the hill for 1.7km until you come to a 1600m **pass** with great views of the three villages of the Poqueira valley and the top of Veleta, at 3394m.

From the pass, you start the descent to Capilerilla and Pitres. Just after the pass, the path crosses a wide track and continues downhill southeast, ignoring a right turn and heading into pine trees as the path becomes a forestry track. Cross over another track, continuing straight on past two left turns back.

Another 1km from the pass, turn right down a track and then almost immediately left onto a small path heading into the trees. This widens out to small track and you get views of Pórtugos ahead and glimpses of Pitres below you. Pass through cherry trees and, by a fountain off to your left, come into the hamlet of **Capilerilla** (1440m, **F**) 2.4km from the pass by a sign to Pitres (0.5km). Turn left through the houses and then, on the other side, right to head round and downhill on a track with somewhat incongruous lampposts to arrive in **Pitres**.

Pitres (1250m, pop. 800) ☜ 🏛 🍴 F ▲ € ☎ ✉ ✚ ⓘ 🚌 🖥

Bustling and extremely pretty, Pitres perches high on the hillside overlooking Altabéitar and the other smaller villages of La Tahá, the municipality of which it is the capital. It is a lively place with lots going on and a sizeable community of British expats (evident from the marmite, Hellmann's mayonnaise, baked beans and Bisto section in the supermarket).

Accommodation and food

Balcón de Pitres (adult/tent/dorm bed in *albergue*/cabin € 5/5/from 31/from 45) large, shady campsite to the northwest of the village with restaurant, shop, laundry service and swimming pool, and information on local walks, about 500m out of the village (Caratera Orgiva-Ugívar, Km52, ☎ 958 766111, info@balcondepitres.com, www.balcondepitres.com)

Hostal San Roque (s/d en suite inc breakfast € 30/42) friendly hotel and restaurant at entrance to village (☎ 958 857 528)

For more information

Town hall: Pza Ayuntamiento 1, ☎ 958 766 061

Pitres – Trevélez

Distance	15.7km
Time	5h45
Height gain	720m
Height loss	560m
Highest point	1740m

Head east out of Pitres on the bottom road past the Hotel San Roque and before leaving the village turn right down Calle Agua Agria (there is a post for a GR7 sign but the sign itself was missing at the time of writing). The street rapidly turns into a dirt path as you leave the houses behind. Pass through a gateway in an old wall and then take two left turns to go down to a stream, **El Bermejo**. Cross over it on a little bridge and then, a short distance on, 400m from the start, cross a second stream surrounded by lush vegetation.

Leave Pitres on a path through lush vegetation past streams, passing through the tiny hamlet of Atalbéitar to climb to Pórtugos. Visit the colourful iron-rich spring then take the oak woodland route to Trevélez.

The meaning of the hamlet's name comes from the Arabic word *Haratalbaitar* which means veterinarian's neighbourhood. It was apparently once the home of a wise man known throughout all of the La Tahá area for his extensive knowledge of the healing properties of plants and herbs.

Follow the path round and up to the right and after 300m it brings you to a small tarmac road along which you turn right. Ignore a turning to the right to a ceramic workshop shortly after, following the road into **Atalbéitar** (1250m, pop. 40 ⦿ **F**), which is now in sight (1.5km, 30min). ◀

Leave Atalbéitar to the east by the laundry on a small path (signposted Pórtugos 30min). After 200m, the path crosses a small bridge over the Barranco de los Castaños and carries on through figs and broom. Another 300m later, when you come to a T-junction, turn left onto a wider track.

Almost immediately turn right and then left again after another 200m to bring you back onto a small path by an old sweet chestnut tree. Climb for another 300m to arrive at a big wall on the edge of **Pórtugos**. To the left you can see the rear of the Hostal Nuevo Malagueño. The route heads right and up to the road and a viewpoint which looks back towards Pitres and down to the other villages of La Tahá. Turn left along the road and take the first right to enter the centre of the village.

Pórtugos (1300m, pop. 600) ⤳ ⦿ F ▲ € ☎ ⊠ ✚ 🚌
Pórtugos started life as a Roman settlement. It is famous for its red waterfall, El Chorreon, which is worth a short detour even if you're not stopping here. If you have more time to spend make sure you stroll through its three plazas: La Nueva, La Vieja and La Churriana, the last with a waterfall and laundry inside a cave.

Accommodation and food
The village has plenty of hotels and restaurants:
Mirador de Pórtugos (s/d en suite €35/47) central with balconies looking down onto Plaza Nueva, with lively restaurant with an €8 menu of the day (☎ 958 766 014)
Hostal Nuevo Malagueño (s/d en suite €40/67) smart hotel and restaurant on Calle Sierra Nevada where the GR7 exits the village (☎ 958 766 093)

For more information
Town hall: C/Sierra Nevada, ☎ 958 766 001
Taxi: ☎ 958 766 006

Pórtugos – Busquístar (1.7km, 30min)

If you went into Pórtugos (or are starting from here), the route out leaves from the centre opposite the bank at a GR7 sign (Busquístar 45min) and heads southwest to rejoin the road which you turn left along.

The road passes by the **Agua Agria de Pórtugos**, possibly the most famous mineral water spring in the Alpujarras. Just down off the road to the left, its iron-rich water is red, orange and yellow. It is supposed to be very good for you but the taste is not unlike drinking liquid rust! You then pass a small, shady **picnic area** to your right before leaving the road after 700m for a small track off and up to the left.

Where the track divides just soon after you join it, take a small path to the right running below the right fork in the track. It follows the edge of fields and a hedge and, after only 200m, the village of **Busquístar** comes into sight.

When the path divides stay on the lower of the two branches to walk in front of a house. The path then becomes a track which takes you down onto the road. Turn left along the road to come to Busquístar entering the Albaycín – the Barrio Alto of Busquístar. The route continues up to the left and the village is down to the right.

Busquístar (1150m, pop. 400) ⤳ ◉ F ⚓ ☎ ⌂

Beautiful and tranquil, Busquístar is situated in the Río Trevélez valley, opposite the imposing rock faces of the Sierra de Mecina. It has typically Alpujarran Berber-style whitewashed buildings, slate roofs and steep narrow streets. Sites of interest in the village include the 15th-century parish church (earlier than most in the area) and the remains of an ancient mosque.

Accommodation

Casa Sonia (s/d en suite €38/50) very comfortable rooms with rustic charm, some with balconies, breakfast included and dinner sometimes available (on C/San Francisco at the bottom of village, ☎ 958 857 503, www.casasonia.eu/es/index.html)

Hotel Alcazar ★★ (s/d en suite €65–75/80–90) luxury rooms with breakfast, air conditioning, swimming pool and restaurant and even more luxurious suites and apartments available, overlooking the village and hills (C/Paraje los Álamos 1 (instead of going into village, turn left along the main road for 200m), ☎ 958 857 474/486 794, www.alcazabadebusquistar.com)

Other information
Town hall: C/Mesquita, 1, ☎ 958 766 031
Taxi: ☎ 958 766 036

Busquístar – Trevélez (11km, 4h)

Leave Busquístar on a small path heading north off the main road. It takes you round the front of a building and then right to come to a concrete road and the village's basketball court. Turn left up the concrete road which rapidly turns into a dirt track. When it divides take the right fork.

The track gets smaller and divides again, 500m from leaving the village. This time you go left through chestnuts and oaks and cross the Acequia de Busquístar on a small bridge. This has water all year round and is a lifeline for the village.

You head right and uphill on the other side and, 1.5km on, the path comes to a wide track. Head left and then turn left at both of the next two divides, as you pass through some oak trees. A further 500m on (2.4km from the start), ignore a track off to the right, but take the next small path to the right soon after. Throughout the relatively young oak woodland there are rich smells of lavender, oregano and thyme. ◄

You will come across rock roses, gorse and Spanish broom.

Climb for 100m then, where the path splits, take the right fork to level out and contour around the hillside through trees. After about 1km you will emerge into a more open brushy landscape with views of the Sierra Nevada beginning to appear. The path then crosses a small track and heads along and down through pine trees to a gully. Cross over it and climb, steeply at first and then more gently.

The path follows the edge of the pine forest for a kilometre before arriving at a loftily located *cortijo* 5.5km from the start. Here cross over the track and stay on the small path heading in the same direction as before, taking a left fork when it divides almost immediately.

After 500m on this path you come to a wide forestry track on the Parque Nacional de la Sierra Nevada boundary along which you turn right. After 300m, turn off the track onto a small path to the right which heads steeply downhill into oak trees. The path zigzags down for 400m through the

Trevélez, nestled in the hills of the Sierra Nevada

oaks to meet an old *acequia* which you cross straight over and then continue downhill for another 400m to come to a stream – the **Barranco de la Bina**, a permanent water source which flows into Río Trevélez. Cross the stream and begin the climb up the other side.

Soon afterwards you pass through two gates and then behind a **ruined farmhouse**. Just after this take the left and higher of two paths which goes steeply uphill heading north. As you climb, the path splits many times. You turn left at four divides in a row, the last of which is 600m on from the barranco. Then 200m later take the right turn.

This takes you back into pine trees and much more gently uphill. Pass through a further gate and across a dry streambed taking the left of two paths just afterwards, to come through the woods and out onto the open shoulder of the hillside. Head north and through a final gate to take a right fork among some striking rock formations.

One of the many pretty streets in Trevélez's old town

This path brings you back to the forest track 3km after you left it and Trevélez can be seen just down to your right. Walk along the track for 500m then start to lose height, turning off onto a small path downhill to the right.

Another 400m further down cross over the track for the last time and keep descending, the path now heading through fields. Ignore a small path off to the left after 300m then turn right just after you cross a footbridge over the **Río Chico de Trevélez**, named after the larger Río de Trevélez which the route crosses in its next section.

Arrive at the top edge of Trevélez, the *barrio alto* at 1600m, by a GR7 sign pointing back to Busquístar. This area is home to the best-conserved traditional Alpujarran architecture in the village. From here, head down Calle Charquilla and between the houses to come to a wider street. Turn left along this to enter the main part of the village.

Trevélez (1400m, pop. 1150)

Vegetarians should be warned that Trevélez seems to be the ham capital of the world with ham-curing specialists on almost every street and few restaurants or shops not adorned by multiple legs of ham hanging from the ceiling. While similar to the other beautiful Berber-style villages in the area, it is larger and more touristy than those you'll have already passed through. Notable, though contested, as the highest village in Spain, it is an excellent starting point for climbing in the Sierra Nevada, especially Mulhacén.

Accommodation and food
A good number and range of hotels including:

Camping Trevélez (adult/tent/2/3/4/7-person cabin €4.5/€4–5/19–77 plus €8.50 per person) pleasant, terraced site which is open year-round with friendly owners, great views and a restaurant (1km southwest of the village on the main road, ☎ 958 858 735, www.campingtrevelez.net)

Hostal Fernando (s/d en suite €20/27) offering straightforward, reasonably priced rooms near the top of the village (C/Barrio Medio, ☎ 958 858 565)

Hotel la Fragua (s/d en suite €25/35) a simple, friendly guesthouse with a popular restaurant and great views over the village from its roof terrace (C/San Antonio, ☎ 958 858 626/512, www.hotellafragua.com)

For more information
Town hall: C/Carcel 2, ☎ 958 858 501

Trevélez – Cádiar

After a steep climb out of Trevélez, this is an attractive, gentle route on forestry tracks and little paths which winds its way between sleepy hamlets passing through beautiful oak woodlands, pine forest and fertile market gardens.

NB: throughout this section the unconventional red arrow markings do mark the correct route.

Distance	18.2km
Time	6h
Height gain	300m
Height loss	780m
Highest point	1660m

Leave on the bottom road out of Trevélez crossing the river on a road bridge. Then, after 130m, take a left turn up a little GR7 signposted path (Juviles 3h) surrounded by plane trees. Climb steeply, initially next to an *acequia*, then up through gardens. Cross a wide *acequia* and a little stone bridge after 500m then turn left at a split 600m later into pines. The track flattens out a bit here heading downhill gently and then up less steeply, looking down on Trevélez to your right.

After 1.2km, leave Trevélez behind as you round the edge of the hill and head into landscape of scrubby gorse with some solitary oaks dotted around and pine trees ahead of you. Continue on the same path gently undulating, but contouring around the hillside heading south into the valley.

A further 300m on, ignore a little path back to the right and continue on the same path for another 300m to cross the **Barranco de los Castaños** on a little wooden bridge. At the split immediately after it, head left uphill under a walnut tree (there are no marks here). The path then splits again, but either branch is fine as they shortly rejoin. Cross another dry streambed on a cobbled path and climb, passing through oaks to pine trees to meet a forestry track, now 3km from the start.

Turn right along the forestry track and right again when it meets another track. Beware, you will come to what appears to be a new GR7 post 500m after you join the track directing you uphill to the left on a small path. This is not actually the route of the GR7, just another route which uses the same markings. Ignore it and carry on along the main track.

After 500m pass another track back to the left, continuing along the main track, which runs through the firebreak, until it reaches a crossroads 1km on. Here you go straight on into more open countryside. After a few metres turn right down a small track with a faint mark on a rock, then

almost instantly onto a small path to the left which heads
southeast.

This takes you into brushy landscape with yellow flow-
ering shrubs in spring. After you cross over a gully take the
right-hand one of the two small paths. Descend on this path
for about 2km until you meet a wider dirt track and cross
over it heading in the same direction as before.

The path brings you to a junction of two tracks, but you
cross over them staying on the same small path in the same
direction and then across another track shortly afterwards.
This brings you down to join the track just before an *acequia*
and a water tank.

Head downhill round the left side of the **water tank** to
meet another track along which you turn right and then,
very soon after, leave on a little path down to the left into
gardens and orchards. The path is cobbled in parts and
passes through lush vegetation including mint, figs, brambles and broom alongside an *acequia*. It comes out at a
small white building which you go round to the left and then
turn right onto a concrete track heading steeply downhill.
Pass a fountain and laundry, then descend further to arrive
on the main street in Juviles. If you want to go to the bar with
accommodation, turn right along the road; otherwise head
left for the other bars and to carry on along the route.

Juviles (1255m, pop. 150) ⤵ 🍴 F ▲ ☎ ✚ 🚌

A small village with great views down from its chestnut-surrounded plateau. It
was important in the Arab era when it was capital of a group of villages in the
area. You can see the ruins of the 18th-century castle which was an important
refuge for inhabitants of surrounding villages in times of danger.

Accommodation and food

A few bars with food and one with beds. (Note that there are no longer rooms
available in the two other bars on main road that still have signs advertising beds.)

Bar-Pensión Tino ★ (s/d en suite €20/33) friendly family-run bar with rooms
above, slightly set back from the main street through the village (C/Altillo
Bajo, ☎ 958 769 174)

For more information

Town hall: C/Carretera 23, ☎ 958 769 032
Taxi: ☎ 958 753 038

Juviles – Timar (1.7km, 40min)

Leave Juviles heading left along the main street and come to a GR7 sign (45min to Timar) pointing you down to the right at the edge of the village as you pass a supermarket on your left. The road out is also signposted to the Fuerte de Juviles and Fuente Agria. Take a left fork just after this onto a dirt track which heads downhill to a little stream (**Barranco de la Umbría**).

The route crosses over this, but you can also take a short diversion to the left to the Fuente Agria. At the next divide take the lower right path alongside a high dry stone wall passing olive and almond trees on a shady little path. At the split just after this, keep right again through cherry trees.

Where the path widens into a small track, take the left fork and continue on the same path round the hillside with crags above you to the right, brambles and broom bordering the path on both sides and lush green vegetation in the valley below.

Walk up to pass between two rocky crags with panoramic views across olive-clad hills. Below, the roofs of the first houses of the village are visible. Take either the left or right fork down the other side (the lower left fork is shorter but more scrambly). They rejoin and you descend into the top of **Timar** (950m, pop. 50 **F**).

Timar – Lobras (1.5km, 30min)

Head west from the plaza (which has a drinking fountain in front of the church) and come to a GR7 signpost (35min Lobras). Go down the concrete street and continue along it as it turns to tarmac, with the last houses of the village on the right and fruit trees on your left. When you come to ruins on your right, turn left down a dirt track off the road.

Continue round an *era* (a circular stone threshing floor typical of the region) on a track to the right, and pass a small turning up to the right into a field 250m further on. At the next junction keep right and then turn off onto a small track.

This takes you steeply downhill and you turn right onto a little path just as you get to the valley floor. Look behind you for good views back to village above. Cross the valley floor and continue on the other side, zigzagging uphill to meet a path next to an *acequia* as a street lamp comes into view ahead, a sign that you are nearing the village. Continue

On the route between Juviles and Timar

Looking back up at Timar

round this path which is green with figs, almonds and fruit trees. Ignore a track down to the right and continue round the hillside onto a tarmac road and into **Lobras** (930m, pop. 150 🍴 **F**).

Lobras – Cádiar (5km, 2h)

Continue downhill through Barrio el Chorro to a fountain and laundry. A GR142 sign down to the left opposite the fountain points you to Cádiar (2h). Ignore it and carry on down the street with wooden handrails until you come to the GR7 sign (pleasingly only 1h15). There is also a sign here for a **PRA292** Sendero Ventilla which is marked with yellow signs.

Follow these yellow signs to continue along the tarmac road out of the bottom of

Map 23

Southern Route: Juvile
Posada de los Arrieros

Bérch

Barranco de la Umbría   Alcúta

Juviles

Timar

Nieles   Lob

PRA292

the village. Just at the edge of the village come to a signpost with another estimate of 1h45 to Cádiar. Here there is a right fork off to the PRA292. You stay on the road and turn left off it at the last house, 200m from the GR7 signpost.

Head up the dirt track into almond trees and then, 100m on, turn right down an unmarked path. Descend and after another 500m pass a ruined *cortijo* on your right. Here there is a profusion of signs, none of them for the GR7 in the direction you are going, but continue straight on and then keep left ignoring a track heading steeply uphill to the right.

After another 300m, cross straight over a track onto another little path which goes round and down into the valley of the **Río Cádiar**. When it splits, take the right fork to follow alongside an *acequia* on the right.

Cross over the *acequia* passing a ruined building and at the crossroads just next to it continue straight on across the stream. For a 500m diversion for food or

219

a bed follow the sign to the **Alquería de Morayma** hotel-restaurant.

Once across the stream, there is an *acequia* running alongside the path first on the right and then on the left. Pass through figs and vegetable and fruit plots with raspberries and kiwis. Ignore a track back to the right and continue with bamboo and the river on your right.

When you come to a split in the path, go right and walk alongside the river passing a couple of log bridges and then a fallen larger wooden bridge before the track becomes tarmac and crosses the river. Turn left and walk alongside the river until you pass a football ground where you turn right to enter **Cádiar** near the centre.

Cádiar (919m, pop. 2000) ⤴ 🍽 F ▲ ☎ ✚ 🚌

Cádiar is divided into an older area with traditional architecture, including the 16th-century parish church, and a *barrio alto* with new buildings. It is one of the most commercial villages in the area. The 3rd and 18th of each month are usually the market days and you will see farmers from all around coming into town.

Accommodation and food

A few options for beds and food, the Alquería de Morayma restaurant, supplied by its own kitchen garden, is something special:

Hostal Cadi (s/d en suite €12/24) basic cheap accommodation in small en suite rooms, bar downstairs (C/Real, ☎ 958 768 064)

Ruta de la Alpujarra ★★ (s/d en suite €40/60) comfortable place with good restaurant (Ctra Ugijar, ☎ 958 768 059)

La Alquería de Morayma (s/d en suite €43–47/49–59 self-catering apartments also available) lovely family-run complex with courses including massage and relaxation, set amongst organic almonds, vines, figs, olives and fruit trees, 2km walk out of the village (Ctra A-348, Cádiar-Torvizcón, ☎ 958 343 221, www.alqueriamorayma.com)

For more information

Town hall: Pza España, 12, ☎ 958 768 031
Buses: ☎ 958 768 006

Distance	17.7km
Time	4h50
Height gain	960m
Height loss	800m
Highest point	1440m

Cádiar – Narila (1.8km, 20min)

Head northwest from the church passing along Calle Cristal to a small plaza with a fountain and a palm tree. Turn right out of the plaza, heading north between stone walls, then turn left to come to a refurbished mill and a GR7 post where the road becomes a track.

After 200m the track ends at a field and you take a small path to the right crossing over an *acequia* to follow the line of the wall and the edge of the fields north for 200m. After this it arrives at a track by a water tank beside the riverbed.

Follow the track to the right alongside the river bed and cross a small stream twice. Stay on the track for another 400m and then, as you become level with the first buildings of Narila at a large open area of ground, take a small unmarked path to the right. This takes you up a partially cobbled path across an *acequia* between walls and into **Narila** (980m, pop. 170 **F**). ▸

Narila – Berchules (3.2km, 1h)

Head out of Narila by the plaza next to the church following a sign west to Agua Agria. Stay on the main street which comes around the side of a gorge on Calle Pajares which brings you to a sign (Alcútar 1h) 250m from the plaza.

This sign directs you west along a small concrete road and you go left when it divides soon after. It then becomes a dirt track and you carry on, ignoring a turning down to the left. When it divides again, a sign points you to Agua Agria (5min) and you go left (signpost Alcútar 50min) and cross the river on stepping stones (avoiding a precarious bridge) 1km from the start.

Turn right at a divide soon after and continue through almonds as the track becomes a path and starts zigzagging

Another day where you never stray far from civilisation, picking your way over and around hillsides and across streams to reach a string of little white villages. There is a steep climb and descent between Bérchules and Mecina Bombarón that takes you from one river basin into another.

If you have time to wander round the village, its claim to fame is being home to the ruins of the Moorish King Aben-Humeya's house.

uphill. At a small divide 500m from the river go right. The path is now cobbled in parts. A further 250m on, you stay on the main path, ignoring one off to the left into the fields. Then cross over a track and keep climbing until you come to a wider track after 400m.

Turn right along the track, but quickly leave it again on a path up to the left. Ignore a left turn just after this and then climb steadily to meet a wider track at gates to a garden and turn right along it.

Climb to meet a concrete track and take it uphill, ignoring a little path to the right and looking back on increasingly good views of Narila and Cádiar as you gain height. Head left into **Alcútar** (**F**) climbing the street past the laundry and fountain.

Alcútar is a satellite settlement of the larger Bérchules which is just 700m and 10min away. The signs to leave Alcútar are a little confusing. At the laundry a large metal sign indicates that the GR7 is right up a little path, contradicting a red and white mark on the wall directing you up to the left through the village. Ignore the signpost and follow the marks steeply upwards to Calle Churre, then head right and uphill along Calle Real and then Cantera to the church plaza.

There's a fountain in front of the church (17th-century Iglesia Santa Maria la Mayor). The route just heads up the short stretch of tarmac road to **Bérchules** which is visible ahead as you set off. On entering the village, pass Fuente de los Carmelos and continue up the same road into the centre.

Bérchules (1322m, pop. 800) ⏦ 🍴 F ▲ € ☎ ✉ ✚ 🚌

A beautiful old village which is the capital of the municipality. It has a great vantage point with views across the surrounding area. Important in Moorish times, it was once a centre for the silk trade and there are some lovely examples of traditional Alpujarran architecture. There are other walks in the area detailed on information boards in the village.

Accommodation and food
A few good choices for places to stay and eat:

Hotel los Bérchules ★★ (s/d en suite €37/€45) the first hotel-restaurant you come to, up to the left as you enter the village, good value but luxurious-feeling place to relax, with friendly owners, a pool, balconies and shared terrace with great views and a cosy lounge (☎ 958 852 530, hot.berchules@interbook.net, www.hotelberchules.com)

La Posada casa rural run by friendly Dutch couple with homecooking available (Pza de Abastos 7, ☎ 958 852 541)

Apartments and *Café El Mirador de Bérchules* attractive 2/3/4 bedroom apartments in a complex offering activities including horseriding, meals also available (Pza de Zapata 1, ☎ 958 769 090, elmiradordeberchules@wanadoo.es)

For more information
Town hall: Pza Victoria, ☎ 958 769 001/958 852 548

Bérchules – Mecina Bombarón (7km, 2h)

Head out of Bérchules northeast on Calle Agua, a little concrete street that turns to dirt as you come to a GR7 sign (Mecina Bombarón 2h). The GR7 and the Sendero Veréica Misa follow the same route through lush greenery beneath figs, hazels and chestnuts until you come to the first split where you head left and the circular route turns right.

You then cross a wider track under a large chestnut tree and cross over a stream heading downhill on a shady path into the gorge. After crossing another little stream surrounded by ferns, you descend to the river, looking out at the dramatic rock face to your right.

Cross the river on a **bridge** to begin climbing steeply up the other side of the gorge on a rocky path. Where the path divides into a few little goat tracks about 500m further on you can take either, as they rejoin, and continue climbing. While stopping for breath, enjoy great views back towards Bérchules and Alcútar.

At the next divide in the path 250m on, take the right fork and pass a ruined stone building. The path then joins another flanked by dry stone walls and comes to a wide track heading right about 750m further on which you take, now ascending less steeply.

After nearly another kilometre you meet another track and again head right, curving round and passing smaller side tracks off into the pines and two wide tracks off to the right, the first after 300m and then another 500m further on.

After the second right turn, watch out for a barely visible path about 400m later heading into an almond grove.

This takes you down a dry stream bed between trees. It may be hard to spot the route but keep going southeast and aim for the house below and you should emerge next to the house and a post.

Continue in the streambed in the direction you've been going and it brings you down to a path that runs alongside a cool and shady *acequia*. Follow this left and you soon come to a track to the right which you take, leaving the *acequia* behind. Descend past a building on your right and **Mecina Bombarón** should come into view to your left. Continue down to the road and turn left onto it to enter the village.

Mecina Bombarón (1110m, pop. 1200) ⟋ ◉ F ▲ € ☎ ⊠ ✚ 🚍

Another village established by the Berbers, Mecina Bombarón has a bloody history. It is thought to have been home to Abén Aboo, the last Moorish King in Spain, who assassinated his cousin the previous King Aben Humeya to become ruler of the Moors for a short period before he himself was assassinated by Philip II. Lots of circular walking routes start from the village.

Accommodation and food
There are a few places to eat but accommodation is in short supply unless you want to rent one of the many *casas rurales* in the area. A good choice is:

El Benarum (2/4 bedroom € 55/85) a range of well-equipped little houses, with activities on offer (C/Casas Blancas, ☎ 958 851 149, informacion@benarum.com, www.benarum.com)

Others include: www.molinomonfi.com, www.casasblancasmecina.com, www.molinoabenhumeya.com, www.molinoabenabo.com, www.altas-vistas.com

For more information
Town hall: Avda Jóse Antonio 30, ☎ 958 851 001

Mecina Bombarón – Yegen (5.7km, 1h30)
Leave Mecina Bombarón down the street to the south which leaves from the middle of the main street, signposted to Los Macabes. After passing the school, turn left and go down the hill on a small concrete road, Calle Santa Teresa. Turn right at a T-junction and continue on downhill going left around a building. The road soon becomes a dirt track and you see the hamlet of Golco ahead.

After 200m, when you meet a **stream**, ignore a left turn and continue straight on along the lamppost-lined track. Cross an *acequia* then take a small unmarked path to the left that zigzags downhill before running parallel to the main track then along an *acequia*.

The route between Mecina Bombarón and Golco

After a short distance you come back up on the main track then take the left fork at a divide. Pass another two turns, one off to the right and then to the left, to come into **Golco**, a tiny hamlet notable for its large church which is one of the oldest in the region. A sign directs you downhill on a small concrete road to **Montenegro** (50min).

Follow the small road downhill, turning left where it divides. It takes you very steeply down to a small picnic area before becoming a dirt track. After 600m, pass by a path and a track to the left and, 100m further on, take a path to the right, with fruit orchards on your left.

This little path heads east passing an *era*, on your left, before heading downhill to meet another track. Go left along the track, ignoring another left and continue downhill. Shortly after it becomes concrete, you take a small path off it

225

Distinctive barren rock gullies on way into Yegen

to the right just at the gate to what look like new holiday cottages (1km from Golco). Cross the small **Río de Mecina** and continue on the same path through poplars. After another 100m cross a dry stream and then pass a **ruined building**. The landscape here is barren and almost desert-like with vividly coloured scree slopes and dry brushy vegetation.

Pass another abandoned building on your left 1.5km from Golco, still on the same path, with **Montenegro** now visible ahead. After 300m at a crossroads of small paths, go straight on to come to a T-junction. Right will take you to the **Ermita Fatima de Abén Aboo** in Montenegro, an abandoned *cortijo* which is thought to have belonged to the Moorish king. Left takes you on the continuation of the route to Yegen (30min).

Take the left track and at a split soon afterwards turn left to pass over a little stream and under a weeping willow where there is a mini **picnic area** with little child-sized seats. Another 700m on you see the white walls of Yegen's **cemetery** above you. Climb to join a concrete road and follow it into **Yegen** passing a fountain and a GR7 sign at the entrance.

Yegen (1087m, pop. 500) 🚶 ⊙ F ▲ ☎ ✚ 🚻

Yegen's main claim to fame is having been home to the British writer Gerald Brenan (1894–1987) whose work, including *South from Granada*, gave a detailed account of life in the village in the 1920s. His house, just off the main plaza, now has a plaque outside and there is a walking route named after him leaving the village on a path below the road.

Accommodation and food

There are a couple of options for accommodation and food:

Pensión la Fuente (s/d en suite €12/14) straightforward, good value accommodation just off the plaza (C/Real 46, ☎ 958 851 067)

Hostal el Tinao (s/d en suite €15/30, pp inc dinner €20) run by a slightly eccentric but very friendly Irish lady, it has clean, cheap rooms with great views over the valley and the option of a Guiness in the bar (La Carretera, ☎ 958 851 212/626 967 102)

El Rincon de Yegen (d en suite €36) a hotel-restaurant which has whole *casas rurales* to let as well as individual rooms, on the main road as you leave the village (Camino de las Eras, ☎ 958 851 270/276, elrincondeyegen@telefonica.net, www.aldearural.com/rincondeyegen)

Yegen – Laroles

Distance	18.3km
Time	5h10
Height gain	660m
Height loss	640m
Highest point	1300m

Leave Yegen and pass some remarkable fizzy natural springs, then loop in and out of gullies and ravines to visit three of the four villages of the municipality of Nevada and arrive in its capital Laroles.

Yegen – Válor (4km, 1h)

Leave Yegen from the top of the village, the Barrio de Arriba where Gerald Brenan lived. The GR7 follows the road heading east out of the village. As you go along the road you will pass a GR7 mark on a tree and post which look as though they want you to go up a track to the left here but don't. Instead stay on the road, which then crosses the **Barranco de las Eras** and climbs gently for just over 1km.

At this point, just after a bend when the road begins to go downhill, and opposite a big plane tree, take a track off to the left (there is a small GR7 mark on a rock) then almost instantly turn right onto a smaller track heading towards Válor which you can now see ahead of you.

The slightly overgrown track takes you downhill between fields for 200m before crossing the road and continuing on, as a path, in the same direction. It takes you through grasses and wildflowers between almond groves.

Pass a **ruined building** 500m after crossing the road and continue downhill gently to come to the **Cuestra Viñas** fountains, four natural springs with varying degrees of natural fizziness and iron 300m later.

From the fountains, head left uphill and follow the track as it bends round to the right passing beneath the houses which make up **Cortijo de Doña Loreto**. Climb on this track through almond groves to the concrete road, ignoring tracks off to either side. At a bend in the road 500m on from the fountains, turn right onto a dirt track.

Pass turnings to the right and then left, and when you reach a T-junction take the left fork and then the next two lefts to carry on along a dirt track, still walking through almond and olive trees.

Finally you meet another track with the road visible up to the left and you turn right and then down to the left to cross an old stone **bridge**, the Roman Puente de la Tableta. Beneath it is another *agua agria* fountain. Climb to enter **Válor** on the other side.

Válor (909m, pop. 850) 🔁 🍴 F ▲ ☎ ✚ 🚌

As the birthplace of Aben Humeya who lead the 1568 revolt against the Christians, Válor was an outpost of Moorish resistance until the beginning of the 17th century. The village's annual Moros y Cristianos festival, a lively recreation of battles between the Moors and the Christians, held in September, is one of Spain's most famous. There are a couple of other marked walking routes around the village including three circular routes which are described on an information board.

Accommodation and food

A few bars/restaurants with outdoor seating and a couple of accommodation options:

Hostal-Restaurante los Perdices ★★ (s/d en suite €25/35) comfortable little *pensión* with restaurant below serving good home cooking including a leek cake with goats cheese highly recommended for vegetarians bored of egg and chips, on the route out of the village (Ctra de Trevélez, ☎ 958 851 821, www.lasperdicesvalor.com)

Balcón de Válor (4/6 person apartments €80/100) *casas rurales* with the same owner as Los Perdices, a little out of the village on the GR7 route (www.balcondevalor.com)

For more information
Town hall: ☎ 958 851 812

Válor – Nechite (1.5km, 35min)

Head through the village on the road until you come to Hotel los Perdices where you turn left and pass the hotel heading up to the left on the road signposted to Ermita de la Torrecilla, but not signposted for the GR7 till a little further up (Nechite 35min).

Climb on this road which turns to gravel as you pass the **Balcon de Válor** *casas rurales*. Pass two tracks off to the right, staying on the same gravel track, which becomes concrete again as it goes round the left-hand side of a few buildings.

Then, about 400m from the GR7 sign out of the village, take a little path off to the right that passes between fields, leaving the village behind. It is marked with yellow posts for the Sendero del Agua circular route, and with sparser, less obvious GR7 posts and marks.

Immediately after turning onto the little path, pass little paths off to either side and, as you head uphill, also pass a small track off to the right. Cross over a drive leading to some gates and keep ascending. The path levels out as you follow the line of an *acequia* and then turn left between walls.

Walk along the edges of fields, following yellow posts and taking in the views back down over the valley. Join another *acequia* and come to a water tank after about 700m on the little path. Here the path becomes a track and when it divides you go right and then pass another path off to the right. Continue on in the same direction, again next to an *acequia*, passing beneath shady chestnuts.

As you pass the first house of Nechite with the rest of the village visible down to the right, ignore little paths off to either side. Cross over a track at a small electricity substation and come to the cement road and a GR7 sign pointing back the way you've come. Cross over this road and go down to the left to the village passing the Fuente Martín drinking fountain. (Don't be confused by the metal sign here which seems to direct you up to the right to the fountain – you can actually see it down below.)

Nechite (980m, pop. 100 **F**) has three neighbourhoods clearly separated by pretty gardens, vegetable plots and a ravine full of vegetation. The only accommodation available is a whole house available for longer lets (Casa Jasmine, ☎ 958 851 516/699 599 227, www.casa-jasmine.co.uk).

Nechite – Mairena (4.8km, 1h15)

Continue down into the village till you come to a sign to the Fuente Rojo where you turn left to pass in front of a small ruin and come back onto a little path which curves round next to a wall, heading north into the gorge. Pass one track

The view down to Mecina Alfahar from the route

off to the right which ends at a gate, and another back to the left just after 200m.

Once you've left the village behind, the path turns into a track. Continue straight on (don't take the right fork) and you meet another track along which you turn right at a GR7 signpost (Mairena 1h15). Stay right at the next divide immediately after this and ignore a driveway up to the left. The track becomes a path again and you cross a stream by a waterfall heading down into the ravine and across the **Río Nechite** on a small bridge.

Zigzag up the other side of the ravine. ▶ Continue south, then east, parallel to the valley, reaching the highest point after nearly 3km. After 200m, the path becomes a track and you turn right to keep heading east with the town of Ugíjar visible down to the right.

Once you're high up there are great views back over Nechite (and the village of Mecina Alfahar below).

After 400m, cut a corner off the track by turning off to the left on a small marked path, with an almond orchard on the left. Rejoining the track a few metres on, you bend round to go uphill to the left and keep going in the same direction on another path, crossing a small stream beneath a sweet chestnut tree. Continue along the path to come steeply down to the road at the entrance to **Mairena** just before you cross the bridge and go left into the village.

Mairena (1082m, pop. 300) ↵ ⦿ F ☎ 🚌
Mairena is also known as El Balcón de las Alpujarras because of its stunning panoramic views, and as the gateway to the high Alpujarras. Like other villages in the area, it was inhabited since long before the Islamic era, but it is the Moors that have left their mark on it.

Accommodation and food
There is one option for food and accommodation:

Las Chimeneas (s/d en suite/studio apartment €40/65/65) B&B in beautiful old house and little apartments, with packed lunches and friendly dinner round shared big table available on request (C/Amargura 6, ☎ 958 760 352, www.alpujarra-tours.com)

Mairena – Júbar (1km, 15min)

Head up through Mairena to the church and then east along Calle Iglesia to meet the road, along which you go left. A small path marked with a post leaves the road at the bend just after you join it. Head uphill steeply on the path, which is partially cobbled, and when it divides go right on a wider track under fig trees. It meets another track and you take it to the right to come back to the road. Again go left along it and then take the road turning to the left signposted Júbar 0.5km.

A small path takes you off to the left of this road at the first bend. Head up it steeply and turn right to climb more gradually and come round the hillside to a wide track. Cross this track twice carrying on in the same direction on the small path, the Camino de las Eras, to enter the village of **Júbar** (1140m, pop. 60 🍽 **F** 🚌) by the old laundry and fountain.

Júbar – Laroles (7km, 2h)

Head for the church, the Iglesia de Santo Cristo de la Columna XII, one of the oldest in the Alpujarras and notable for having traces of the three main religions of the area in its architecture: its roof has a Christian cross and a Jewish star of David and its main doorway is of the traditional Hispanic-Muslim style.

Take the track up to the left before the church as you enter the plaza, passing a GR7 signpost (Laroles 1h15) and continuing up this track. A further 200m on, pass a left turn and then a right turn climbing uphill and over an *acequia*.

After another 350m, at the brow of the hill, Laroles comes into view. Pass a left turn and then continue straight on at a crossroads of tracks heading away from Laroles north into the gorge. Another 350m on from your first view of Laroles, pass a right turn, then a left a further 100m on and then two rights, the second marked with yellow and white signs by Cortijio de las Encinas.

At a split just after passing the *cortijo* turn right and cross a stream. Keep heading north into the gorge with Laroles now behind you. Pass a left turn, 800m after the *cortijo,* and at an abandoned farmhouse turn off the track onto a little path down to the right towards a big chestnut tree.

Now heading back towards Laroles, the path continues down into a lush valley full of poplars and chestnuts. You come to a stream next to a waterfall surrounded by ferns.

Cross the stream 600m down the little path and continue along the same path up the other side. Climb up the other side of the valley, with views of another waterfall opposite and the road below you.

Climb more steeply and, 600m on from the second waterfall, Laroles comes into view again. Join a track 200m further on and head left along it walking on mica-rich rocks. When you come to an old ruined mill turn off to the right onto a little path which rejoins the track after 100m. After 200m the track then meets the road at a GR7 sign on the edge of the village. Turn left up the road to enter **Laroles**.

Laroles (1100m, pop. 750) ⤴ 🏕 🍽 F ▲ € ☎ ✉ ✚ ⓘ 🚌

A bustling little place, Laroles is one of the oldest settlements in the Alpujarras and capital of the Nevada municipality. It has a variety of craft workshops making and teaching handicrafts including *esparto* grass work, wickerwork, tapestry and rug making. For architectural interest visit the 16th-century parish church with its 18th-century red brick Mudéjar tower and take a look at some of the grand old *casas señoriales*.

Accommodation and food
A touristy place with a handful of options for food and beds including:

Alpujarras Camping (person/tent/log cabin for 4 € 4/4/75–81) about a kilometre out of Laroles (signposted from village centre), lots of space with good plots separated by trees, swimming pool and bar-restaurant (Ctra la Puerta, ☎ 958 760 231, www.laragua.net)

Refugio de Nevada ★★ (en suite s/d/suite with lounge € 45/55/70) a small family hotel with 12 rooms, 7 with fireplace and small lounge, breakfast included and bed for third person added for an extra fee, swimming pool and garden (Ctra Mairena, ☎ 958 760 320)

Balcon de Alpujarras restaurant, rooms and apartments on the route out (Ctra Puerto de la Ragua, ☎ 958 760 217)

Villa Rural la Ragua (2–4 person apartments from € 60) apartments for rent near campsite, minimum 2-night stay (☎ 950 483 703/646 740 902, www.aldearural.com/villalaragua)

For more information
Tourist information: Pósito, 1, ☎ 958 760 007

Laroles – Puerto de la Ragua

Climb up to Bayárcal and cover the 12km of route in Alméria, passing back in to Granada province before you reach the highest point on the GR7 in Andalucía at a pine-forested pass.

Distance	16.5km
Time	5h45
Height gain	1120m
Height loss	220m
Highest point	2000m

Laroles – Bayárcal (4.5km, 1h30)

Come out of the village on the road heading west taking the turning to the right signposted to Cherin on the appropriately named Camino de Bayárcal then, just past the Balcón de Alpujarras restaurant, turn off to the left onto a track with a GR7 sign (Bayárcal 1h30).

After 600m, at a divide in the track where there is a dry stone building above you built into the rocks, turn right into orchards and olive groves. The village of **Bayárcal** comes into view above you ahead, and you pass a right turn (which may have a chain across it) and a left turn just afterwards and continue, heading through holm oaks. There are no markings for this section.

Where the track bends up to the left, about 2km from setting off, you leave it on a little path to the right, passing a GR7 signpost of an unfamiliar type as you cross the province boundary into Almería (Bayárcal 1h15).

Leave the path soon afterwards to head down a little dry streambed to the right between two walls. It turns into an attractive little path taking you steeply down to the bottom of the valley where the vegetation is lush and green with ferns and poplars.

You pass a small building hidden in the undergrowth 200m from where you joined the little path and cross the **Río Bayárcal** on big boulders. Climb up the other side on a path that becomes cobbled and, at the split 100m on, take the left fork still climbing uphill. Emerge out of the trees at a small water storage reservoir and head left onto a wide track which is concrete in places.

Just after an apple orchard turn left onto a path next to a dry stone wall. You climb on this up to some ruined buildings, passing a left turn and continuing straight on uphill.

Turn right at the next fork to come to the village laundry and fountain, and head steeply past them uphill to the left into **Bayárcal**.

Bayárcal (1255m, pop. 300) 🚶 🍴 F ▲ ☎ ✚ 🚌

Like many villages in the area, Bayárcal was a Arab settlement which was severely depopulated and destroyed when the area was 'Christianised' in the 16th century. There are still ruins of an Arab castle. Also worth a visit is the 16th-century Mudéjar-style church which was destroyed during the Alpujarran rebellions but reconstructed by the end of the same century by the Archbishop of Granada.

Accommodation and food
There are a couple of straightforward *hostales* but they are not always open off-season:
Hostal Restaurante Hermanos Navarro a simple *hostal* (C/José Antonio, ☎ 950 512 873)
Sol y Neive another simple *hostal* on the route out of the village (C/Granada 3, ☎ 950 512 813)

For more information
Town hall: Pza de Generalísmo 1, ☎ 950 512 848
Taxi: ☎ 950 512 813

Bayárcal – Puerto de la Ragua (12km, 4h15)

Leave Bayárcal heading north uphill on the road. After 400m, just before you come to a dry stone building and ruins, there is a big sign for the Puerto de la Ragua Punto de Informacion directing you onto a path off to the right. Behind it is a smaller, and, at time of writing, broken, GR7 sign (Puerto de la Ragua 4h15).

Follow this path up behind the building, zigzagging uphill to meet a track which you follow to the left to rejoin the road. Leave the road again on a signposted track (4h) to the left 200m on.

When the path divides after a further 200m, take the lower left path staying next to the wire fence with orchards behind it. Pass between gardens, orchards and buildings following the line of the gorge and pass below a stone farmhouse on a little undulating path.

You then start climbing more steeply with great views back into the gorge. At a divide 200m after the farmhouse, head left on the lower path which begins to level out a bit passing through old holm oaks. A further 200m on, the path divides again and this time you take the upper right path under some craggy rocks.

You emerge from the trees and at the point when you can see a dry stone building on the other side of the gorge take the right fork at a divide. Bend up to the right and, before you get to another dry stone building built into the crags ahead, climb steeply northwest on an unclear path, but with lots of marks to follow. This takes you up past an *era*, and back into holm oaks. Climb more gently through these coming up close to the road which is above you on the right.

Stay on the same path as it levels out more and comes out of the trees at a profusion of signs. A new wooden post points uphill to the right on a zigzagging route to the road but you continue straight on to pass below a ruined building to a GR7 sign just past it (2h back to Bayárcal). Beware, the new wooden post is the first of many in this section which, although they have the red and white markings, are not for the GR7.

Pass above another *era* and descend below more crags with beautiful pools in the river down to your left. Another 300m on from the GR7 sign you come to a divide; the left, marked with the new posts, takes you down to a **bridge** over the river, but don't go this way. Instead, take the unmarked path up to the right to continue through brambles and under crags along and up the gorge, with the edge of the road visible ahead.

This brings you up onto the road (the **A337**) just before the **Posada de los Arrieros** at 1800m. Head for the hotel-restaurant built on the site of the ancient resting point, the Venta del Zamburino on the Camino de los Arrieros which was an important trading route from the 16th century onwards between the Alpujarras and the Almerian coast.

The Posada (s/d en suite/luxury suites €50–59/ 55–65/100–130) offers 20 comfortable bedrooms, three lounges with fireplaces and a restaurant serving up traditional dishes. Winter adventures sports are available (☎ 952 583 945/472 494, www.posadadelosarrieros.com).

At Puerto de la Ragua – the GR7's highest point

A GR7 sign (Puerto de la Ragua 1h40) directs you through the gate of the Posada and onto a little path around the left-hand side of the building. Follow it along the line of the gorge, now on the left bank of the river. The path is very pretty with hawthorn, elder, brambles and dog roses. After 1.2km briefly enter shady pines coming out at a meadow to cross the stream for the first of many times heading up the gorge. From here you simply follow the line of the stream all the way to **Puerto de la Ragua**.

The path takes you for 1.7km past a dry stone building and through cow pastures and in and out of pine trees on both sides of the stream. After this you then begin to climb above the stream going in the same direction, but slightly higher up, coming close to the road on the other side of the stream.

Don't cross over to the road but continue uphill, still following line of gorge, with a small natural stone arch up to your right. The path here is less clear, but posts direct you along and the route levels out as you begin to approach the pass. 1.5km on you come to the **picnic area** of Puerto de la Ragua, through which the path passes. On the other side of the road here there is the **Pilas de las Yeguas** fountain. Continuing along the path through the picnic tables you come to the *albergue* and information centre at 2000m, the highest point of the whole GR7 in Andalucía.

Puerto de la Ragua (2000m) ⤳ ▮ F ☎ ①

A mountain pass and hub for a range of outdoor activities, especially cross-country skiing in the winter. A network of walking routes spans out from here including a 13.5km, 5h route to Doctor where there is a refuge; and a 9.7km, 3.5h route to Dilar along an old *camino real* between Dilar and the Alpujarras. There is also a circular route to the Laguna Seca and an alternative route back to Laroles on forest tracks on the other side of the gorge (7h, 18.3km).

Accommodation and food

Puerto de la Ragua Albergue (€12.80pp dorm bed) is the only place to stay at the pass itself, it is worth checking that this youth hostel accommodation is open before you go as it tends to be at its busiest in winter when people flock to the pass for skiing. It is run by the same people as the campsite in Laroles (☎ 958 345 528, correo@laragua.net, www.laragua.net). Otherwise, you may need to camp or carry on to La Calahorra.

For more information
www.puertodelaragua.com

Distance	11.6km
Time	2h50
Height gain	100m
Height loss	900m
Highest point	2060m

A couple of hours' descent on paths and tracks through pine forest and farm land bring you to Ferreira, and from there it's a gentle amble to La Calahorra, dominated by its impressive castle.

Puerto de la Ragua – Ferreira (8.6km, 2h20)

Pass the *albergue* and head down along the road to the right, turning left off it after just a few metres to cross a wide wooden **bridge**, made of old railway sleepers, and enter the pine forest. At the edge of the forest you come to a GR7 signpost (Ferreira 2h) directing you down the forest track. Follow the track out and back into trees where a signpost (not GR7) marks two routes to Ferreira. You take the one to the right, climbing gently on the track then leaving it for a small path off to the right marked by a GR7 post, 600m from the start and just before the track bends to the right.

Follow the path down into and then out of a small ravine to go round the hillside heading south above the road. ▶ After 600m, the path comes down to cross over the road (marked on either side with GR7 posts).

On the other side of the road head north downhill, and after 300m you come to a **cow shed**. Go round the right-hand side of it, then head straight on to some **ruined buildings**. Keeping the ruins on your left, head downhill to the right on a path which runs alongside a wall. Stay on this path going through rocky and scrubby landscape for 600m before entering a firebreak in the pine forest (no marks in this section but the occasional post). Keep to the left edge of the trees to come to a wide track lined with poplars.

Turn right along the track and then take the first left soon after, the village of Ferreira now visible down and ahead in the distance. At the first bend of the new track head off onto a small path which takes you back over to the edge of the pine trees and then bends to the right to go down the side of them.

Follow this path as it heads down between trees into the gorge and comes to a stream, the **Arroyo Chico**, on the left

Breaks in the trees here give amazing views over to the mountains of the **Parque Natural de la Sierra de Baza**, through which the GR7 continues.

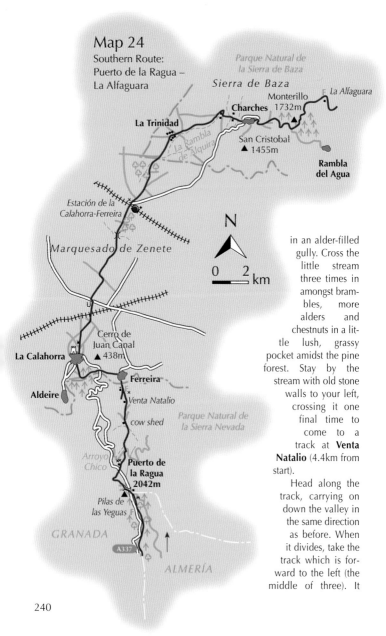

Map 24
Southern Route:
Puerto de la Ragua – La Alfaguara

Parque Natural de la Sierra de Baza

Sierra de Baza

Monterillo 1732m

Charches

E La Alfaguara

La Trinidad

San Cristobal ▲ 1455m

La Rambla de Alquira

Rambla del Agua

Estación de la Calahorra-Ferreira

Marquesado de Zenete

N

0   2 km

Cerro de Juan Canal ▲ 438m

La Calahorra

Ferreira

Aldeire

Venta Natalio

cow shed

Parque Natural de la Sierra Nevada

Arroyo Chico

Puerto de la Ragua 2042m

Pilas de las Yeguas

GRANADA

A337

ALMERÍA

in an alder-filled gully. Cross the little stream three times in amongst brambles, more alders and chestnuts in a little lush, grassy pocket amidst the pine forest. Stay by the stream with old stone walls to your left, crossing it one final time to come to a track at **Venta Natalio** (4.4km from start).

Head along the track, carrying on down the valley in the same direction as before. When it divides, take the track which is forward to the left (the middle of three). It

240

soon becomes more path-like and enters the woods, passing a small white building on the left.

Continue along this path, joining a track which carries on in the same direction, and take the left fork when it divides, onto a smaller path again. (There are no markings from Venta Natalio to this point.) Another 300m on, the path divides and you stay left to pass in front of some ruined buildings, carrying on along the path which then goes between some walls and crosses an *acequia*.

Soon afterwards, you arrive at a wider track which you turn right along, passing the pretty Virgen de la Cabeza church on your left and a fountain on your right. Just at the church the track becomes a tarmac road and you stay on it until it meets another at the start of the village beside a GR7 sign. Go left along the road to enter the village of **Ferreira** (pop. 320 🍴 **F** ▲ ☎ 🚌).

Ferreira is so named because of large iron deposits found here. It is built on the site of a historic passing place of travellers. If you have time, visit the prehistoric burial site and the 14th- to 15th-century Arab baths in the north of the village.

Ferreira – La Calahorra (3km, 30min)

Leave Ferreira on the small road to La Calahorra. A little ceramic sign names it as the Ruta de Múzar but there are no GR7 markings. Stay on the road as it passes between almond fields and you'll come across some GR7 marks on the walls.

Then, after 1.2km where it meets a larger road, follow the signs for the Huénega – La Calahorra cycle route. These take you off the road to the left onto a forestry track which runs alongside pine trees. The **castle** of La Calahorra dominates the horizon to your right and some of the Sierra Nevada peaks are visible ahead.

Stay on the cycle route heading east with more and more of the village coming into view as you progress. Turn right after 2km to head northwest down another track passing a track to the left which ends at large metal gates with horses on it to arrive in **La Calahorra**.

La Calahorra's famous castle

La Calahorra (1192m, pop. 800) ⤴ ⑩ F ▲ € ☎ ✚ 🚌

La Calahorra is famous for its huge fairytale castle which was built in the 16th century for the Marquis de Zenete as a palace and a fortress. It is worth going inside to see the well-conserved and ornate decorations. It was the last castle built in Spain before more sophisticated weaponry made this style of fortress redundant.

Accommodation and food

There are a couple of reasonably priced *hostales* in town, both with restaurants, and there is a more luxurious option on the outskirts:

Hotel Manjón (s/d en suite €20/35) nice rooms with air conditioning and bar/restaurant downstairs and information on outdoor activities in the area (C/Los Caños 20, ☎ 958 677 346)

Hostal Labella ★ (s/d en suite €22/35) spacious rooms with air conditioning some with large balconies above a good bar/restaurant (C/Aldeire, ☎ 958 677 241, labellhrr@hotmail.com, www.hostallabella.com)

Hospedería del Zenete ★★★★ (s/d en suite €61/82) a grand establishment on the edge of the town, with luxury flats and jacuzzi, gym and sauna available (Ctra de la Ragua, ☎ 958 677 192, reservas@hopederiadelzenete.com, www.hospederiadelzenete.com)

For more information

Town hall: Pza Ayuntamiento, ☎ 958 677 132
Taxis: ☎ 958 677 062

La Calahorra – Narváez

Distance	49km
Time	13h10
Height gain	1060m
Height loss	900m
Highest point	2000m

NB A tent is essential should you want to break
the journey.

This is a walk full of contrasts. You leave the Sierra Nevada behind to cross the flat, dry plains of the Marquesado de Zenete before re-entering more rugged countryside in the Parque Natural de la Sierra de Baza, heading deep into woodlands of pines, oaks, maples and juniper then descending to the Hoya de Baza. (Note that there is no accommodation, but wild camping is permitted in two areas of the park.)

To leave La Calahorra turn off the main street onto Calle San Anton just opposite Meson la Orca. At the end of the street turn right. The street soon becomes a gravel track and leaves the village.

Follow the gravel track, turning left when it divides soon after and then ignore tracks off to either side, the right-hand one of which passes between farm buildings. After the buildings, ignore another track to the left, taking the right turn towards the last farm before the plains. From here there is a large flat expanse between you and the foothills in which Charches sits and the walking is along long, straight farm tracks.

After 1.4km you come to a crossroads and turn right. Then 700m later, go straight across another crossroads. You cross the **railway line** at a pedestrian crossing 400m later, and another 600m on pass beneath a major road, turning left after the **underpass** onto a small tarmac road. It goes alongside the major road for 100m before you take the first right turn onto a long, straight track.

After 1.2km the track ends at a T-junction where you go left and, 200m later, right. Another 2.4km on, still on same track, cross a concrete bridge and continue straight on passing a couple of little tracks off to the right and then going straight over a crossroads. ▸

Come to a small tarmac road and a level crossing at the **Estación de la Calahorra-Ferreira**. Then, 100m after crossing the tracks, turn off onto a track to the left just after a red brick **ruined building** covered in bird boxes. This wide track,

Fruit trees in the fields to your left mark the first real change in vegetation all day.

Leaving La Calahorra

which looks as though goats use it more often than people, heads north and you ignore a track off to the left. After 1km the track splits and you take the left fork and then turn left again 200m on.

Another 1km in amongst fruit trees brings you to a right turn which you ignore to come to the **Rambla de Alquira**, a dry riverbed. Go left along it briefly and then take the track up to the right finally beginning to leave the flat plains behind.

Come to another track and turn right along it with the hills now closer up ahead. Follow this track through the almost abandoned hamlet of **La Trinidad** and, when it divides 200m later, take the track to the left and head right up the dry riverbed. Follow the course of the riverbed until you meet another track and then turn right along it.

This takes you east and around behind some farm buildings. After these, turn off to the left onto a very small unmarked path heading directly for Charches. At points the path is unclear but keep going towards the buildings. It brings you down and across a dry riverbed after 250m and then up onto a wider track. Head between two farm buildings onto another unmarked, unclear path still heading in the direction of the village.

SIERRA DE BAZA NATURAL PARK (536km²)

One of the lesser-known natural parks, the Sierra de Baza is part of the Cordillera Penibética. It is known for its dramatic limestone and dolomite geology of jagged crags. The porous limestone results in a lot of underground water, which emerges at many fountains and springs.

The whole area is known as a 'climatic island' with up to 1000 litres of rain per square metre falling every year in sharp contrast with its hot, dry surroundings. It is a verdant landscape between two arid plains – the Llanos del Marquesado (which the route crosses to reach the park) and the Hoya de Guadix.

Wildlife
There are thought to be 100 plant species endemic to the southern Iberian penisula in the park. The vegetation ranges from cultivated cereals at lower altitudes to pine forest (including patches of native woodland) and, in the highest parts, tough thorny shrubs. Other notable trees in the park include holm oaks, gall oaks and junipers. There are also patches of deciduous forest with Italian maples and Lusitanian oaks and lots of Mediterranean scrub which includes Kermes oaks, laurel and sloes. You're also likely to catch the scents of thyme, lavender, marjoram and rosemary.

The park is rich in animal life including impressive big birds of prey such as golden eagles, hawks and Egyptian vultures; over 100 other bird species including woodpeckers and turtle doves in the woodland areas; and hoopoes, crested larks and red-legged partridges in cultivated fields. About 30 species of mammals have been catalogued in the park, amongst the most common being: deer, badgers, genets, beech martens, wild cats and foxes. You are also likely to see game animals including roe deer and, if you're lucky, wild boar.

Camping
From May to November, camping is allowed at the Tablas and Fuente del Pino picnic areas (but banned in summer because of the risk of forest fires). You need to apply for permission in writing from the Consejería de Medio Ambiente, C/Marqués 1, Granada, ☎ 958 026 000.

For further information
The Centro de Visitantes de Narváez (☎ 958 002 018), which the route passes, has lots of information on the park and on walking routes, many of which leave from the centre.

The path becomes much clearer after you've crossed two fields and then it rejoins a wider track to come down to cross another dry riverbed. Go up the riverbed to the left and then take another very small path uphill to the right heading straight for Charches. Pass between farm buildings to come out on a wide track. Head uphill as the track turns to concrete to enter **Charches** (1426m, pop. 2400 🍴 F ▲ ☎ 🚌) which sits on the edge of the Parque Natural de la Sierra de Baza (see box above).

Leave Charches on the road heading east past a fountain and laundry and follow the road until it turns into a track and divides. Take the right fork signposted to La Rambla del Agua, La Fraguara Encinar Pino Mediteráneo and Gor. You come across the first GR7 signpost of this section here (Prados del Rey 5h).

Take the left fork at the first and second divides, staying on the main track. After almost 1km, pass another turn to the left, climbing steadily, the track taking you higher into the Sierra de Baza through scrub vegetation.

After 3km, pass a turning down to the right to the small hamlet of **Rambla del Agua**, and 450m further on the track levels out as you enter pine trees. As you continue, pass a track off to the left with yellow and white markings for the PRA116 Rambla del Agua – Charches route.

Flat, dry plains of the Marquesado del Zenete

The route winding its way through the Sierra de Baza

You pass a stone cattle shed and **ruined building** on your right, 5.5km after leaving the village, and come to the **Fuente La Alfaguara** on your left beneath a weeping willow. Pass a left turn just after it and then ignore the continuation of the **PRA116** which goes down to your right.

Pass by a further track up to the left, this one small and very steep near an unlikely hand-painted sign to Arizona, and continue on to the next fork in the main track. The fork to the right would take you to the **Casa Forestal el Raposo** (4km); you take the left fork to continue on the route. There are no marks at this junction or the next.

Less than a kilometre on you come to another major divide in the track (now 10.5km from Charches). Here the right fork would take you to the **Mirador de Barea** (10km), Caniles (36km) and Escullar (37km). The left fork, which you take, is signposted to Los Prados del Rey, but its distance of 20km seems to be excessive.

Begin to descend with the hills and rocky outcrops of the natural park all around you. After 250m you pass another fountain and, at the next junction, 2km from the last, you turn right. GR7 markings reappear here and you begin to climb again.

Leaving Prados del Rey

Pass two turnings off to the left after 1.2km and then, 600m after that, continue uphill. A kilometre on you pass a turning to the right just before crossing a bridge, then 700m further on also pass a smaller turning to the left which goes to the **Cortijo de los Pollos**. Just opposite this turning there is a water fountain on the right side of the main track.

The route continues along the forestry track passing a left turn 1.2km from the fountain to come to a well-marked junction. A signpost here pointing left indicates it is 3.5km to Los Prados del Rey, 11km to the picnic area at La Canaleja and 15km to Narváez. You will pass through all three before arriving in Baza. Right is the route to the **El Pinarillo** picnic area (7km).

Take the left to head uphill on a long, straight and enthusiastically marked section of track, ignoring a track down to the left to the Casa Forestal el Cascajar (3km). Pass a little **house** on your right and then **mine workings** and some enticing caves down to your left.

From here the path levels out and you enter an area of natural pine woodland. Pass by a turn on your left that leads back to the caves and a right turn just after. A few hundred metres on, a small side track down to the right leads to a fountain (which does not always have water).

Staying on the main track, ignoring a further track to the left, you come to a GR7 signpost indicating that you've arrived at **Los Prados del Rey** and the highest point of the route at almost 2000m and 22km from Charches. A track up to your left would take you into ancient natural pine woodland of great ecological importance. This area is a great place to look out for birds including raptors.

The signpost directs you along the main track still to Narváez (2h15) and then on to Baza (4h30). The track now heads downhill with great views opening up before you over the peak of Jabalcón and the *altiplano* through which you are about to walk. After going down the track for

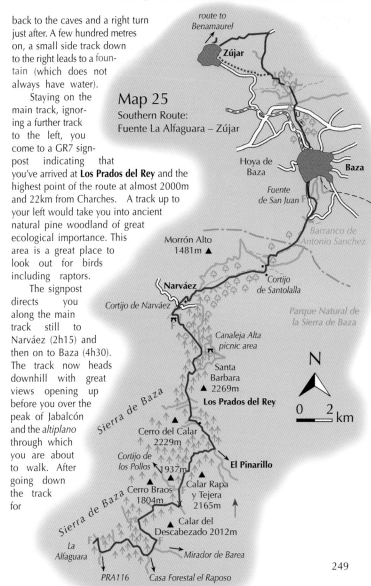

Map 25
Southern Route:
Fuente La Alfaguara – Zújar

249

almost 1.5km, turn off to the left onto a tiny path just after a stone **bridge**. There is a post, but it is a little difficult to spot so be careful not to miss it.

Descend steeply on a well-marked and pretty little path through pines, zigzagging down for 1km before levelling out slightly and then arriving at the Canaleja Alta **picnic area**, a pleasant shady spot to stop with picnic tables and a fountain. You are now 7h from Charches.

Head left around the picnic area, now briefly back on the main track, before taking a little path off up to the left after 200m (signposted Narváez 1h30). This takes you uphill through pines, levelling out a bit after 1.5km and entering some hawthorn, oaks and dog roses as well as pines.

The path emerges into a firebreak which you follow down to the right before re-entering trees on the other side. Continue on the small path as it goes down the left side of another firebreak and, 3km from the start of this path, a large building comes into view ahead and below you. This is the **Cortijo de Narváez** which now houses an information and education centre for the park and a tourist complex with outdoor activities. You are heading for it, although not in a direct line.

At the next junction, take the left fork passing by, or making use of, stone and wooden benches, then descend further on what becomes a wider track. Ignore a track down to the right and continue on past the **Fuente del Olvido** passing more picnic benches, crossing over a small stream and around a hillside.

Ignore another track down to the right and continue for 500m before turning down to the right into the trees onto a small path just beside an open water storage tank. This brings you down to a tarmac road just to the right of a **bridge** (almost 5km from the Canaleja Alta).

Cross over the road and onto a wide gravel track where there is a GR7 sign (Baza 2h15) – 2h50 is a more realistic estimate. A park sign directs you up the next track to the visitor centre, but you can also get to it by taking the first right turn off the track you are following. (Cortijo de Narváez (dorm bed/wood cabins 2–12 people €15/60–200) the hostel also runs a range of outdoor activities and there is a bar-restaurant (Ctra de Murcia Km175, ☎ 958 342 035/675 262 920, informacion@cortijonarvaez.es).)

Distance	25km
Time	5h20
Height gain	200m
Height loss	800m
Highest point	1400m

Narváez – Baza (14km, 2h50)

Next to the centre are the starting points of three marked walks including the Sendero Mirador de Narváez, a gentle 1km walk to a viewpoint along a fire break. To continue along the route to Baza stay on the main track passing the turning into Cortijo Narváez.

Ignore a right turn for one of the other walking routes after 700m, but do take a right at the next divide just over 1km further on. Pass a right turn almost immediately and cross a dry stream beside a small concrete **building**. The route then continues through small oak trees and bushes and you pass three more right turns before the track turns into a small path 3.5km out of Narváez.

The path follows the course of a dry stream, crossing it for the first time after 500m and then recrossing it a further nine times in the next 1.3km before ending up on a wider track on the left-hand side. This track heads uphill past a dam, then back down and across the streambed. After passing a small white **building** on your right you arrive at the **Cortijo de Santolalla** (now 5km from Narváez).

Follow the track round to the right between the buildings of the *cortijo*. Take the left fork when it divides just beyond the buildings before turning off to the right almost instantly onto a smaller track heading north. Another 400m further on turn right onto a small path which goes along the edge of a field then brings you to the dry riverbed of the **Barranco de Antonio Sanchez** where the path continues up and along its right-hand side.

As with the streambed, the path then re-crosses the riverbed several times for the next 600m before ending up on the left-hand side. From here it climbs and the riverbed becomes more of a gorge. You get your first views of the

Through the sprawling city of Baza and then into the unique landscape of the Subbética, walking towards and then a little way round the distinctive mountain Jabalcón which rises above the gullies and ravines of the high plateau below.

outskirts of Baza and go through a gate and along the top right edge of field before descending back into the riverbed, along which you turn left.

Ignore two tracks out but take the third which heads uphill to the right. When it meets a crossroads, go straight across heading directly for **Baza**. Cross the riverbed for the last time then follow the track between almond trees until you arrive at a tarmac road and a pizza restaurant. Turn right off the road onto a gravel track soon after to cut off a section of road only to rejoin it at the **Fuente de San Juan** and carry on into the town.

Baza (847m, pop. 22,000) ↴ ◉ F ▲ € ☎ ⊠ ✚ ① 🚌 ▣

Now a busy town and the capital of the Hoya de Baza region, Baza has been an important settlement from prehistory up to Christian times and many cultures have left their mark there. Visit the archaeological museum to see examples of finds from the 3rd- to 4th-century Bastetan civilisation which founded the town, then Ciudad Basti. The ruins of a Moorish castle and surrounding neighbourhoods are reminders of its past as a frontier town in the time of the Nasrid kingdom, and the town's 10th-century Arab baths in the old Jewish quarter are among best preserved in Spain.

Accommodation and food
There's a good range of hotels and a choice of places to eat ranging from pizza places and typical bar fare to more upmarket restaurants including seafood:

Pensión los Hermanos ★★(s/d en suite €25/40) serviceable rooms with dated décor, air conditioning, TV, restaurant downstairs and free internet access (Ctra de Murcia, Km176, ☎ 958 701 880, www.hostalloshermanos.com)

Hotel-Restaurante Anabel ★★ (d en suite €50) reasonable rooms with comfortably long beds, not particularly good value for the price and not the friendliest service (C/Maria de Luna 3, ☎ 958 860 998)

Cuevas al Jatib Hospedería Troglodita (caves of different sizes and facilities from €85) a cave village with Arab baths, tea house and a cave for children (Arroyo Cúcar, ☎ 958 342 248/667 524 219, info@aljatib.com, www.aljatib.com)

For more information
Tourist office: Pza Mayor 1, ☎ 948 861 325

Baza – Zújar (11km, 2h30)

Leaving Baza, with Jabalcón in the distance

The GR7 leaves Baza along the road to the cemetery reached by going down Calle Ingeniero Guiterrez Segura from the bus station and then left along Carretera de Granada. The road to the cemetery leaves the Carretera de Granada at the final roundabout.

Go down the small concrete road between olive trees and buildings ignoring all side roads. After 1.5km you pass the cemetery and carry on as the road becomes more track-like. Just over a kilometre further on you come to the motorway and go through an **underpass**.

Where the track divides into three on the other side, you take the right fork and then turn left when it splits again to go around the edge of a field heading towards the prominent lone peak of Jabalcón, which this section of the GR7 skirts. At 1496m it is a popular spot for paragliding and the starting point for a popular pilgrimage of La Virgen de la Cabeza from the chapel of the same name on top.

253

The Embalse de Negratín and open plains between Baza and Zújar

Almost 1.5km further on, the track crosses a dry riverbed and divides again. You take the middle of the three options to head uphill between almond trees. Another 600m on, turn left at a crossroads onto a smaller track edged with more almonds and fields. Follow it and climb to reach a wider track along which you turn right. When it comes to a junction take the middle of three tracks again, heading straight ahead and ignoring a much smaller track off to the right soon after.

Almost 7km from the start, the track brings you to an unmarked T-junction with a sign pointing back the way you've come and you can see Zújar ahead and the road into it down to your left.

Here take the right track heading steeply uphill. This takes you up in a roundabout way to the tarmac road which goes up to the top of Jabalcón. You join it on the south side of the hill and follow it down to the left for just over 2km all the way into **Zújar**. If you have time and energy for an extra climb, it is worth heading right and going to the top for stunning views across to the Embalse de Negratín.

(A shorter route into the village involving less climbing and tarmac would be to turn left at the junction and then right onto a dirt track which follows the line of the road all the way into Zújar.)

Zújar (760m, pop. 2900) 🚏 🍴 F ▲ € ☎ ✉ ✚ 🚌

Parts of Zújar are modern with a lot of new housing, but it also has a historic centre where many Arab-style buildings survive. There are also many cave houses. Although the limestone landscape here is bare and dry, the centre of Zújar lies in an area rich in subterranean waterways. The many springs have encouraged the development of a lush area of fertile land.

Accommodation and food
A couple of hotels and several café/bars to choice from:

Hostal Restaurante Jaufil a family-run restaurant with 11 rooms, all with air conditioning and TV (Ctra Pozo Alcón, ☎ 958 716 191, www.altipla.com/jaufil/)

Hostal-Café Bar Jabalcón a simple *hostal* (Avda de los Baños 27, ☎ 958 716 043)

For more information
Town hall: C/Jabalcón 10, ☎ 958 716 017, www.altipla.com/zujar
Taxi: ☎ 958 716 105

Zújar – Benamaurel

Distance	20km
Time	4h45
Height gain	260m
Height loss	300m
Highest point	920m

Heading out of the village turn right off the main street onto the Camino del Pasillo (the second turn on the right along the main street if you entered Zújar on the GR7). This turns into a track as you pass the last houses of the village and heads into fields of olives and walnuts. Where the track forks at a stone wall, take the left fork and stay left on the main track next to a wire fence and around a farmyard. After 500m, at a fork after passing vines on the left, pass the first turning to the right, but take the second, ignoring another track off to the left just after a house.

A gentle climb out of Zújar soon rewards you with stunning views of the Embalse de Negratín. You descend to the spa on the reservoir and then climb again for a panoramic view across the Hoya de Baza flanked to the north by the Sierra de la Sagra. Track walking through strange dry landscape and then a road walk bring you to Benamaurel.

255

Continue straight on beside an *acequia* and then stay on the main track as it bends round to left and across another *acequia*, ignoring a track off to the right.

From here you stay on the main track, ignoring smaller ones off into fields. Stay left at a wider fork after 500m where El Chopo Camino los Baños is written on the wall and then take the right fork at the next junction. ◄

There are beautiful views ahead here of the Sierra del Pozo, the Sierra Harana and the Sierra Mágina.

This brings you to a confusing GR7 post which is marked with a cross and seems to indicate that you should turn off the main track to the left. Don't – the route continues along the main track.

You start to climb here heading further up the western slope of Jabalcón with the **Embalse de Negratín** coming into view. This huge reservoir has the third largest capacity in Andalucía. You can also see the deep ravines and sharp-edged ridges which give this area its unique character.

As the track begins to level out, pass by a right turn and come up to meet another track which you go left along. Pass another left then continue straight on at a staggered cross-roads, heading uphill towards pines. There are no markings here but stay on the main track and soon it begins to descend, passing another right turn. Here you see more of the reservoir and, below you, a **power station** and a **large greenhouse**.

Continue down the same track, taking the left fork at the junction just as you're

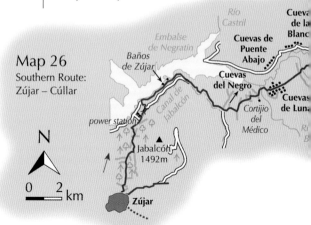

Map 26
Southern Route:
Zújar – Cúllar

N

0   2 km

passing above the greenhouse. This brings you down and across the canal on a small concrete **bridge** to descend on the track on the other side. Follow it down until you reach the road and then continue right along the road to **Baños de Zújar** (8km, 1h30).

Approaching the Embalse de Negratin

The thermal waters, which are heated by hot air under the

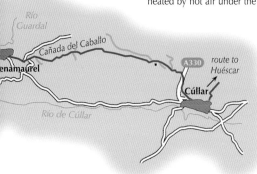

ground beneath the volcanic **Jabalcón**, have been in use since Roman times. There is now an outdoor spa where for just €2 you can experience the healing waters (closed Mondays). There is also a friendly bar/restaurant.

Continue along the road past the Baños de Zújar and the last GR7 marking, passing a large mansion down to your left. The road climbs, leaving behind the shores of the Negratín and gaining views down to where the **Castril, Guardal** and **Baza** rivers join the huge reservoir.

After 1.4km the road joins the one which runs alongside the canal and you continue along in the same direction (now with the canal on your right). From this height you can see Jabalcón's north side and a wide panorama over the Sierra de la Sagra and the other mountains of the national park.

The road leaves the side of the canal briefly 2km on, but returns to it after 600m. From here stay on the road for just over a kilometre more before turning off to your left, where there are two tracks. The left track is signposted with an alternative route to Benamaurel, **Cuevas del Negro** and Cortes to Baza. You take the right of the two, signed to **Cortijio del Médico**, which heads downhill into a strange landscape of scrub and heavily irrigated agricultural plains.

Ignore a track off to the left after 400m and another off to the right 500m further on. Stay on the main track between the fields, ignoring smaller ones, and at a divide 600m later take the right fork, with the hamlet of Cuevas de Luna now straight ahead. Another 500m on, stay right and then left when it forks, soon after making your way across the maze of farm tracks.

Go right at a crossroads then left and across a small **bridge** to leave the fields behind. The track bends up to the right and then splits. The right fork takes you into **Cuevas de Luna**, which as the name suggests is made up almost entirely of cave dwellings and set in such arid surroundings that it could be the moon. The unusual terrain and climate in this area has led to a cave-dwelling lifestyle.

The left fork is the continuation of the route and takes you the remaining 4km (45min) to **Benamaurel** on the road, which soon becomes tarmac. To your left you will pass some of the other cave hamlets of Benamaurel: **Cuevas de Puente Abajo**, San Marcos, **Cuevas de la Blanca** and Huerta Real.

CAVE HOUSES

Cave dwelling has been common in the northeast of the Granada province since the Moors arrived in the eighth century. It is especially common around Baza and across the *altiplano*.

In the recent past (up until the 1950s) the caves tended to be used by farmers as temporary accommodation during harvest times, or for housing livestock. However, in the last few decades they have become more and more popular as homes and holiday homes. Many are being renovated, and there are architects and estate agents specialising in cave renovation rental and sales.

Apart from their current popularity, the appeal of cave dwelling has a lot to do with the ability to self-regulate their temperature to a comfortable year-round 18–20°C. Their thick limestone walls and vaulted shape offer perfect insulation from heat and noise and make them a very environmentally friendly form of housing.

Benamaurel (720m, pop. 2500) ⌁ ◉ F ▲ € ☎ ✉ ✚ ☗

A historic village set on an outcrop with great views down on the bizarre contrast of the lush valley of the Río Guardal and the desert-like plains. There are many ancient cave houses here. Some of them date from 12th century. Try to make time to visit the ancient Almohad cave dwellings in Las Hafas del Salto where there are caves containing a beautiful Roman *columbarium* and a dovecot dug into the rock face.

Accommodation and food
There are a couple of options for eating out, including a pizzeria and one cave complex to stay in:

Casas Cuevas de San Marcos (€18 per person with discounts for longer stays) cave accommodation conveniently near the central plaza with very friendly owners, comfortable 2/3/5 bedroom caves with living rooms with open fires and TV, kitchen and patio with BBQs (Ctra Castillejar, Barrio San Marcos, ☎ 958 704 175/629 594 826, www.altiplanodegranada.org/cuevajabaluna.htm)

For more information
Town hall: Pza Mayor 1, ☎ 958 733 011, aytobenamaurel@telebase.es

Benamaurel – Cúllar

A stretch of flat, easy walking through more bizarre lunar landscapes brings you to the Río Cúllar valley with the Sierra de Ocre as a beautiful backdrop.

Distance	12km
Time	2h15
Height gain	140m
Height loss	20m
Highest point	900m

Leave from the bottom of the village on the road past the plaza and the park and come to a left turn at the end marked with a GR7 sign (Cúllar 2h15) and a sign for a walking route to Puente Arriba.

Turn up to the left along this small tarmac road and stay on it, ignoring turnings up to the left to houses, including some interesting cave houses. Then at a U-bend after about 400m, leave the road, taking a gravel track to the right. This takes you along next to small flat fields bordered by low hills covered in scrubby undergrowth and, at a divide after 300m, you take the right fork.

Leaving Benamaurel

Pass another right turn soon after, then stay on the same track, the **Cañada del Caballo**, heading east. The peaks of the Sierra de Orce are visible in the distance ahead and you continue through the yellows and greys of the dry hills and *esparto* grass. ▸

Esparto, which is a local crop, has been used in handicrafts since prehistoric times.

After 3km you pass a right fork and then a left about 200m on. Stay on the same track, which is easy, fairly flat walking, and look back for views of Jabalcón. Then 3.7km later meet another track and head right, leaving behind the small hills and walking through open farmland.

Just over a kilometre further on you come to a **farm** and continue straight on past it. At the next junction just beyond it, turn left. After passing another farm to the left you soon come to a tarmac road. Turn right onto it towards the outskirts of the town which are visible ahead, and when this road meets a bigger road, the **A3330**, turn right onto it and follow it into town.

This road turns into Avenida Andalucía, which is the main street across the bottom of the town and contains most of its accommodation. If you want to head into the centre, turn left turn onto a smaller road with a GR7 mark as you enter **Cúllar**.

Cúllar (890m, pop. 5000) ﹏ ▮ F ▲ € ☎ ✉ ✚ ⛢

A historic village with an architectural legacy from many different cultures since prehistoric times. There are many Paleolithic and Neolithic archaeological remains including the major Bronze Age archeological site El Malagón, where the Idolo de Malagón, a fine ivory figure carving thought to date from 2700–2300BC, was found. It is now in the archaeology museum in Granada. Almost half of the population live in cave houses. At the end of April, the Fiesta de los Moros y Cristianos is an impressive sight.

Accommodation and food
A few eateries and hotels to choose from:
Luna Mar a *hostal* with 8 rooms with air conditioning (Juan Pérez, ☎ 958 731 120)
Hostal Ventas del Peral a small *hostal* on the street of the same name (Ventas del Peral 50, Bajo, ☎ 958 730 288)
Villa Milo a *casa rural* (Pza Barranco 32, ☎ 958 732 473)

For more information
Town hall: ☎ 958 730 225

Cúllar – Orce

Easy walking, although very poorly marked, along farm tracks skirting the edge of the dry plains with good views of the Sierra de Orce and back to Jabalcón, arriving in Orce after a brief road walk.

Distance	21.6km
Time	4h
Height gain	200m
Height loss	160m
Highest point	1020m

Leave Cúllar from Calle Vieja, the old road, at the top of the village. Heading east along it, take the second track on the left past the large red-and-white pylons/antennae just opposite a large farm shed, the last building on the road.

The track takes you downhill and towards fields. After 400m, pass a track off to the right as the track bends round on itself. Then, when you join another track 200m on, turn right along it passing both a left then a right turn. Continue on the same track heading uphill and east through broom with an impressive panorama of the **Sierra del Periate** ahead and corn fields and olives all around.

Take the left at a divide, 800m after joining this new track, and then turn right at a crossroads 300m further on, heading along a dry riverbed. A track comes off the riverbed 900m along and you take it up to the right. It crosses the riverbed a couple of times, following its course, and then at the crossroads of the riverbed and a track 400m further on, you head left uphill towards a **rubbish dump**.

You pass the tip 3km after leaving **Cúllar** and, at the next junction, take the right fork. Continue with young olive groves on your right and young pines on your left. A further 1.3km on, go straight over crossroads heading east, and 500m later, when you meet another track, turn left and shortly come to a large abandoned *cortijo*.

Carry on between the buildings of the *cortijo*, now heading north along a tree-lined track. When you come to the next *cortijo* 1km on, head straight on again behind the buildings and, where the track forks just beyond, take the left fork. Continue along this track, which bends round to head north, parallel to the road a couple of kilometres to the left, and alongside the Sierra del Periate, now to the right. Jabalcón is still visible to your left.

You stay on this main track now almost all the way to Orce ignoring all turnings off for 10.5km. You pass two large **greenhouses** and eventually arrive at the tarmac road to Orce, 1.2km from a warehouse and 16.6km

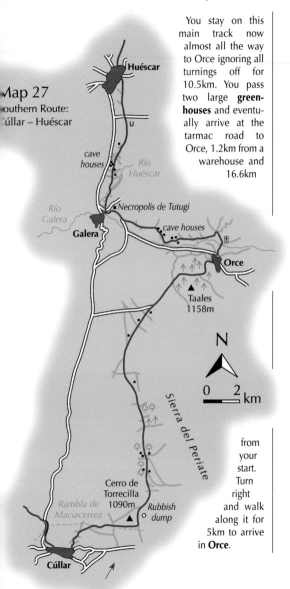

Map 27
Southern Route:
Cúllar – Huéscar

Huéscar

cave houses

Río Huéscar

Río Galera

Necropolis de Tutugi

Galera

cave houses

Orce

Taales
1158m

N

0   2 km

Cerro de
Torrecilla
1090m   Rubbish
dump

Rambla de
Maciacerrea

Sierra del Periate

Cúllar

from your start. Turn right and walk along it for 5km to arrive in **Orce**.

263

A lone pine, an example of the sparse vegetation along this section

Orce (928m, pop. 1350) ⏻ ◉ F ▲ ☎ ✚ 🚌

Orce claims to have been inhabited by the first ever human beings in Europe, by virtue of a piece of bone found in 1982 which is thought to be a one to two million-year-old fragment of the skull of the famous 'Hombre de Orce'. Although

Orce church

this is disputed, Orce is unquestionably one of the most important prehistoric sites in Europe. Stone remains and fossils of a wide variety of animals have been found here and many of them can be viewed in the museum in the Arab castle, the Alcazaba de las Siete Torres.

Accommodation and food

A couple of places to stay, a few bars with food and great, good value meals on offer at the *albergue*:

Albergue Villa de Orce (pp dorm room/private room €11/16, breakfast/lunch/dinner €2/6/6 or €23 full board) great new youth hostel in centre with option of a private room, friendly staff and good home-cooked food including vegetarian fare

(C/Mercedes Ortiz 6, ☎ 625 341 725/619 481 121)

Turismo de Orce (2/3/4/5/6 person cave €65–80/90–120/120–140/130–155/150–180) fully-equipped caves in a restored cave village, panoramic views, BBQs and garden furniture, mountain bike hire (☎ 958 746 281/678 869 121, www.cuevasdeorce.com)

For more information

Town hall: ☎ 958 736 101

Orce – Huéscar

The route as far as Galera crosses the *vega* (fertile plain) following a little oasis-like channel in the arid landscape as you walk next to reed-filled *acequias* and green crops. After Galera, you return to crossing arid landscape with patches of cultivation to enter the historic town of Huéscar.

Distance	17km
Time	3h45
Height gain	140m
Height loss	100m
Highest point	950m

Orce – Galera (9km, 2h)

Leave the Plaza Nueva heading towards the castle and turn down to the right past the church, continuing down Calle Chalud as it leaves the village which brings you to a GR7 sign (Galera 2h10).

Stay on the tarmac road for 300m until you come to the white walls of the **cemetery** then turn left just before it to go along the road for 150m before turning left onto a gravel track heading north. Pass through fields of crops with craggy hills ahead then, after 550m, turn left at a crossroads. Now walk alongside reed-filled irrigation channels passing more crops including sunflowers with the village up to your left. After 1.2km you come to a divide and go left, passing another turn down to the left, and then at the next divide keep left.

Pass by some abandoned **cave houses** 4km from the start and, at the junction just afterwards, keep left heading towards some buildings with the road down to your left. Continue between the buildings and beneath a rock face on your right. Another 400m later, when the track divides again, continue straight on.

Stay on the same track as it turns into a path. After about 500m it passes through a farmyard. Stay to left of the farm buildings to re-emerge on a track along which you turn right passing a grand, but now empty, cave house, before it becomes a small path again. Descend on this small path heading around the hillside, passing more abandoned cave houses, before meeting another wide track along which you turn left, 1.3km after the farm buildings.

Go downhill gently to meet another track and follow it round to the right ignoring a little turn up to the right soon after. Continue along main track parallel to the Cúllar–

On the route to Galera

Huéscar road which is on your left. The village comes into view just around the corner, and at the junction just after some newly renovated caves turn left to come down to the road passing the Molino de Morillas at a GR7 sign. Now 7.8km from start, turn right along the road and follow it past a turning to the **Necrópolis Ibérica de Tútugi** to your right. After 900m turn left down into **Galera**.

Galera (830m, pop. 1500) ⇡ ⦿I F ▲ ☎ 🚌

Like Orce, Galera boasts important prehistoric and Iberian archaeological sites of which the most important is the Necrópolis Ibérica de Tútugi, where the Phoenician Goddess La Dama Ibérica de Galera was found (now housed in el Museo Arqueológico Nacional in Madrid). You can also visit the Mudéjar church, declared a national monument, and the cave museum.

Accommodation and food

Several cave accommodation options and a couple of bar-restaurants:

El Molino de Morillas (2/4 person €60–82/152–164) lovely apartments in renovated old flour mill, indoor and outdoor swimming pool, pool room and internet room (C/Iglesia 4, ☎ 958 739 068/608 459 645, www.molinomorillasgalera.com)

Cuevas la Morada (up to 4/up to 6 €65/90) 5 caves with 2–8 rooms, fully
    equipped with kitchens, wood fires, TV, minimum 2-night stay, meals to
    order, visits in 4x4 arranged (C/San Isidro 30, ☎ 660 862 044,
    cuevasgalera@yahoo.es, www.lamoradagalera.com)
La Pisá del Moro (2–6 person €50–120) 5 recently refurbished caves, air condi-
    tioning, wood fires, fully-equipped kitchens (Avda Nicasio Tómas 6, ☎ 958
    739 061/689 503 664, lapisadelmoro@worldonline.es,
    www.altipla.com/lapisadelmoro)

For more information
Town hall: ☎ 958 739 115

Galera – Huéscar (8km, 1h45)

Take the first right off the road on which you entered the village, going up to and across a bridge over the big road. Just
at the end of the bridge take an unmarked track off to the
left. Follow this dirt track, and come to what at the time of
writing was the one and only post you see all the way to
Huéscar.

Ignore a couple of turnings off to the left to houses and,
after about a kilometre on the same main track, continue
straight on, passing a track downhill and a right uphill. Then,
at a divide immediately after, where Huéscar's 15th-century
church spire comes into view briefly in the distance, take the
left fork.

Cross over a little bridge and at the next junction just
over a kilometre further on, take the left fork. Then at a
divide just after this take the right fork at an impressive walnut tree. Stay on this same track passing a couple of **houses**
to the right then, 400m after joining the track, a turn steeply
up to the left (marked no entry).

After another 300m and a line of pines with a row of
basic **cave entrances** behind them, another track joins yours
from back to the right and you continue to the left and pass
another house. Ignore a right turn down to farm buildings,
but then at the next fork, 250m after the house, turn right.

Stay on this main dirt track, ignoring more minor tracks
off to both sides and 400m further on come to a T-junction
with a big **house** up to the left. You go right, staying next to
the *acequia*. Again stay on this main track ignoring small

turns off to either side and heading generally northeast then east.

After 2km come to a major road and pass through an **underpass**, continuing straight on the other side on a track that heads towards **Huéscar**, now clearly visible ahead. At the divide a kilometre on, take the right fork and meet a small tarmac road after 450m. At the next divide turn right again back onto a gravel track which brings you up to the village. It becomes concrete and you turn left where you meet the road, then right into the Paseo de San Cristo to head into the centre of town.

Line of pines with a row of basic cave entrances behind them between Galera and Huéscar

Huéscar (953m, pop. 9500) 🚶 🍴 F ▲ € ☎ ✉ ✚ ⓘ 🚌 🖥
Huéscar is rich in history. The area around it has been inhabited since prehistoric times and it was an important settlement in Roman times and then a frontier town, changing hands between Christians and Muslims for several centuries. There are a few sites worth visiting, including the ruins of the castle and its 15th-century watchtowers, some of the grand residential palaces, churches, the Santo Domingo Convent, and the 16th-century chapel which was converted into a

theatre in the 19th century. Make time to visit the thermal baths which make use of a natural source of hot water at 18°C.

Accommodation and food
A range of places to eat and a few hotels to choose from. For longer stays, there are also many good caves and *casas rurales* on the outskirts:

Hotel Rural Patri (s/d en suite €30/€55) hotel-restaurant with 17 smart, comfortable rooms set around sunny central patio area, all with TV, air conditioning and heating, restaurant with good range of dishes including a daily set menu for €9 (Avda de Granada 18, ☎ 958 742 504, www.hotelpatri.com)

Ruta del Sur Avda ★★ (s/d en suite €20/26) pleasant clean rooms with satellite TV and air conditioning and a restaurant downstairs, friendly English-speaking owner (Avda Granada 41, ☎ 958 741 289)

For more information
Town hall: ☎ 958 740 740
Taxi: 958 740 729/958 741 260/958 742 313
www.huescar.org
www.comarcadehuescar.com

Huéscar – Puebla de Don Fadrique

A 15km walk along the cyprus-lined Carretera de las Santas followed by a delightful forested climb and descent into the final village on the Andalucian GR7.

Distance	23.5km
Time	6h
Height gain	540m
Height loss	340m
Highest point	1480m

Leave the centre of Huéscar heading north along Calle Mayor. When you get to the edge of the town take the Carretera de las Santas marked with a road sign and a broken GR7 post. Going along this small tarmac road you immediately enter cyprus trees which line either side of the road for 10km and stay on the road for this whole distance getting good views of hills on either side as you climb gently. (The road is pleasant and quiet and your only other option is a taxi.)

Pass a sign for **Piedra del Letrero** where there are cave paintings (shut for conservation work at the time of writing). Further on there is a solitary, strangely shaped rock popularly known as the Salto del Moro, the Moor's jump. Ahead is the **Sierra de Jurena** and, to the right, the **Sierra Bermeja**. The valley opens up and becomes the **Campo de Jurena** with fruit plantations and fields.

After 10km you come out of the trees into more open landscape but stay on the road as it climbs more, crosses several small bridges and enters pine trees. Another 5km further on, you finally leave the road for a forestry track off to your right. A large GR7 signpost here tells you the **Ermita de las Santas** is 30min further along the road and that **Puebla de Don Fadrique** is 3h45 up the forestry track. The Puente de las Tablas picnic area is also less than a kilometre further.

Turn up the track heading into the pine forest ignoring a left turn after 300m. Another 600m on, pass by a **semi-ruined *cortijo*** with the buildings on your left and fields of almonds to

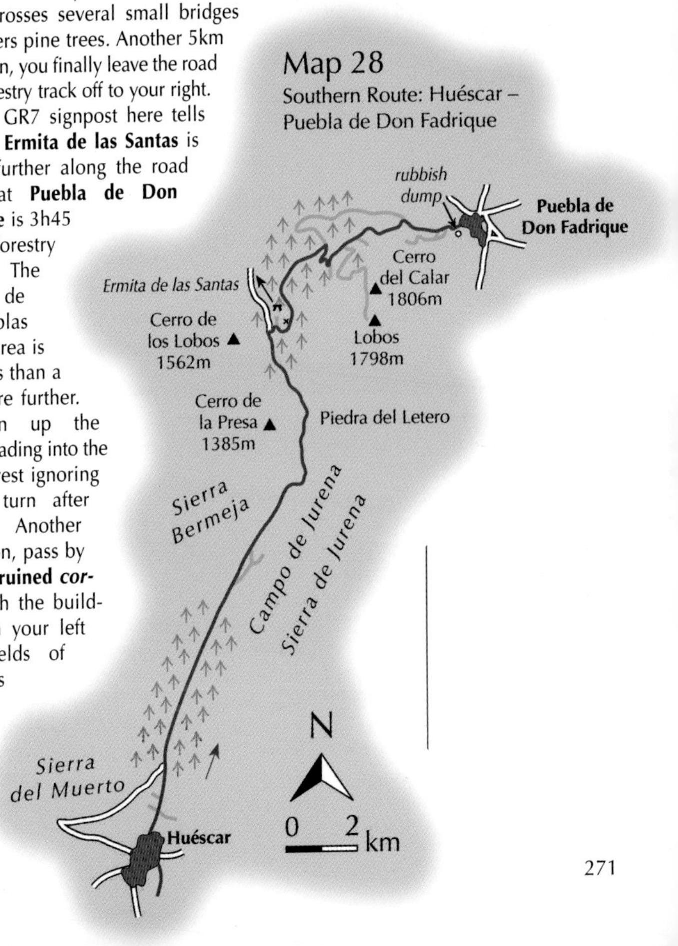

Map 28
Southern Route: Huéscar – Puebla de Don Fadrique

rubbish dump

Puebla de Don Fadrique

Ermita de las Santas

Cerro del Calar ▲ 1806m

Cerro de los Lobos ▲ 1562m

Lobos ▲ 1798m

Cerro de la Presa ▲ 1385m

Piedra del Letero

Sierra Bermeja

Campo de Jurena

Sierra de Jurena

Sierra del Muerto

N

0   2 km

Huéscar

Walking on to the last stop on the GR7 in Andalucía

your right. From here stay on the main track still heading uphill.

The track levels out as you pass a stone picnic table on your left 1km on from the *cortijo* and you get great views over the hills. Almost 2km on, the track divides and you take the right fork to climb again, heading part way up the north side of **Lobos**, which stands at 1798m. Ignore a track off to the right a kilometre on. A further 800m on the track divides again. The right fork would take you all the way to the top of Lobos, but you take the left to begin the descent to Puebla de Don Fadrique.

Head downhill with the views opening out ahead of you, but Puebla de Don Fadrique still hidden. At the next divide stay on the main track to the left leaving the pines behind for scrub and pasture land, now in the foothills of the **Cerro del Calar** and passing almond trees on your right.

Approaching Puebla de Don Fadrique

At the next junction, 2km from the start of the descent, take a right turn and keep left, ignoring a right turn heading uphill. The town comes into view a kilometre later, sitting in a big valley surrounded by hills.

Ignore another right turn 500m later to head downhill straight for **Puebla de Don Fadrique**, past a **rubbish dump** to your right, then turn off the track to your left to follow a small path down alongside a stone wall to arrive in the town on Calle Ramblica. Follow this down and into the town where you'll find a GR7 signpost pointing you on to the continuation of the route into Murcia or celebrate the end of the route in Andalucía at the strange roundabout in the centre of the town which has used GR7 posts to prop up its 'keep off the grass' signs!

From Puebla de Don Fadrique there is a daily bus (on weekdays only) to Granada (3h45) and Málaga (5h15).

Puebla de Don Fadrique

Puebla de Don Fadrique (1164m, pop. 2500) 🚶 🍽 F ▲ € ☎ ✉ ✚ ⓘ 🚌
A pleasant little town with white houses and its 16th-century church of Santa
María surrounded by fields of cereals and almonds. It has a rich past, first as a
Muslim settlement and later a Christian one.

Accommodation and food
The hotel is the main place to stay and eat although there are a few bars.

Hotel Puerta de Andalucía ★ (s/d en suite €20/€40) spacious, bright but characterless rooms, with bar and restaurant downstairs (Ctra Granada-Valencia 1,
☎ 958 721 340/958 721 076, p.andalucia@ribernet.es,
www.ribernet.es/hostal_puerta_de_andalucia)

Apartamentos Don Fadrique well-equipped tourist flats with kitchens, heating
and TV (Ctra Granada, behind petrol station, ☎ 958 721 116)

For more information
Town hall: ☎ 958 721 001

Route	Refreshment/ accommodation at end point	Height gain/ loss	Highest point	Distance	Time	Description	Page
	Where symbols are in brackets the facilities require a small detour to a nearby town or village.						
Part 1							
Cádiz province (6–9 days, 155.5km, 46h)							
Tarifa – Los Barrios (2 day section with tent)	F	560m/ 500m	240m	41.5km	12h	Beach walk followed by a gentle climb up into the green hills. Worth **wild camping** to split in two.	45
Los Barrios – Castillo de Castellar (optional 2 day section, but no tent needed)	F	400m/ 180m	244m	34km	10h30	Hill tracks and a road walk ending at the hill-top castle of Castellar. A km detour at Almoraima on the route would take you to Castellar de la Frontera and shorten the route by 4km and 1h30 or you could stop at hotel along route.	50
Castillo de Castillar – Jimena de la Frontera	F	160m/ 200m	244m	18km	6h	Flat route along a railway line through pretty rural landscapes.	55
Jimena de la Frontera – Ubrique (optional 2 day section with tent)	F	720m/ 600m	860m	36km	10h	Small paths passing over lofty passes and through cork trees. **Wild camping** permitted.	57
Ubrique – Montejaque		900m/560m	1060m	26km	7h30	Steep climbs over limestone crags and beautiful paths though the spacious valleys of the Sierra de Grazalema natural park.	60
Ubrique – Benaocaz	F			3.5km	1hr		
Benaocaz – Villaluenga del Rosario	F			4.5km	1h20		
Villaluenga del Rosario – Montejaque (optional 2 day section)	F en route			18km	5h10		

Route	Refreshment/ accommodation at end point	Height gain/ loss	Highest point	Distance	Time	Description	
Málaga province (7–8 days, 113km, 34h30)							
Montejaque – Arriate		360/440m	740m	17km	5h30	Steeply up and over the El Puerto pass and across the wide valley floor to Arriate. Worth splitting to spend time in Ronda.	68
Montejaque – Ronda	⛺ 🏠 🍽 F ◀						
Ronda – Arriate	⛺ 🍽 F ◀						
Arriate – Ardales (2 day section)	⛺ 🍽 F ◀	700m/840m	840m	38km	11h	Very long route through remote hilly landscapes and beneath rocky outcrops which **can be split** by taking a detour to spend a night in nearby **Cuevas del Becerro**.	72
Ardales – El Chorro	⛺ 🏠 🍽 F ◀	380m/620m	600m	13km	6h	Cross hilltops and then descend a zigzagging mountain path.	76
El Chorro –Valle de Abdalajís	⛺ 🍽 F ◀	580m/440m	700m	10km	3h	A long steep climb up beneath the Sierra del Huma.	78
Valle de Abdalajís – Antequera	⛺ 🍽 F ◀	640m/400m	780m	20.5km	5h	Easy route with some road walking and views of El Torcal.	80
Antequera – Villanueva del Cauche	⛺ 🍽 F ◀	320m/200m	900m	14.5km	4h	Small, pretty paths make up for an early uphill road walk.	83
TOTAL FOR PART 1		5720m/ 4980m		268.5km	80h30	**13–17 days**	

Part 2: Northern Fork

Málaga province (5–6 days, 88km, 24h30)

Route	Icons	Ascent/Descent	Max	Distance	Time	Notes	Page
Villanueva del Cauche – Villanueva del Trabuco		160m/160m	760m	14km	4h10	Gentle route between fields and olive groves with mountains on the horizon.	87
Villanueva del Cauche – Villanueva del Rosario	F ◄			10km	3h		
Villanueva del Rosario – Villanueva del Trabuco	F ◄			4km	1h10		
Villanueva del Trabuco – Villanueva de Tapia *(optional 2 day section with tent)*	F ◄	320m/360m	940m	28km	8h	Loop around village then through open farmland and olives. **Wild camping** is possible to break the day up or there is an option to cut the route shorter.	90
Villanueva de Tapia – Villanueva de Algaidas	F ◄	500m/620m	920m	17km	4h30	Pretty undulating tracks through seemingly endless olive groves.	93
Villanueva de Algaidas – Cuevas de San Marcos		100m/280m	540m	27km	7h	Overgrown route alongside a riverbed.	97
Villanueva de Algaida – Cuevas Bajas	F ◄			18.5km	5h		
Cuevas Bajas – Cuevas de San Marcos	F ◄			8.5km	2h		
Cuevas de San Marcos – Rute	F ◄	460m/180m	700m	10.5km	3h	A beautiful section crossing from Málaga into Córdoba.	100

Route	Refreshment/ accommodation at end point	Height gain/ loss	Highest point	Distance	Time	Description	Page
Córdoba province (3 days, 57.5km, 14h40)							
Rute – Priego de Córdoba	🍴 🍽 **F** ◀ 🏕 en route	580m/560m	920m	22.5km	6h30	Magical woodland paths passing through pine and oak.	104
Priego de Córdoba –Almendinilla	🍴 🍽 **F** ◀	120m/140m	740m	10km	2h40	Through trees and rocky landscape then into olives.	109
Almedinilla – Alcalá la Real	🍴 🍽 **F** ◀	860m/540m	1100m	25km	5h30	Small section of road walking followed by a steady climb through olive groves before a lovely descent.	111
Jaén province (13–15 days, 297.5km, 72h40)							
Alcalá la Real – Frailes	🍴 🍽 **F** ◀	140m/280m	1020m	9km	1h50	Gentle route through open countryside.	118
Frailes – Carchelejo *(optional 2 day section with tent)*	🍴 🍽 **F** ◀	1280m/ 1240m	1500m	35km	9h30	A climb in beautiful wild hills then through a rocky gorge. (Worth **wild camping** to divide this section.)	120
Carchelejo – Cambil	🍴 🍽 **F** ◀	160m/200m	840m	15km	3h30	Half road walk, half riverside stroll.	124
Cambil – Torres	🍴 🏕 🍽 **F**	1000m/ 880m	1650m	26km	6h45	A beautiful stretch in the heart of the Sierra Mágina.	127
Torres – Bedmar		480m/740m	1250m	16.5km	5h30	A climb to the Albánchez pass then around the Sierra Mágina foothills.	131
Torres – Albánchez de Úbeda	🍴 🏕 🍽 **F** ◀			5.5km	2h		
Albánchez de Úbeda – Bedmar	🍴 🍽 **F** ◀			11km	3h30		
Bedmar – Jódar	🍴 🍽 **F** ◀	480m/500m	1133m	7km	2h20	One of the GR7's steepest climbs.	135

Stage		Ascent/Descent	Max alt.	Distance	Time	Description	Page
Jódar – Quesada	F ◄	420m/320m	728m	34.5km	8h	A long road walk then an easy, pretty stretch though grassland and olive trees. You can **wild camp** in Hornos de Peal.	137
Quesada – Cazorla	F ◄	500m/380m	1180m	17.5km	4h30	Dramatic rugged mountains of the Cazorla natural park.	142
Cazorla – Vadillo de Castril	F ◄	680m/560m	1400m	16km	5h30	Wide tracks through vast pine forests and below rocky crags.	147
Vadillo – Coto-Ríos	F ◄	480m/800m	1400m	38km	7h	Forest tracks bring you out next to the pretty Río Guadalquivir.	151
Coto-Ríos – Pontones	F ◄	1140m/440m	1700m	34km	7h	Ascent into peaceful pine woodlands and rocky peaks.	154
Pontones – Santiago de la Espada	F ◄	340m/340m	1620m	15km	3h15	A gentle pretty route following tiny paths in open farmland.	158
Santiago de la Espada – Puebla de Don Fadrique	F ◄	540m/720m	1664m	34km	8h	Nice route to Cortijo de las Cuevas then very long road walk.	161
NORTHERN FORK TOTAL		**11,700m/10,840m**		**443**	**111h50**	**21–24 days**	

PART 3: Southern Fork

Málaga province (2 days, 43km, 11h30)

Stage		Ascent/Descent	Max alt.	Distance	Time	Description	Page
Villanueva del Cauche – Riogordo	F ◄	480m/780m	1160m	18km	5h	Unmarked, but fairly easy to follow, section over a high pass. (**B&B** sometimes available in **Riogordo** but if not you can go to nearby **Colmenar**.)	165
Riogordo – Ventas de Zafarraya	F ◄	720m/200m	940m	25km	6h30	8km road walk then along an old railway in lovely scenery.	169

Route	Refreshment/ accommodation at end point	Height gain/ loss	Highest point	Distance	Time	Description	Page
Granada province (22–23 days, 408.3km, 107h55)							
Ventas de Zafarraya – Alhama de Granada		340m/420m	1040m	20km	5h30	Pass into Sierras de Tejada, Almijara and Alhama natural park.	176
Alhama de Granada – Arenas del Rey		300m/280m	1100m	20km	6h	Beautiful route through a dramatic gorge and cork oak groves.	181
Arenas del Rey – Jayena		300m/260m	1060m	15km	4h	Forestry tracks back through pines in the natural park.	183
Jayena – Albuñuelas (optional 2 day section with tent)		580m/740m	1300m	31.5km	7h15	Remote pine forest track into the hills with great views. (You could split this by **wild camping**.)	186
Albuñuelas – Nigüelas		460m/260m	950m	14km	3h30	Pretty, winding path orange groves and along ancient irrigation channels.	190
Albuñuelas – Restábal				4km	55min		
Restábal –Nigüelas				10km	2h35		
Nigüelas – Lanjarón		360m/660m	1280m	15km	3h30	Forest tracks high up through pines then a long descent.	195
Lanjarón – Soportújar		460m/240m	1040m	12.8km	4h50	Zigzags round ravines passing Cáñar and across a dam, Dique 24.	198
Lanjaron – Cáñar				7.8km	2h50		
Cáñar – Soportújar				5km	2h		
Soportújar – Pitres		740m/460m	1600m	13.9km	3h45	Pass between villages, through the stunning Poquiera Valley, with views of the Sierra Nevada.	202
Soportújar – Pampaneira				7km	2h		
Pampaneira – Bubión				1.4km	20min		
Bubión – Pitres				4.5km	1h25		

Pitres – Trevélez		720m/560m	1740m	15.7km	5h45	Through lush vegetation past streams to climb to Pórtugos then on up through beautiful oak woodland. 207
Pitres – Pórtugos	◄			3km	55min	
Pórtugos – Busquístar	◄			1.7km	30min	
Busquístar – Trevélez	◄			11km	4h	
Trevélez – Cádiar		300/780m	1660m	18.2km	6h	Gentle route on forestry tracks between sleepy hamlets through beautiful oak woodlands. 214
Trevélez –Juviles	◄			10km	2h50	
Juviles – Timar				1.7km	40min	
Timar – Lobras				1.5km	30min	
Lobras – Cádiar				5km	2h	
Cádiar – Yegen		960/800m	1440m	17.7km	4h50	Walk round hillsides and over streams to reach a string of beautiful white villages, 221
Cádiar – Narila				1.8km	20min	
Narila – Bérchules	◄			3.2km	1h	
Bérchules –Mecina Bombarón	◄			7km	2h	
Mecina Bombarón – Yegen	◄			5.7km	1h30	
Yegen – Laroles		660/640m	1300m	18.3km	5h10	Pass some amazing fizzy natural springs then loop in and out of gullies and ravines to each of the villages. 227
Yegen – Válor	◄			4km	1h	
Válor – Nechite				1.5km	35min	

Route	Refreshment/ accommodation at end point	Height gain/ loss	Highest point	Distance	Time	Description	Page
Nechite – Mairena	⟲ ⦿ F			4.8km	1h15		
Mairena – Júbar	⦿ F			1km	15min		
Júbar – Laroles	⟲ 🏕 ⦿ F ◀			7km	2h		
Laroles – Puerto de la Ragua		1120m/ 220m	2000m	16.5km	5.45	Along the 12km of route in Almería, through its highest village then further up to the highest point of the GR7.	234
Laroles – Bayárcal	⟲ ⦿ F ◀			4.5km	1h30		
Bayárcal – Puerto de la Ragua *(may need tent)*	⟲ ⦿ F			12km	4h15		
Puerto de la Ragua – La Calahorra		100m/900m	2060m	11.6km	2h50	A pleasant descent on paths and tracks through pine forest and farm land.	239
Puerto de la Ragua – Ferreira	⦿ F ◀			8.6km	2h20		
Ferreira – La Calahorra	⟲ ⦿ F ◀			3km	30min		
La Calahorra – Narváez *(2 day section with tent)*	⟲ ⦿ F	1060m/ 900m	2000m	49km	13h10	Across the flat dry plains of the Marquesado del Zenete then climb through the green rugged hills of the Sierra de Baza. (**Wild camping** permitted in two areas of the park.)	243
Narváez – Zújar		200m/800m	1400m	25km	5h20	Through the sprawling city of Baza and then on towards and round the distinctive mountain of Jabalcón.	251
Narváez – Baza	⟲ ⦿ F ◀			14km	2h50		
Baza – Zújar	⟲ ⦿ F ◀			11km	2h30		

Route				Ascent/Descent	Altitude	Distance	Time	Notes	Page
Zújar –Benamaurel	⛺	🍴	◀	260m/300m	920m	20km	4h45	Twinkling reservoir, great spa baths then strange arid area.	255
Benamaurel –Cúllar	⛺	🍴	◀	140m/20m	900m	12km	2h15	Flat easy walking through odd lunar landscapes.	260
Cúllar – Orce	⛺	🍴	◀	200m/160m	1020m	21.6km	4h	Gentle walking, though terribly marked, along farm tracks.	262
Orce – Huéscar				140m/100m	950m	17km	3h45	Following oasis-like channel next to *acequias* and green crops.	266
Orce – Galera	⛺	🍴	◀			9km	2h		
Galera – Huéscar	⛺	🍴	◀			8km	1h45		
Huéscar – Puebla de Don Fadrique	⛺	🍴	◀	540m/340m	1480m	23.5km	6h	15km road walk then lovely forested up and down to the end.	270
SOUTHERN FORK TOTAL				**11,140m/ 10,820m**		**451.3km**	**119h25**	**22-25 days**	

Appendix 2:
SPANISH–ENGLISH GLOSSARY

A few useful walking-related words which you may see on maps or signs.

Spanish	English	Spanish	English
acequia	irrigation channel	garganta	ravine
agua (potable/ no potable)	(drinking/ non-drinking) water	hoya	hollow/plain
		iglesia	church
albergue	hostel	laguna/lago	lake
alcazaba	castle	lavadero	laundry
aldea	hamlet	llano	plain
arroyo	stream	minas	mines
ayuntamiento	town hall	mirador	viewpoint
atalaya	watchtower	montaña	mountain
baños	baths	parque natural	natural park
barranco	gully/ravine	parque nacional	national park
Calle (abbreviated to C/)	street	plaza (plza/pza)	square
camino	path	prohibido el paso	no entry
Carretera (Ctra)	road	puerto	pass
casa forestal	park house	rambla	watercourse/stream
castillo	castle	río	river
cerro	hill	senderismo	walking/cycling
comarca	region	sierra	mountain range
cordillera	mountain range	tajos	cliffs/cleft
cortijo	farmhouse	torre	tower
coto privado de caza	private hunting reserve	vega	fertile plain
cruz	cross	venta	country inn
cuesta	hill/slope		
cueva	cave		
desfiladero	gorge		
embalse	reservoir		
era	threshing circle		
ermita	chapel/hermitage		
estación	station		
fábrica	factory		
finca	farm/estate		
fuente	fountain		

Appendix 3:
FURTHER INFORMATION

Useful websites
www.andalucia.com a good all-round information source on the region

www.andalucia.org the region's official tourist information site

www.andalusia-web.com a useful site with information and advice on travelling in the region

www.ecologistasenaccion.org Andalucía's main environmental group

www.era-ewv-ferp.com European Ramblers Association

www.fedme.es The Spanish mountain and climbing sports federation – responsible for the GR routes in Spain (Spanish)

www.iberianature.com a wealth of information on Spanish nature, environment and wildlife

www.juntadeandalucia.es site for the Regional Government (Spanish)

www.paginas-amarillas.es Spanish Yellow Pages, useful to look up accommodation and facilities

www.wild-spain.com lots of information on the environment and travel in Spain

Additional reading
Alastair Boyd *The Sierras of the South: Travels in the mountains of Andalusia* (Harper Collins, 1992)

Gerald Brenan *South from Granada* (1st edn 1957, Penguin Books, 1992)

Washington Irving *Tales from the Alhambra* (1st edn 1832, Editorial Everest, 2005)

Chris Stewart *Driving over Lemons* (Sort Of Books, 1999)

LISTING OF CICERONE GUIDES

BACKPACKING
The End to End Trail
Three Peaks, Ten Tors
Backpacker's Britain Vol 1 – Northern England
Backpacker's Britain Vol 2 – Wales
Backpacker's Britain Vol 3 – Northern Scotland
The Book of the Bivvy

NORTHERN ENGLAND LONG-DISTANCE TRAILS
The Dales Way
The Reiver's Way
The Alternative Coast to Coast
A Northern Coast to Coast Walk
The Pennine Way
Hadrian's Wall Path
The Teesdale Way

FOR COLLECTORS OF SUMMITS
The Relative Hills of Britain
Mts England & Wales Vol 2 – England
Mts England & Wales Vol 1 – Wales

UK GENERAL
The National Trails

BRITISH CYCLE GUIDES
The Cumbria Cycle Way
Lands End to John O'Groats – Cycle Guide
Rural Rides No.1 – West Surrey
Rural Rides No.2 – East Surrey
South Lakeland Cycle Rides
Border Country Cycle Routes
Lancashire Cycle Way

CANOE GUIDES
Canoeist's Guide to the North-East

LAKE DISTRICT AND MORECAMBE BAY
Coniston Copper Mines
Scrambles in the Lake District (North)
Scrambles in the Lake District (South)
Walks in Silverdale and Arnside AONB
Short Walks in Lakeland 1 – South
Short Walks in Lakeland 2 – North
Short Walks in Lakeland 3 – West
The Tarns of Lakeland Vol 1 – West
The Tarns of Lakeland Vol 2 – East
The Cumbria Way & Allerdale Ramble
Lake District Winter Climbs
Roads and Tracks of the Lake District
The Lake District Angler's Guide
Rocky Rambler's Wild Walks
An Atlas of the English Lakes
Tour of the Lake District
The Cumbria Coastal Way

NORTH-WEST ENGLAND
Walker's Guide to the Lancaster Canal
Family Walks in the Forest Of Bowland
Walks in Ribble Country

Historic Walks in Cheshire
Walking in Lancashire
Walks in Lancashire Witch Country
The Ribble Way

THE ISLE OF MAN
Walking on the Isle of Man
The Isle of Man Coastal Path

PENNINES AND NORTH-EAST ENGLAND
Walks in the Yorkshire Dales
Walks on the North York Moors, books 1 and 2
Walking in the South Pennines
Walking in the North Pennines
Walking in the Wolds
Waterfall Walks – Teesdale and High Pennines
Walking in County Durham
Yorkshire Dales Angler's Guide
Walks in Dales Country
Historic Walks in North Yorkshire
South Pennine Walks
Walking in Northumberland
Cleveland Way and Yorkshire Wolds Way
The North York Moors

DERBYSHIRE, PEAK DISTRICT, EAST MIDLANDS
High Peak Walks
White Peak Walks Northern Dales
White Peak Walks Southern Dales
Star Family Walks Peak District & South Yorkshire
Walking In Peakland
Historic Walks in Derbyshire

WALES AND WELSH BORDERS
Ascent of Snowdon
Welsh Winter Climbs
Hillwalking in Wales – Vol 1
Hillwalking in Wales – Vol 2
Scrambles in Snowdonia
Hillwalking in Snowdonia
The Ridges of Snowdonia
Hereford & the Wye Valley
Walking Offa's Dyke Path
Lleyn Peninsula Coastal Path
Anglesey Coast Walks
The Shropshire Way
Spirit Paths of Wales
Glyndwr's Way
The Pembrokeshire Coastal Path
Walking in Pembrokeshire
The Shropshire Hills – A Walker's Guide

MIDLANDS
The Cotswold Way
The Grand Union Canal Walk
Walking in Warwickshire
Walking in Worcestershire
Walking in Staffordshire
Heart of England Walks

SOUTHERN ENGLAND
Exmoor & the Quantocks
Walking in the Chilterns
Walking in Kent
Two Moors Way
Walking in Dorset
A Walker's Guide to the Isle of Wight
Walking in Somerset
The Thames Path
Channel Island Walks
Walking in Buckinghamshire
The Isles of Scilly
Walking in Hampshire
Walking in Bedfordshire
The Lea Valley Walk
Walking in Berkshire
The Definitive Guide to Walking in London
The Greater Ridgeway
Walking on Dartmoor
The South West Coast Path
Walking in Sussex
The North Downs Way
The South Downs Way

SCOTLAND
Scottish Glens 1 – Cairngorm Glens
Scottish Glens 2 – Atholl Glens
Scottish Glens 3 – Glens of Rannoch
Scottish Glens 4 – Glens of Trossach
Scottish Glens 5 – Glens of Argyll
Scottish Glens 6 – The Great Glen
Scottish Glens 7 – The Angus Glens
Scottish Glens 8 – Knoydart to Morvern
Scottish Glens 9 – The Glens of Ross-shire
The Island of Rhum
Torridon – A Walker's Guide
Walking the Galloway Hills
Border Pubs & Inns – A Walkers' Guide
Scrambles in Lochaber
Walking in the Hebrides
Central Highlands: 6 Long Distance Walks
Walking in the Isle of Arran
Walking in the Lowther Hills
North to the Cape
The Border Country – A Walker's Guide
Winter Climbs – Cairngorms
The Speyside Way
Winter Climbs – Ben Nevis & Glencoe
The Isle of Skye, A Walker's Guide
The West Highland Way
Scotland's Far North
Walking the Munros Vol 1 – Southern, Central
Walking the Munros Vol 2 – Northern & Cairngorms
Scotland's Far West
Walking in the Cairngorms

Walking in the Ochils, Campsie Fells
    and Lomond Hills
Scotland's Mountain Ridges
The Great Glen Way
The Pentland Hills: A Walker's Guide
The Southern Upland Way
Ben Nevis and Glen Coe

IRELAND
The Mountains of Ireland
Irish Coastal Walks
The Irish Coast to Coast

INTERNATIONAL CYCLE GUIDES
The Way of St James – Le Puy to
    Santiago cyclist's guide
The Danube Cycle Way
Cycle Tours in Spain
Cycling the River Loire – The Way
    of St Martin
Cycle Touring in France
Cycling in the French Alps

**WALKING AND TREKKING
IN THE ALPS**
Tour of Monte Rosa
Walking in the Alps (all Alpine areas)
100 Hut Walks in the Alps
Chamonix to Zermatt
Tour of Mont Blanc
Alpine Ski Mountaineering
    Vol 1 Western Alps
Alpine Ski Mountaineering
    Vol 2 Eastern Alps
Snowshoeing: Techniques and Routes
    in the Western Alps
Alpine Points of View
Tour of the Matterhorn
Across the Eastern Alps: E5

**FRANCE, BELGIUM AND
LUXEMBOURG**
RLS (Robert Louis Stevenson) Trail
Walks in Volcano Country
French Rock
Walking the French Gorges
Rock Climbs Belgium & Luxembourg
Tour of the Oisans: GR54
Walking in the Tarentaise and
    Beaufortain Alps
Walking in the Haute Savoie, vol. 1
Walking in the Haute Savoie, vol. 2
Tour of the Vanoise
GR20 Corsica – The High Level Route
The Ecrins National Park
Walking the French Alps: GR5
Walking in the Cevennes
Vanoise Ski Touring
Walking in Provence
Walking on Corsica
Mont Blanc Walks
Walking in the Cathar region
    of south west France
Walking in the Dordogne
Trekking in the Vosges and Jura
The Cathar Way

PYRENEES AND FRANCE / SPAIN
Rock Climbs in the Pyrenees
Walks & Climbs in the Pyrenees
The GR10 Trail: Through the

French Pyrenees
The Way of St James –
    Le Puy to the Pyrenees
The Way of St James –
    Pyrenees-Santiago-Finisterre
Through the Spanish Pyrenees GR11
The Pyrenees – World's Mountain
    Range Guide
The Pyrenean Haute Route
The Mountains of Andorra

SPAIN AND PORTUGAL
Picos de Europa – Walks & Climbs
The Mountains of Central Spain
Walking in Mallorca
Costa Blanca Walks Vol 1
Costa Blanca Walks Vol 2
Walking in Madeira
Via de la Plata (Seville To Santiago)
Walking in the Cordillera Cantabrica
Walking in the Canary Islands 1 West
Walking in the Canary Islands 2 East
Walking in the Sierra Nevada
Walking in the Algarve
Trekking in Andalucia

SWITZERLAND
Walking in Ticino, Switzerland
Central Switzerland –
    A Walker's Guide
The Bernese Alps
Walking in the Valais
Alpine Pass Route
Walks in the Engadine, Switzerland
Tour of the Jungfrau Region

GERMANY AND AUSTRIA
Klettersteig Scrambles in
    Northern Limestone Alps
King Ludwig Way
Walking in the Salzkammergut
Walking in the Harz Mountains
Germany's Romantic Road
Mountain Walking in Austria
Walking the River Rhine Trail
Trekking in the Stubai Alps
Trekking in the Zillertal Alps
Walking in the Bavarian Alps

SCANDINAVIA
Walking In Norway
The Pilgrim Road to Nidaros
    (St Olav's Way)

EASTERN EUROPE
The High Tatras
The Mountains of Romania
Walking in Hungary
The Mountains of Montenegro

CROATIA AND SLOVENIA
Walks in the Julian Alps
Walking in Croatia

ITALY
Italian Rock
Walking in the Central Italian Alps
Central Apennines of Italy
Walking in Italy's Gran Paradiso
Long Distance Walks in Italy's Gran
    Paradiso
Walking in Sicily

Shorter Walks in the Dolomites
Treks in the Dolomites
Via Ferratas of the Italian
    Dolomites Vol 1
Via Ferratas of the Italian
    Dolomites Vol 2
Walking in the Dolomites
Walking in Tuscany
Trekking in the Apennines
Through the Italian Alps: the GTA

**OTHER MEDITERRANEAN
COUNTRIES**
The Mountains of Greece
Climbs & Treks in the Ala Dag
    (Turkey)
The Mountains of Turkey
Treks & Climbs Wadi Rum, Jordan
Jordan – Walks, Treks, Caves etc.
Crete – The White Mountains
Walking in Western Crete
Walking in Malta

AFRICA
Climbing in the Moroccan Anti-Atlas
Trekking in the Atlas Mountains
Kilimanjaro

NORTH AMERICA
The Grand Canyon &
    American South West
Walking in British Columbia
The John Muir Trail

SOUTH AMERICA
Aconcagua

HIMALAYAS – NEPAL, INDIA
Langtang, Gosainkund &
    Helambu: A Trekkers' Guide
Garhwal & Kumaon –
    A Trekkers' Guide
Kangchenjunga – A Trekkers' Guide
Manaslu – A Trekkers' Guide
Everest – A Trekkers' Guide
Annapurna – A Trekker's Guide
Bhutan – A Trekker's Guide
The Mount Kailash Trek

TECHNIQUES AND EDUCATION
The Adventure Alternative
Rope Techniques
Snow & Ice Techniques
Mountain Weather
Beyond Adventure
The Hillwalker's Manual
Outdoor Photography
The Hillwalker's Guide to
    Mountaineering
Map and Compass
Sport Climbing
Rock Climbing

MINI GUIDES
Avalanche!
Snow
Pocket First Aid and Wilderness
    Medicine
Navigation

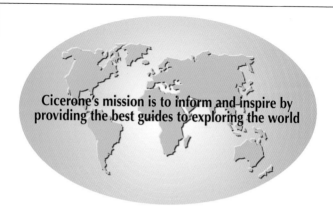

Cicerone's mission is to inform and inspire by providing the best guides to exploring the world

Since its foundation over 30 years ago, Cicerone has specialised in publishing guidebooks and has built a reputation for quality and reliability. It now publishes nearly 300 guides to the major destinations for outdoor enthusiasts, including Europe, UK and the rest of the world.

Written by leading and committed specialists, Cicerone guides are recognised as the most authoritative. They are full of information, maps and illustrations so that the user can plan and complete a successful and safe trip or expedition – be it a long face climb, a walk over Lakeland fells, an alpine traverse, a Himalayan trek or a ramble in the countryside.

With a thorough introduction to assist planning, clear diagrams, maps and colour photographs to illustrate the terrain and route, and accurate and detailed text, Cicerone guides are designed for ease of use and access to the information.

If the facts on the ground change, or there is any aspect of a guide that you think we can improve, we are always delighted to hear from you.

Cicerone Press
2 Police Square Milnthorpe Cumbria LA7 7PY
Tel:01539 562 069   Fax:01539 563 417
e-mail:info@cicerone.co.uk   web:www.cicerone.co.uk